Adharanand Finn is the author of *Running with the Kenyans* (2012) and *The Way of the Runner* (2015). The first of these was the *Sunday Times* Sports Book of the Year, won Best New Writer at the British Sports Book Awards and was shortlisted for the William Hill Sports Book Award. *The Rise of the Ultra Runners* (2019) was also shortlisted for the William Hill Sports Book Award. He is a journalist at the *Guardian* and also writes regularly for the *Financial Times*, the *Daily Telegraph*, *Runner's World*, *Men's Health* and many others.

Further praise for *The Rise of the Ultra Runners*:

'Finn gives us an inside view of the mind-boggling world of long-distance running, and perfectly captures the ebb and flow of a long race; the moments when you feel you can't take another step, chased by those fleeting periods when you believe you might run for ever.' Emily Chappell, *Guardian*

'This book will resonate with any ultra runner.' Jasmin Paris

'[A] tale of transcending boundaries and facing one's frailties head on.' *Financial Times*

'A stirring and quietly moving genre-blurring book.' *Irish Times*

'A thrilling and passionate insight into the world of ultra running and what motivates people to push themselves to the limits of endurance. Through challenging himself to take part, Adharanand brilliantly portrays the roller coaster of emotions and the importance of the power of the mind in these merciless events. A very exciting read demonstrating the strength of the human spirit' Jo Pavey

'Thrilling, exhilarating and truly inspirational. This is sports writing at its very best as Finn takes us through the world of ultra-distance running to show not just what it takes to cover immense distances, but also how rewarding and how fun it can be. A must-read for anyone who has ever laced up a pair of shoes and wondered where their journey might take them.' Robin Harvie, author of *Why We Run*

'The go-to book for anyone undertaking the challenge of an ultra' Tom Evans

'A thoroughly researched, astute and highly enjoyable expose of the weird and wonderful world of ultra-running' Damian Hall

'I felt like I was there. Mind-blowing!' Ronnie O'Sullivan

by the same author

The Rise of the Ultra Runners

A Journey to the Edge of
Human Endurance

ADHARANAND FINN

First published by Guardian Faber in 2019
Guardian Faber is an imprint of Faber & Faber Ltd,
Bloomsbury House, 74–77 Great Russell Street,
London WC1B 3DA

This paperback edition first published in 2020

Guardian is a registered trade mark of
Guardian News & Media Ltd,
Kings Place, 90 York Way, London N1 9GU

Typeset by Faber & Faber Ltd
Printed and bound by CPI Group (UK) Ltd, Croydon CR0 4YY

A CIP record for this book
is available from the British Library

ISBN 978–1–783–35133–6

10 9 8 7 6 5 4 3 2 1

'We should always be struggling to know. Know, then, thyself.'

Geoff Oliver, age eighty-five, after running 77 miles at the
Tooting 24-hour track race in south London

Prologue

I'm slumped on the ground, my back against a mound of sand, staring out through smudged, yellow sunglasses. All I can see, as far as the sky, is sand. Sand with scratches of dry grass. A wasteland. A faint trail runs through it. Tyre tracks that suggest civilisation can't be far away. But I'm not moving. My legs are like two bits of rusted machinery I've been dragging along with me for days. It feels good to put them down. My groin, right where the front of my left leg fuses on to my body, screeches and grinds with each step when I run, but sitting here, it becomes a faint, almost pleasurable pain.

My thoughts seem to exist outside myself. My essence, my core being, is just sitting here, melting into the sand, too exhausted to think. But the officers in my head, those left in charge of making sure I stay alive, are in frantic discussion.

I can't sit here all day. I'm low on water. The sun is too hot. I've come too far. Think of all that distance you've run. Countless miles across this soul-sapping sand. You can't stop now. The end, the beach, the sea is only a few miles away. You can do it, one small step at a time. You didn't come all this way to quit this close to the finish.

I recall vaguely the various strategies I've used to keep myself going up until now. When things first got tough, around Day Two, I got myself pumped up. 'Come on, tough guy,' I told myself. 'You can do this. You show them. The desert may be tough, but it won't stop Mr Finn.' I actually called myself Mr Finn. The race was already twisting my brain.

By Day Five, though, the bravado had been replaced by tenderness as I cajoled myself along through the night stage. 'It's OK, don't worry, you'll make it. You're going to be fine, just keep moving.' The night lay dark and still around me. The sand under my feet brutally soft. But I got through it. Twenty-six miles in seven and a half hours. But I got there.

But now, so close to the end, my will has run dry. The voices in my head are futile. I'm not moving.

'That's what you're supposed to do, get up and drag yourself to the finish. But why? Who set up these stupid rules? You don't have to play along like some prize poodle.' This is interesting. I shuffle myself around so the grass is less spiky, stretching my legs, pushing my feet out in front of me. My shoes are full of sand, like they're about three sizes too small. I've been coping with it like this for days. It's a minor irritant, among everything else.

'The really courageous thing to do, right now,' the genius in my head continues, 'would be to listen to yourself, not everyone else. Everyone else will tell you that you have to finish, that nobody quits this close to the end. But you're different. You play by your own rules. You have nothing to prove. If you want to stop, you just stop.' Sitting here, not moving, is beginning to feel like the ultimate act of rebellion. I'm quickly turning into the James Dean of desert running. Someone will come and find me eventually. They'll try to egg me on to the finish, but I won't play ball. I'll show them. I play by my own rules.

'Hey, Finn!' I look up. An elderly German couple in their sixties are standing over me. I can't quite tell if they're smiling or grimacing.

'Are you OK?' Gudrun asks me kindly. She looks in shock.

'Come on, get up,' barks Hansmartin. 'Follow us.'

Before I know it I'm hauling myself up and we're walking off in single file. Wading through the sand again, my groin wincing. Everything, my clothes, my backpack, my headscarf, is stuck to me with sweat. For days the sun has had me in its vice, slowly squeezing, wringing both my body and spirit dry. But now I'm up and moving again, following Hansmartin's commanding footsteps. Nobody speaks. They're nearly as exhausted as I am, but we plough on. It's only walking, although they have poles and are striding along fairly seriously. I watch Hansmartin's lolling backpack as he picks his way through the tufts of sand. And, eventually, I begin to recover. I begin to feel a tiny spasm of life return to my legs. My head starts to clear. Without even meaning to, I start to trot.

'Ah, good, good,' he says. 'Go. We will see you at the finish.' And with that I begin to run. The dunes are rising up like mountains now, the biggest dunes of the race, but I can almost smell the sea. I take off my glasses and shove them in my pocket. The sand is white. I scale the giant, shifting slopes, skipping and stumbling down the other side. I imagine I'm a child, excited, running for the sea.

A few times I think I'm there, but another dune looms up before me. But I'm high on adrenaline now. I can sense the finish, calling to me. And then, suddenly, I'm there. An arc of balloons. Tents. People lolling in the waves. I'm almost the last finisher and most people are already relaxing in camp, cooking food, washing their clothes. A couple of Dutch runners spot me crossing the line and offer me a muted round of applause, but they've long since lost their enthusiasm for cheering people across the finish. A bored photographer steps out from his seat in the shade and points his camera at me. He asks me how I feel. For the race video, he says.

I don't know what to say. After everything I've been through I should be bubbling over with emotion, but instead I feel strangely muted.

'That was hard,' is all I can muster. 'Bloody hard.' And with that I unclip my backpack and stumble down the beach and walk straight into the cool waters of the Sea of Oman, collapsing into the waves.

I am never doing anything as stupid as that ever again, I say to myself.

1

The Oman Desert Marathon was my first ultra marathon. It was just over 100 miles (165km) across the baking sand. I didn't really want to do it. It only came up as an idea when an editor from the *Financial Times* contacted me and asked if I would write an article about it. My initial response was a firm no.

I've always considered myself something of a purist when it comes to running. I would have as much admiration for a person who could run a mile in less than four minutes as I would for someone who has run around the entire world. To run the entire world would take determination, bloody-mindedness, good planning skills and a lot of spare time. But to be fast, really fast, that took skill, dedication, the careful honing of a precious talent over many years. To watch athletes like Mo Farah, David Rudisha or Eliud Kipchoge in full flow was to witness something poetic, at once combining the depths of human effort with incredible grace, balance and power. It was running made beautiful.

Ultra running, on the other hand, was to bludgeon running until it was close to death. Backpacks, poles, food, head torches – they all muddied the water. It became something else. Admirable and courageous, sure. Mad and insane, perhaps. But it was no longer running.

It secretly annoyed me when people who asked about my running were more impressed with how far I ran than how fast. To me, the distance was irrelevant if you didn't know the speed. In my head, anyone could run far if they jogged, or walked even. There was little merit in that.

One day I was getting a cup of tea in the office in London when a colleague who knew I did some running broached the subject.

'You do triathlons, don't you?' he asked.

'No,' I replied.

'Oh. Ultra marathons?'

'No,' I said. He looked confused.

'Just marathons?' he said.

To run a marathon used to be a big deal. People used to be impressed. They would sometimes even ask your time, and if you had run under three hours you would get a satisfyingly impressed raise of the eyebrows. But that water-cooler sentiment that wanted to shake its head at how mad some people were, that wanted a quick hit of 'bloody hell, that's crazy, rather you than me', but didn't want to get bogged down in the details, had got used to bigger, more extreme things. Marathons were now small fry. It seemed we had entered the age of 'just marathons'. Now running had to come with the overblown prefix 'ultra'. One hundred miles across the desert? Wow. Everyone could be impressed by that.

Except me, it seemed. Whenever I watched a video on an ultra race website and saw people walking, my heart sank. I read a blog called 'The A to Z of UltraRunning' and under W it said: 'Walking: A mode of travel rarely acknowledged but commonly used during ultra marathons. We've even named it "powerhiking" to save some face.'

To me, in my world of fast 10Ks and Tuesday track sessions with my athletics club, ultra marathons – any race longer than a standard 26.2-mile marathon – only impressed people who didn't know anything about running. But I did know about running. So I said no to the Oman job.

It was my wife, Marietta, who got me to rethink.

'Don't people pay a lot of money to do races like that?' she said. 'And you're getting invited to do it. I thought you liked running?'

Yes, these big stage races, set over a number of days, were not cheap. Then you needed the equipment. It was a huge personal investment, with lots of time away from home and work. Why did people do that? It surely wasn't simply to impress their colleagues at the tea-point.

The more I thought about what it actually entailed, the more I realised that, while perhaps as a runner this wasn't my kind of race, purely as an experience it would be an amazing adventure: to run across the desert; to sleep under the stars; to cross a hundred miles of wilderness under my own steam. Put like that, it felt suddenly enticing, epic even. I jilted my runner-geek self aside for a moment. This was an opportunity to connect with nature, the planet, to spend some time out in the wild. Who knew what it would be like and what I would discover out there under the baking sun? I might come back a changed person. And besides, I'd hardly lose any fitness for my 'real' running. I'd be a lean, mean machine by the time I got home. It was win-win. So I called the editor back.

'I know it looks a bit mental,' he said. 'It's over six days, but you could just do two or three if you preferred.'

No, I now wanted the full experience. The idea had suddenly gripped me and was slowly dragging me in. I wanted to feel what it was like to take on such a challenge and make it out the other side. It couldn't be too difficult, I reasoned, for a real runner like me.

I arrived in Muscat at one o'clock in the morning on a flight with around ten other runners – including the German couple Gudrun and Hansmartin, whom I had met on the plane. We were expecting to be taken straight to a hotel, so when the organiser meeting us said that instead we would be waiting in the airport until the bus came at 9 a.m., I got a little annoyed.

'Sit in the café,' he suggested flippantly, as though he was brushing away a child. His English wasn't great and I wondered if perhaps I was misunderstanding him.

'Sit in the café? For *eight* hours?' I asked, my voice rising a little too much. Surely he wasn't serious. We were about to run 100 miles across the desert. We needed our rest. But he just shrugged and pulled down his cap, pretending not to understand.

I was on the point of telling him that I was from the *Financial Times* and that this just wasn't good enough. I turned around to look for support from my fellow runners.

But there was no one there. It was just the empty arrivals hall. Where had they all gone?

As I skulked away, I realised that while I had been stamping my feet and remonstrating, the other runners, on hearing of the delay, had all calmly whipped out their roll mats and sleeping bags and found somewhere to sleep on the airport floor. For a moment I stood there confused. Did they know something I didn't? Or was this somehow an ultra running thing?

In the event, the bus arrived three hours early and we were all shipped off to a comfortable hotel oasis in a narrow valley between mountainous sand dunes. But the reaction of the other runners to this small setback was something I would think about many times over the next few years as I went on to tackle one crazy ultra race after another.

At the hotel oasis, the dunes were so high that you could hire snowboards for racing down them, although the locals seemed to prefer driving up and down in their shiny 4x4s. The runners, of course, used their legs, with everyone from the race walking up to the top of the dune that evening, having emerged from our rooms one by one, to catch the sunset. We stood in small awkward groups, still getting to know each other, the sky big and clear, the air warm on our skin. Then we raced back down in the dark laughing and tumbling through the sand.

Tomorrow we would be doing it for real, for hours, in the heat of the day, with everything we needed for six days strapped across our backs.

I'd been sold this race by the organisers – via the *FT* editor – as a 'manageable' first ultra marathon. It was like a shorter, easier version of the famous Marathon des Sables, they told me. The MdS was one of the most famous races in the world, 156 miles across the Sahara desert. It billed itself as the Toughest Footrace on Earth, though I had it on good authority from a number of ultra runners that it was no such thing. But regardless of the hyperbole, the MdS was a serious undertaking. It wasn't the kind of thing I was planning to go anywhere near, so I was pleased to hear that this race in Oman was an easier option. 'MdS-lite', as I heard someone describe it. It was in the desert, sure, but we would not be running on soft sand, the organisers told me, but on hard-baked earth. And 100 miles over six days, well, that wasn't too bad either. It would be like a hot-weather training camp.

So, standing on the start line in the small town of Bidiyah, I felt fairly relaxed. This was not a race, but an adventure. For the first time in my running life I wasn't worrying about my speed. I was just here to enjoy the experience. This took the pressure off. Without the need to push the pace, I could just jog, and part of me seemed to believe I could jog for ever. Really, how hard could it be just to keep your feet churning over gently? I was a little worried about the heat, and at the back of my mind I was concerned that the required kit for the race included an anti-venom pump, a knife and a signalling mirror. While I had been enjoying telling people, in the weeks leading up to the race, that I was off to run across the desert, as though I was some sort of action hero, the thought suddenly hit me that I may actually have to deal with a dangerous situation. Would I be able to cope if something happened?

In the town square, the local people had come out to wave us off. We were given a ceremonial dance and the village bustled happily with men in long, white robes, expensive daggers and iPhones tucked into their belts.

Among the hullabaloo, a Swedish woman, Elisabet Barnes, stood not watching the dancers, but serious, with the air of someone focused on the job at hand. I had befriended Elisabet in the oasis hotel the evening before. She lived in England and had recently won the famous Marathon des Sables. I asked her for some tips as we sat on cushions eating couscous and grilled vegetables at low tables.

'Have you stitched or glued your gaiters to your shoes?' she asked. Elisabet owned a specialist ultra running shop in Essex. She knew her stuff. My gaiters clipped on to my shoes. Wasn't that enough? They came like that. I thought it was quite nifty.

'Oh,' she said, trying her best not to look concerned. 'You'll probably be OK. How much sand running have you done?'

Er . . . none. But the race was on mostly hard-baked earth, that's what I was told.

She was smiling like she was not sure. 'Maybe,' she said. 'How much does your bag weigh?'

I had no idea. She took a deep breath. I told her the organiser had tried to scare me by telling me not to bring any pictures of my family. 'You'll end up burying them in the sand,' he had said. 'People even trim their toothbrushes to save weight.' She didn't say anything, but carried on eating.

'That's not true?' I said. 'That's ridiculous. Right?' But the look on her face told me that she didn't think so. I suddenly felt way out of my depth.

'Of course, it's not necessary,' she said. 'It's as much about getting in the right frame of mind, knowing you have done everything possible to be light, that you have left no stone unturned. It helps you mentally to feel ready.'

So I hadn't trained on sand, my gaiters were useless and my bag was probably too heavy. And I hadn't trimmed my toothbrush. But how hard could this be? Gudrun and Hansmartin were in their sixties, and there was a blind Frenchwoman in her late fifties in the race. As long as I controlled my pace, kept jogging, shuffling along, I would be fine.

And so we trotted off out of Bidiyah, past the waving children and the last trees we would see for six days. I was careful to take it slowly, running in the middle of all the bobbing backpacks. It was barely running. I watched my shadow, the pillow I'd snaffled off the flight strapped on to the top of my bag. That was a stroke of genius. It weighed almost nothing, but it would help me sleep. I may only have clip-on gaiters, but I had a pillow.

There were only about seventy-five runners in total and the field soon began to spread out. For the first hour we made our way along a flat, sandy plain until, after the first water stop, the route headed up into the sand dunes. Here the sand was soft, sloping, wind-blown. It was difficult to walk through it, let alone run. These were the dunes of Tintin books, made of the fine sand that finds its way into your shoes no matter how tight your gaiters are fixed. And mine were not tightly fixed at all.

The temperature was also rising – getting close to 40°C by the time we were up in the dunes. I struggled on, sinking with each heavy step, getting slower and slower. I kept expecting the more experienced runners to come by me, but no one appeared. They must have been having similar difficulties.

With relief, after a few hours of trudging and cursing, we rolled down one long final dune and on to a flat section to the finish. But it had been a tougher first day than I had expected.

I somehow convinced myself, sitting in the Berber-style tents in the camp that afternoon, that they had sent us through the dunes on the first day to give us a sample of what it was like, to get things off to a crazy start, but that the rest of the race would be mostly on the promised hard-baked earth that ran here and there between the dunes.

It must have been what everyone else was thinking too, because at about 4 p.m. a cry went up around the camp. What was it? People were pointing, coming out of their tents, shaking their heads. 'It must be a joke,' someone said. 'Impossible,' said another.

On top of the highest dune opposite, sat the first course marker for the next stage. We were going to have to start

Day Two by running straight up there. This wasn't going to get easier.

And so it went. Each day I was sure that was it, that the next day we would get some respite. But each day was harder than the last; the endless sand, the heat squeezing the life out of me. I got moments of energy, of inspiration. On Day Four I realised I was ranked in the top twenty and, suddenly inspired to compete, I decided to try to do the whole stage without walking. It almost worked. Rather than walk, when the sand got really soft I just slowed to a pitter-patter shuffle. It was slow, but easier and quicker than walking. Less sinking in. As the dunes rolled, I rolled with them. I was getting this. I wasn't going to be defeated.

I finished Day Four with a fist pump and went to sit among the fastest runners, waiting for the others to complete their weary way. The good thing about running faster was that you spent less time out in the stranglehold of the heat. It was, in some ways, easier to go faster. And the next day, the organisers told us, the course would be flatter and the sand would be firmer. I don't know why, as they said this every day, but this time I really believed them. I could even picture it in my head, a firm road to the finish. I was going to cruise this.

Day Five was the longest stage of the race – exactly a marathon – and was to be run mostly at night. The top twenty runners were to start two hours after everyone else. That afternoon we all gathered around and they did a roll call, reading out the names of the top twenty. I was on it, number seventeen. Tough guy Finn. Don't mess. I tried not to look too chuffed with myself as we went back to our tents. Seasoned ultra runners were talking about how hard this race was. But, half prepared, I was still going strong.

Lots of people do these races in part for the camaraderie of the other competitors. Running together through the desert for a week, you begin to form close bonds. In Tent Two, as we became known, we were a group mainly of Italians – one the mother of a Premier League football player – as well as a Belgian bioengineer, a bubbly South African woman and a fellow Brit, Rob, who was in the army.

A couple of the others in Tent Two were also in the top twenty, but my buddy Dino had just missed out. He seemed happy, though. He didn't care about his position, he was there for the experience, to chat, and to take photographs. He held court in our tent most afternoons, once we had all settled down to rest, telling us about all the places he had been – over two hundred countries in all, he said, often listing them – and usually for crazy ultra races. He had stories about scrapes with bandits in Mexico, close calls with crocodiles in Botswana, falling down crevices in Iceland. He told them all with verve, good humour and a generous dollop of pantomime.

Months later Dino sent me a clip of an interview he did about the Oman race on Italian Sky Sports television – this guy was always being interviewed by someone. In the clip he tells the story of how in his tent there was the Italian mother of a Liverpool football player and an English guy from Liverpool. That was me. I wasn't from Liverpool, but I had lived there for three years as a student and I liked the football team. Anyway, he talked about how we spent those long afternoons reminiscing about the Liverpool football legends, the great games, and about the Liverpool anthem, which the fans always sing on match days, 'You'll Never Walk Alone'.

Then, on one of the race stages he found himself alone and tiring, the sun beating down with full force. He had begun walking and humming this song quietly to himself, becoming lost in his own world, so much so that he didn't notice that I had caught him up. Hearing what he was humming, I joined in. He looked across at me through his mirrored sunglasses with a big grin and together we walked on singing 'You'll Never Walk Alone' at the tops of our voices like two merry football fans.

'You know,' he said to the interviewer. 'You go to the crazy places, you meet the crazy people.' I don't know if he meant me or him, or both, but I liked that. Ultra running and the places it took you were indeed crazy, and I was beginning to realise that it attracted a certain type of person. Unhinged, perhaps, but also open, friendly and warm. At least, that's what Dino said.

At about 3 p.m., I joined the top twenty, the crack ultrarunning elite squad, to wave the main group off on their way, Dino at the front. We watched them disappear like scuttling ants across the sand. Then we went back to our tents to prepare.

My bag was getting lighter now, as I ate my way through

my supplies, and it felt easier to carry. I was going to fly, I told myself. Especially with the firmer ground this time.

But the firmer ground never came. And as the night wore on, the endless track of churned-up sand got softer and softer. I felt like I was slowly sinking into the Earth. I realised I had pushed too hard the day before, and my legs were struggling now. My strained groin had been taped up by one of the race doctors, but it began aching for real this time. Both my Achilles were also sore, biting at me with each step.

Of the leading twenty runners, I was by far the slowest on this stage. We set off at dusk like a little hunting party, in chase of the others, but I soon got left behind on my own. I had to run for hours in the headlights of the car that followed the very last runner. It was irritating, hearing it behind me, disrupting the desert silence, but at least it kept me moving.

I eventually began to catch people from the slower group, but by then I was hardly moving any faster than they were. We would talk as I walked along beside them for a while. And then I would summon the energy to run on a little.

As the night went on, I walked more and ran less. I had to keep re-estimating how long I was going to be out there. Five hours. Then six. Then seven. Would I ever get to the finish? A few times I stopped and turned my head torch off and stood looking at the blitz of stars above my head. Here I was, a tiny being alone on the edge of a planet flying through space. It seemed ridiculous to be worrying about my race position. Who cared how slowly I ran? It was a relief to realise that no one did. Not even me. I could just walk and take in the majesty of the expanding universe.

But then, on the other hand, I would be out here all night if I didn't get moving. So I would try to shuffle on again. Eventually I fell into a sort of trance, listening to the water sloshing around in my bottle, running to it like some sort of drum beat, my breathing synchronised with it. The circle of light on the ground in front of me was all I saw, a light at the end of a long, dark tunnel. I ran on, into the light, over and over, slosh, slosh, slosh.

Finally I got there. A marathon in seven hours and 34 minutes. A few months earlier I had run a road marathon in under three hours. That was a big drop-off. My race, as a competitor, as a top twenty guy, was over. I had fallen into a dark pit, but I had made it out alive. I had finished. And right then that was all that mattered. Until the morning. It was 1 a.m. The next stage, the final stage of the race, would begin in eight hours. I needed to get some sleep.

I hobbled back through the quiet camp. I was the last person back to Tent Two that night. I wanted to crawl into my sleeping bag and disappear, but I could barely bend down to take off my shoes. So I just stood there staring into the dark tent, full of sleeping bodies, feeling like some sort of running zombie. Even though they were already tucked up in their beds, Rob and Dino, noticing me standing there, got up to help, Rob preparing a recovery drink, while Dino untied my shoelaces. Neither of them spoke. They, too, had struggled that night. We didn't need to say anything; we had all been through the same thing. The trauma of it was written across our faces.

I was just settling down in a clean T-shirt given to me by Rob – as my only one was drenched in sweat – when we heard a blood-curdling cry. People were shouting, mostly in Italian, torches were buzzing back and forth. I couldn't move. I just lay there in my sleeping bag, still shaking from my run, praying that everything would be OK.

It turned out that one poor guy, after all that, after ten hours pushing his weary body through the sand, had returned to his tent and sat down on a scorpion. I don't know if I could have coped.

The medics were soon on hand to treat him and after a bit of commotion, people darting back and forth in the moon-light, a truck somewhere starting up, he was safe and in the medical tent for the night. Amazingly, a few hours later, as the sun was rising, he joined the rest of us on the start line for the final stage.

I stood at the back of the huddle, the sun already bright. Once more unto the breach, dear friends. But I had no fight left. A Dutch runner had told me at the end of Day Two, after he had stopped trying to run, and had started walking, that 'the light went off'. His desire to race, to get to the fin-ish as fast as he could, just died. Without a reason to be out here, a fire in your belly to push yourself, it was easy to lose the will to continue. I now knew what he meant. My light had gone off. Less than twenty paces into the final stage I decided I couldn't run any more. I was already walking. My energy level was at zero. My legs were shattered, my patched-up groin weeping in pain with each step. And we had 14 miles of soft sand left until the finish.

It was the longest slog of my life. Each step, even at a slow walk, was a torment. The sun was up and burning like a kiln. I kept sitting down, stopping. Why rush, my competition was over. But the finish beckoned. The sea. We were finishing at the sea. I fantasised about splashing and frolicking in the waves.

It was somewhere along that desolate road that Gudrun and Hansmartin found me. And saved me.

Later, after my swim, the atmosphere in the camp was different. People were happy, relaxed. The post-run intensity of the previous days had gone. As we lay on our sleeping bags, staring out to sea, thoughts began to drift back to home, to jobs, to our lives in cities, in houses; to life beyond the hot, inhospitable, engulfing desert. Did I imagine it, or was the happiness, the relief to have finished, tinged with a little sadness?

It turned out that this race was tough for a first ultra. Many of the runners had also run the Marathon des Sables. Most of them thought that this, with its endless soft sand, was tougher.

'The Marathon des Sables is a wellness camp after this,' said Gudrun, now a veteran of both races.

'It was like the Alps at the end,' said the Swedish runner Elisabet. 'Except the mountains were made of sand.' She, it turned out, had won every stage of the race and added the Oman Desert Marathon to her growing list of victories. After my struggles it seemed like another world to be running these races to compete and to win. It was a select group of about five men and women who set out each day with such things on their mind, ready to push hard, worrying about rivals, making moves, employing tactics. The rest of us were just trying to keep alive the will to get to the finish.

After I got home to England, I kept thinking about the appeal of ultra running. I had been attracted initially to the romance and adventure of it all, crossing the desert by foot, but there are easier ways to experience the majesty and beauty of the world. Camel trekking, for instance, or hiking, would be just as much of an adventure, without the straining, cursing and struggle. Yet it seems as though everyone, me included, despite the depths of pain we endured, especially in that endless night stage, felt happy and content afterwards. A tranquil harmony reigned over the camp that day after the final stage. Did we just suddenly forget the pain and the suffering? Or was the suffering part of why we were happy?

One afternoon during the race, one of the Dutch runners had been talking about something the famous ultra runner and author Dean Karnazes had once said, that people mistake comfort for happiness. 'Happiness needs to be earned,' the Dutchman said emphatically. I sat listening, looking around the camp, thinking of the huge effort involved in setting up this race, relocating the camp each night in such an inhospitable place, each runner spending vast sums of money to be there, flying to this far-flung corner of the world, running through the heat, across sand, for hours each day. Was this all so we could feel that we had earned our happiness?

In the midst of the race, and struggling to understand what she was doing there, Gudrun had asked rhetorically:

'Why do we do this? We have such a nice home.'

Standing next to her, her husband, Hansmartin, chipped in: '*Because* we have a nice home.'

If happiness wasn't in comfort, was it somehow to be found in being uncomfortable? Was there some need for those of us with no suffering in our lives, to find some? Because it made us appreciate our homes and our comforts more? Or did suffering a little somehow make us stronger, more fulfilled human beings?

These questions played on my mind as I thought back to that moment when we first arrived in Muscat and were told to wait in the airport for eight hours. After the race was over, I realised that given the same situation again, I too would now be more likely to pull out my sleeping bag and grab some kip. A few hours in an airport no longer seemed such a terrible hardship. After a week running across the desert, something had changed.

2

While I'm not exactly hooked, I find myself being drawn in, intrigued to find out more about this world of ultra running. A few weeks after Oman, I get to meet Elisabet again. I've been commissioned to interview her for an article for the *Guardian*, so she comes to meet me at the newspaper's offices in central London, where we sit on leather sofas, drinking espresso as people queue to buy their lunchtime sandwiches. I ask her how she first started ultra running.

She tells me she used to be a keen marathon runner, fitting her training in around a well-paid job in London's financial district. 'I kept improving,' she says. 'But there came a point when I thought, what shall I do now? I could run a marathon faster – which is, of course, difficult, and a good challenge – or I could go further. And I just thought it would be interesting to explore the going further.'

Her decision to delve into ultra running was accelerated by some unexpected life events. Within a short span of time her father died, her mother was diagnosed with Alzheimer's, and her husband got cancer. 'All of those things,' she says, 'make you realise that life is very short, and you just have to do it, you can't sit and wait.'

So she quit her job in the City and set off in search of

adventure. To fund her way she set up her running shop, but since winning the MdS and now the Oman race, people have started writing articles about her, and sponsorship deals have begun to come her way. This makes it easier for her to travel to races and take on more challenges. What started off as a risky move seems to be paying off.

Listening to her talk, I too feel a stirring. It reminds me of the feeling I had when I first decided to run a marathon. The idea had been hovering on the horizon for years, watching me as I tackled shorter races, wondering what was taking me so long. Suddenly, it was time. Life was moving on. So I ran a marathon.

Ever since then, on the horizon, I keep catching glimpses of a trail up a mountain. A long, winding trail. I'm forty-two years old. I've had a few decent attempts at the marathon. Maybe it is time to explore the going further. To explore just what it is that people find out there on that trail that compels them to run these improbable distances.

It's so intriguing that I'm soon on the phone to my editor. 'I think I've found my next subject,' I say. I've written books about travelling to Kenya and Japan to explore two unique running cultures. This time I'm drawn to investigate a cross-cultural, global phenomenon, which I'm only just beginning to realise is so huge. What is this world of ultra running? Who are the people taking part? What is it all about? The best way to find out, I decide, is to sign up for another race.

Over the last decade, ultra running has grown at a stagger-ing rate, becoming one of the fastest-growing sports in the world.

The website runultra.co.uk lists most of the world's big-gest ultra marathons. Its founder, Steve Diederich, tells me that when he set it up twelve years ago he found 160 races listed globally. He now has over 1,800 races on the site – an increase of over 1,000 per cent. The German ultra running website DUV, meanwhile, lists the results of many smaller races, with its forensic database going all the way back to the first 89km London to Brighton race in 1837. Over the last ten years the site plots a similar 1,000 per cent increase in the number of ultra races around the world.

Andy Nuttall, the editor of *ULTRA* magazine, drilled down deeper into the DUV statistics and found that in the UK the rise of the sport has been even steeper: in 2000, only 595 people finished an ultra marathon in the UK. By 2017, the number of finishers had grown to 18,611.

Everywhere I look, it's a similar story. *Ultra Running* mag-azine in the US collects figures for North America, which show the number of races and finishers increasing every year since 1981. In Asia, too, the number of ultra races has exploded. Nic Tinworth, a race director in Hong Kong, tells me that ten years ago there were six ultra races in the terri-tory, but that there are now over sixty. 'In previous years,' he says, 'you could just turn up on the day in Hong Kong and enter, but now the most popular races sell out in minutes.'

Many of the world's most over-subscribed races, such as the Ultra-Trail du Mont-Blanc in France and the Western States 100 in the US, have had to implement lottery systems to cope with the numbers wanting to take part. Diederich manages the UK entries for the Marathon des Sables. Despite the steep £4,250 entry fee, he says the race sells out each year in a couple of minutes.

What are all these runners striving for? I experienced something transformative in Oman that stayed with me long after the race. But I sense there is more to discover. I fell apart over the last two stages and almost gave up. Imagine if I could stay strong, even in the face of such a challenge.

I remember being struck by a photograph I saw of the Spanish ultra athlete Azara García, who has a tattoo on her leg that reads (in Spanish):

> The Devil whispered in my ear: 'You're not strong enough to withstand the storm.'
> I whispered back: 'I am the storm.'

Is this the appeal of ultra running? To push ourselves to a place where we stand face to face with the Devil, the depths of the struggle, but then to rise up and overcome it? Could I stare into the storm – whatever it may be, whatever is thrown at me – and overwhelm it with the force of my will? It is an enticing thought. And a far cry from the *FT* journalist complaining because his bus to the hotel is late.

I have to admit, this is all very appealing to my ego. I find myself watching a documentary about human evolution and the role running played in it, and a Professor of Anthropology at Hunter College in New York says: 'We even have on record humans who can run 100 miles in one go.' He says it as if it is scarcely credible, like these must be some kind of super-humans. And I spy my ego glancing over at me with that cocksure look that says: you could do that.

As the US comedian and ultra runner Michelle Wolf puts it in an interview with *Runner's World* magazine: 'It does kind of make you feel like a badass.'

Talking to other ultra runners, however, I get the feeling that it isn't only the satisfaction and validation of overcoming the challenge and making it to the finish that appeals to them, but also the feeling of oblivion they get from striding into the midst of the storm in the first place, from teetering so close to the edge. Digging in the pain cave, as seasoned ultra runners describe it with relish.

When I start scouting around for races to enter, I find myself looking at the race profiles, and each time I feel a ripple of fear in my stomach. It seems that every ultra race has to produce a slick, short film with dramatic, sweeping shots and lots of high drama. And always, at some point, it shows someone looking broken, close to tears. The runners look more like survivors of some near-apocalyptic disaster than sportsmen and women. It is telling that these are the images they choose to advertise the race. People want to experience this despair, they want to get this close to their own self-destruction.

Many ultra runners tell me they were inspired to take up the sport after reading Dean Karnazes's first book, *Ultra Marathon Man*. In it he describes in minute detail the process of being broken by a 100-mile race, with one thing after another failing in his body and mind until it seems nothing is left and he is literally crawling along the road on his hands and knees. I read it and I shudder. I don't want to hurt that badly. But other runners say they read that and thought: 'That's what I want.'

So, a little scared, but with my ego convinced that I'm tough enough, I begin to search for a race that will give me the full experience of ultra running, that will deliver me into the heart of this growing sport, that will reveal the secrets and allow me to fully understand what is going on.

It is a big, unwieldy thing to get my head around, a sport morphing in many directions at once. With no central overseeing body or organisation, the races, interest groups and self-appointed guardians of ultra running jostle and fight for control and for a cut of the increasing amounts of money sloshing around. It's a Wild West of a sport, still untamed, with many of the original prospectors fiercely protective of it, pushing back against the encroachment of 'brands' and 'outsiders' – people, they feel, who don't understand the ethos of the sport. For many, part of the appeal of ultra running is its low-key, 'Into the Wild' minimalism, a chance to lose yourself in the wilderness, to cross the toughest, most extreme environments on Earth with little more than a flask of water and a rain jacket.

For some seasoned ultra runners, the influx of newcomers is already too much, and they are turning their backs on the big races in search of more isolated challenges. One outlet for these people, who hate mass starts and goody bags even more than a long night of hypothermia clinging to the side of a frozen rock face, is another growing phenomenon called FKTs (Fastest Known Times). This is where people head off, often alone, to run a set route faster than anyone ever (knowingly) has before. It could be from one end of

New Zealand to the other, or a famous hiking trail such as the Appalachian Trail in the US. Or to the top of Mount Everest.

But I'll find out more about these later. For now I am looking for races. They are OK with me. I have run many races over the years. I'm just looking to run further, that's all.

A word you commonly hear when people talk about ultra races is 'runnable'. Some races are considered more runnable than others. This doesn't necessarily mean you can run the whole way, unless you're one of the sport's superstars, but in theory the trail is smooth enough, the ascents and descents manageable enough, that you can run most of it. Some athletes complain when races are too runnable. These people prefer the opposite, known in ultra jargon as 'technical' races, where the climbs and descents are too steep and the ground too uneven to run freely. Races where you need to watch your step and occasionally use your hands.

I definitely veer towards runnable over technical. Sure, we can walk the tough parts, and I'm OK with some scrambling over rocks, but if I do this, I still want to run.

The world of ultra running is a tree with many branches. The oldest of these, at least in the UK, is fell running, known as hill running in Scotland and mountain running in Ireland. These races can be of any length, from a mile to unfixed ultra distances, and take place across mountains and on mostly unmarked routes, meaning some self-navigation is usually required. The first known fell race took place way back in 1040, when King Malcolm Canmore of Scotland organised one in Braemar in Aberdeenshire to help him select a swift messenger.

Despite its long history, fell running remains a parochial branch of the sport. Its local roots and low-key, no-nonsense character are part of its appeal and are fiercely protected. I'd love to try it, but when I think about taking up ultra running, what I'm really imagining is something more global and all-encompassing. The part of the sport responsible for the boom in numbers.

Another branch of ultra running, and one that is seeing a big rise in the number of people taking part, is the multi-day stage races such as the Marathon des Sables, which are usually held in exotic, inhospitable places: deserts, the jungle, the Arctic Circle. These races are expensive to enter and require lots of planning.

There is disdain in some parts of the ultra running world towards some of these big multi-day races. Part of the resentment is against the cost and the corresponding hype of races such as the MdS. 'A holiday for CEOs' is how one ultra runner described them to me. Having been out there in the desert, I could see it was tough and gruelling, but also we did spend a good part of each day recovering in our tents. And despite being completely unprepared for it, I had been running near the front of the race for much of the time. A holiday may be pushing it, but I'm sure there are tougher, more competitive races out there.

Indeed, another offshoot of the sport includes a whole host of races so tough and extreme that each one seems to occupy its own category. These include races such as the Spine Race, which traverses 268 miles of the Pennine Way in the north of England. Non-stop. In January. Or the Badwater 135, which starts in Death Valley in California, one of the hottest places on Earth, where temperatures in the race have hit 54°C. Or the Barkley Marathons, an extreme 100-mile race on an unmarked route through remote mountains in Tennessee – so tough that in the first twenty-five years of the race only ten people managed to finish it. Or there is the longest ultra race in the world: the Self Transcendence 3100, which is a 3,100-mile race around a single city block in New York City.

I'm looking for something to push me to my limits, but I'm not insane. And I still want to run. You can't run for 3,100 miles. Races like the Barkley Marathons are more about your wits, your mind and your survival skills than running. I want that, too, but I want it to still be, to some degree, a running race.

Another offshoot of the ultra world, one where you can run, are the mostly flat, looped races over accurately measured distances such as 100km, or races that go on for a set time, such as 24-hour races. There are world championships and world records in these races, which bear the closest resemblance to regular marathon running.

These races interest me, but, like fell running, they aren't the reason for the phenomenal rise in ultra running. Little has changed in the participation levels in these events since the 1980s, or the 1950s, or even way back to their heyday in the 1870s.

It's an interesting aside to note that while these fixed-loop ultra races are today among the least glamorous and least heralded of all the ultra running branches, they were once among the biggest sporting events in the world.

It seems strange to us now, but in the nineteenth century, the sport of ultra running was incredibly popular, with huge crowds turning up to cheer on competitors in six-day races around tight indoor tracks in London or at New York's Madison Square Garden. Hefty prizes worth hundreds of thousands of pounds in today's money were taken home by the victors, while the fashionable and well-to-do of the day mingled with the rowdy crowds that turned up to bet, drink and socialise.

The sport rose in popularity in part on the back of the exploits of an American named Edward Payson Weston. It all began when, in 1861, after losing a bet with a friend over the outcome of the 1860 presidential election, he was forced to walk the 478 miles from Boston to Washington DC in ten days, in an effort to make it in time to witness the inauguration of President Abraham Lincoln.

As news of his feat of endurance got out, it stirred the curiosity of people living along the route, and crowds started coming out and lining the streets to see him walk through their town. He caused such a stir that when he got to Washington, although he missed the inauguration by a few hours, he was invited to the president's ball that evening and got to shake hands with President Lincoln.

Encouraged by this reaction, over the next few years Weston undertook a series of ever more challenging routes. By all accounts a showman – he sometimes played a bugle while walking, or walked backwards to entertain the crowds – by the 1870s Weston's fame as a long-distance walker had grown to the point where he decided to capitalise by bringing his act indoors where he could charge people to watch. As a result he set in motion a craze for six-day races – the longest time you could walk and run without encroaching on the sanctity of the Sabbath. Over the next few years he held a series of closely fought and wildly popular head-to-head matches with an Irish American called Daniel O'Leary.

The six-day race reached its pinnacle in 1878 when a British nobleman, Sir John Astley, sponsored five international races for lucrative prize money and a championship gold and silver belt inscribed with the words 'Long Distance Champion of the World'.

Previous incarnations of the sport of pedestrianism, as it was known, are recorded as far back as the early 1700s. While these races, often of 1,000 miles in length, also drew large crowds, they were strictly walking races, with rules about heel-to-toe contact similar to today's walking competitions. In contrast, the six-day races of the 1870s were more akin to modern ultra running, and became known as 'go-as-you-please' matches in which contestants could walk, run or rest whenever they wanted.

The Astley Belt contests were the biggest sporting events of any sort during the period, complete with brass bands, enthusiastic press coverage and substantial betting. The first of the five races took place in London in 1878, in the Agricultural Hall, Islington, and pitted seventeen Englishmen against the Irish-born O'Leary from America – Weston's old foe. O'Leary won the race, covering a total distance of 520 miles.

The second Astley Belt race was held later that year before capacity crowds totalling over 30,000 at Madison Square Garden in New York. O'Leary, the champion, won again to take home the $10,000 first prize (over $250,000 in today's money), plus a portion of the gate and side-bets.

The third race, in March 1879, again at Madison Square Garden, had a first prize of over $20,000. Public interest in the competition was now so intense that hourly bulletins were posted in the city's bar-rooms, barber shops, grocery stores and hotels, and the city's newspapers carried daily reports.

It wasn't until the fourth race that the sport's great pioneer, Edward Weston, finally got his hands on the unofficial world title. With the race back in Islington, London, the American won in a new world best, covering a total of 550 miles over the six days.

Alas, in the 1880s the sport went into decline as other sports began to grow to rival it. Matthew Algeo, author of the book *Pedestrianism: When Watching People Walk Was America's Favorite Spectator Sport*, says the rise of cycling, in particular, was key to the demise of the six-day races.

'Pretty quickly six-day bike races replaced six-day walking matches because they were much more exciting,' he tells me. 'The racing speed went from 4mph to 20mph overnight. And the crashes were more spectacular.'

Despite the dwindling crowds, some hardy practitioners continued to push the boundaries of what was possible. The last great feat of the Victorian era was the 623 miles covered in six days by George Littlewood from Sheffield, in a race in New York. Littlewood's world record stood for an amazing ninety-six years, until it was broken in 1984 by Greek ultra running legend Yiannis Kouros, who seven years later set the current six-day world record of 664 miles.

Despite their brief moment in the sun, lapped ultra races on flat courses are today largely stuck in the back corner of the sport. Instead, the most popular, the most brightly lit branch of the sport, the one with the most bunting and the biggest stars is the mountain ultra trail running world. Here the titans of the sport, such as Kilian Jornet and Jim Walmsley, go head to head in races of up to 100 miles. Unlike Oman, these races are a one-time effort. The gun goes and the first one to the finish wins. No afternoons spent hanging out in Berber tents chatting with Dino. Just go, go, go until you get to the end.

And the biggest race of all, the Super Bowl of mountain ultra trail running, is the Ultra-Trail du Mont-Blanc (UTMB). Each year in Chamonix in the French Alps, the cream of the ultra trail running world come together for the grand finale, the race of races. Win this and you're guaranteed legend status in the sport.

The route follows a famous 105-mile hiking trail around the foot of western Europe's highest peak, passing through Italy and Switzerland along the way. The more I hear about it, and the more footage I see of the mass start with its 2,000-plus athletes, its stirring anthem, the incredible photographs of the dawn breaking, peaks jutting through the clouds, the more I decide that if I am going to run another ultra marathon, this is the one.

So I go online and try to sign up. And that's where the fun begins.

The UTMB is so popular that you can't just enter, you have to first qualify, by running three other ultras designated as qualifying races. And even then, that only grants you entry into the race lottery – which gives you roughly a one in three chance of getting a place in the race.

The UTMB has a list of races it considers qualifying races. The reasoning behind this seems to originally have been to make sure only serious and prepared runners turn up for the race. But this reasonable aim seems to have been lost somewhere along the way, and what is left is a highly contentious system.

The issue many people have is that if you are a race director wishing to get your event on the UTMB's list, you don't have to pass any particular safety test or prove that your route is as tough and arduous as you say, or that you are scrupulous and trustworthy. No, you just have to pay them some money.

'It is no longer about ensuring suitable experience, but is now more about generating income, and about trying to monopolise and control trail racing in Europe,' says Lindley Chambers, chairman of the UK's Trail Running Association (TRA), who is clearly not a fan.

One race director who refuses to pay for his race to have UTMB points – and who didn't want to be named – explains how this situation arose. 'When the UTMB first introduced a points system,' he says, 'almost every ultra in the UK jumped on board. Many races that were awesome and could sell themselves, suddenly became "qualifiers" and sold themselves on being qualifiers, rather than on their own merits.'

Then, he says, once those races became reliant upon UTMB points to attract runners, the UTMB introduced a charge. 'It was small enough that the races would still pay it to avoid losing entries, but large enough that when you add up the races worldwide, it's a pretty large sum of money.'

When races pay to get points they actually pay to become members of the International Trail Running Association (ITRA), which says it is an independent, non-profit body working for the good of the sport. ITRA then awards the UTMB points.

But in the wild world of online ultra running forums, few things get race directors' blood boiling as much as the UTMB points system. One recent post said: 'I would rather scoop out my eyeballs with a spoon than pay UTMB for points for any of my races.'

Not everyone feels the same, however, with many races saying they are happy to pay the fee to accommodate runners looking for points, and many saying it easily pays for itself in increased entries to their races.

Nic Tinworth says he started offering points for his events in Hong Kong because people started asking for them. 'It seemed runners were picking and prioritising their races specifically for the points,' he says.

One issue for runners wanting to take part in the UTMB has been races that have been on the list in previous years, but which then drop off when they fail, or refuse, to pay the annual fee, leaving runners who were expecting to gain the points to find out only after completing the race that they haven't qualified after all.

This came to a head when the Hardrock 100, one of the most famous ultra races in the US, decided it was no longer going to pay to be a UTMB qualifying race. This was particularly pertinent because the biggest star in the sport, Kilian Jornet, a three-time winner of the UTMB, was counting on the points from running the Hardrock

100 for his UTMB entry. The UTMB's rules clearly state that every athlete has to have the points, even the elite athletes, so when they saw that Hardrock had not paid up, ITRA emailed the organisers to politely suggest they cough up so Jornet could race in France.

'We didn't like the system and we felt it was a little distasteful,' says David Coblentz, president of the board of directors at the Hardrock 100. 'They don't come and check out your course, you just send them a GPX file and they upload it to some algorithm and give you your points. It is really just another way to make money.'

He says that even when the course doesn't change from year to year, and the GPX file is the same, you still have to pay the fee annually. 'That really stuck in the craw,' he says.

So the Hardrock 100, along with eight other US races, published a public letter stating their intention not to pay and their reasons why.

ITRA responded with its own public letter, making clear that it was a non-profit organisation, that it was only trying to help the sport develop (through medical research, with safety advice, and by setting a global standard) and that it was independent of the UTMB. But Hardrock refused to back down. 'We never heard anything more,' says Coblentz.

In the end, Jornet was there on the start line of the UTMB that year, despite the stand-off. It seems the biggest race in the sport couldn't live without its biggest star. In its letter, ITRA said it had decided, fee or no fee, to 'add retroactively the race [Hardrock 100], on an exceptional basis, to the list of races allowing runners to qualify'.

The whole furore reveals a lot about the state the sport is in as it grows so fast. Behind the beautiful Instagram accounts and the incredible feats of the runners, a gold rush is taking place, with prospectors jostling for power and control. As well as ITRA and the big races, multinational clothing and outdoor sports brands have moved in, staking out their ground by signing up the biggest events and the star athletes, producing slick advertising campaigns, with viral films of men and women racing across sumptuous landscapes, hurtling down fantastical precipices. Ultra running is still a largely untapped and unregulated market, and there are no signs of its growth slowing. So while the runners are out there digging their way deep into the pain cave, others see an open, unguarded door to a gold mine and are racing in to nail their nameplates to the walls.

Despite all this, I still want to run the UTMB. A few months after interviewing Elisabet, as my interest in ultra running is still being piqued, I find myself watching the start of the race online. It's a Friday afternoon and I'm in the *Guardian* office in London. On my screen, in the main square in Chamonix, hundreds of mountain-chiselled men and women gather together, looking on nervously as stirring classical music plays out, drifting off across the valley. And then they're off, sprinting through the streets and out into the mountains.

After my day in the office ends, I make my way through the busy London streets to Paddington Station and catch the train back to my home in Devon. When I wake up on Saturday morning, after a good night's sleep, I find myself thinking about them all still out there on the mountain, still running.

Then, later, on Saturday evening, I think of them again, still going out there on the mountain. I log on to find out that a thunderstorm has unleashed itself on the race. After over 24 hours running. That is tough. What is going through their minds?

The next morning, Sunday, as I go for a slow 10-mile run around the park, I find myself thinking about them again. It seems insane that they're still out there. And yet, it's somehow wonderful, and I begin to feel a strange, needling envy. I just have to run this race. It feels like the beating epicentre of ultra trail running, the key to unlocking the puzzle. And if I want to be there, I am going to have to play by the rules and run some of the qualifying races on its list.

Over the next few weeks, I while away hours on the internet planning a race schedule, watching race videos; people huddled around nervously at the start, often in the dark, then trundling off into some barren or perilous landscape. The music soars as the camera follows the runners through canyons, desolate tropical beaches, snow blizzards. There are close-ups of people crying, hugging, almost falling over, before it all ends with spine-tingling scenes of exhausted runners crossing the line. Tears of joy this time, children embracing the muddy legs of their parents as the camera pans back across the sky, revealing an epic world, the race logo appearing with a final flourish from the string section.

After a while, the numbers being rattled off begin to seem meaningless; 100km, 200km, 10,000ft of ascent, 36 hours cut-off time. Just numbers. The videos are evidence that it can be done. Just put your name down and work the rest out later.

It's fun to watch people's faces when I tell them I've signed up to do a 100km race.

'It's not that far,' says my work colleague and running companion Kate. 'In a car!' She's right, what am I doing? But the video, watch the video again. These people look normal. There's usually a plucky older guy who makes it. If he can do it . . .

Before I know it my year is filling up with trips to races in California, Italy, South Africa. But the journey begins relatively modestly near my home in Devon in the south-west of England with a 'short' 34-mile ultra along part of England's epic, 630-mile South West Coast Path. It's not that much further than a marathon. It will be a nice easy start.

3

I give myself almost six months to get in shape to tackle the South Devon ultra, which takes place in February, but by Christmas I'm still struggling to build up my training. I haven't yet managed to get out for a run longer than two hours. I need to embrace the early mornings – I see from the increasing number of ultra runners I follow on social media that this is when they train in order to fit it in around the rest of their lives. But it is easy to say. In reality, in the middle of winter, when the alarm goes off at 6 a.m., and you can feel the icy chill outside the duvet, the tiredness rushing back in waves, flooding your whole body, sucking you back down into the bed . . . then it's easy to think: *I'll go later. That will be fine. I need to rest, sleep is important too. Sleep is nice.*

But once the day is up and running, the time gets taken. My three children, Lila, Uma and Ossian, need driving to school, my office expects me to turn up for work, I need to eat, wash up, then I get tired again. I'll go for twice as long the next morning, I tell myself. I'll get up early and go for a big run at 5 a.m. I can do three hours before anyone wakes up.

But I don't. And it repeats.

Of course, I run sometimes. I total around forty miles in

a good week. But it's not enough to start feeling anything like an ultra runner.

This is where I am when my brother, who lives in Edinburgh, challenges me and our other brother to a 25-mile trail race in Scotland. It seems a good chance to test my fitness, to practise running a longish race over rough terrain. It's a good stepping stone to my first ultra. But this is no friendly, 'let's do something together and see if we can get around' type challenge. This is more of a race-to-the-death type challenge.

I'm the eldest of three brothers, all close in age. It was always a tough place to be, forever trying to keep one step ahead. I remember clearly the day in the learner pool, when I was five years old, and my middle brother, Jiva, who was only three, began to swim. In a blur of confused emotions, within five minutes, I too had learned to swim.

The most humiliating moment in my sporting life was the day the swimming club promoted my two brothers to the next-level group ahead of me. I quit swimming that day. And took up running.

I was better at running. Luckily for me, over the years, our sibling rivalry has tended to focus mostly around running. We've completed countless fiercely contested races together. Even our training runs almost always turn into battles by the end. We always agree, before we start, that there will be no racing. But at some point, you just know, someone is going to make a move. I'm not talking about picking up the pace because he feels good, but *making a move*, trying to 'win'. Jiva is especially known for his 'moves', sometimes made right at the start of the run in an effort to catch us on the hop.

My two brothers, Jiva and the youngest, Govinda, are both competent runners. Jiva ran at county level as a school-boy and Govinda has a marathon best of 3hrs 12mins. But I've always had the edge over them. Well, almost. The occasions they've beaten me have gone down in sibling folklore. There was that time in 1997 in Northampton. First Jiva passed me. Then Govinda passed us both. Sure, it was only a friendly Sunday run, but it was the first time I'd ever been beaten by either of them. Over twenty years later, it still comes up regularly at family gatherings.

So when Govinda throws down the latest gauntlet – a race called the Great Wilderness Challenge in the Scottish High-lands – I know it's going to be no picnic. He has recently taken up running through the mountains for fun at the weekends, so I know he fancies his chances. All my previous race victories have come on the hard, sure smoothness of the roads. This race – hilly trail running – is still not my terri-tory. But I have to start somewhere if I'm going to become an ultra runner, and a race against my brothers is the perfect impetus to get me moving.

Suddenly I'm off training in the hills of the nearby Dart-moor national park. My first attempts don't go well. I end up struggling after about 10 miles, barely able to move beyond walking pace. My watch tells me I've been running at a speed I would normally consider a slow jog, but it feels a lot tougher out on the moor. It's not just the hills, but the bumpy, soggy terrain, which jolts you out of any rhythm at every step. I find myself getting annoyed. Occasionally I kick a rock, or one of my legs knocks against the other and I almost stumble, and I find myself cursing. *Whose stupid idea was this?* As soon as I find a bit of road, it feels like coming home, back to what I know. Back to running.

I may be struggling, but Jiva is faring even worse. He lives in London and his job, and moving house, are taking up all his time. And the more we read about the race, the less it seems to be one you can muddle through. Jiva once completed the Edinburgh Marathon with barely any training. But hitting the wall along the seafront in Edinburgh is one thing; it is another to falter out in the Highlands. The race requires runners to carry waterproofs, a map and a compass in case of emergency. This is not a fun run.

In the end he realises he is too unprepared and he pulls out, leaving it as a straight fight, *mano a mano*, between me and mountain man Govinda.

We drive up to the Highlands from Edinburgh the night before the race, arriving in Poolewe, north-west of Inverness, in squalls of driving rain, the mountains hulking silent in the darkness on both sides. The closer we get, the more the wind howls. We both look out the window nervously, not saying anything.

The next morning, the rain is still falling, and when we arrive at the start there is bad news. The weather is so bad that the organisers are changing the route to avoid the most treacherous sections. It turns out that one organiser, while out checking the course the day before, got swept away by a river and is now in hospital. A few weeks later we hear that he has died. The mountains are not to be fooled with, and I for one am not complaining when we are told that instead of a 25-mile run across a section of the Highland's most rugged wilderness, the race has now been cut to a 19-mile out-and-back section, along a route that race veterans are glumly calling the most boring section of the course.

Nobody is happy about the change, and I play along and look disappointed, but I'm secretly thrilled. A flattish 19 miles is much better for me. Not only am I less likely to end up walking, but Govinda's strength is the mountains. He gives me a rueful look – he knows what I'm thinking.

The Great Wilderness Challenge is a small, local race, and so we line up with only around seventy other runners. I'm feeling sprightly as we stand at the start, and looking around I even begin to fancy my chances of winning the overall race. The field doesn't look particularly intimidating.

Govinda is trying to find a quiet moment, taking deep breaths. 'He's stressing too much,' I think, my confidence rising. I have the feeling this is already in the bag.

The beginning of the race is along a narrow trail where, we are told, it is hard to overtake, so we both get out fast. The first mile or so feels frantic, too quick, but Govinda is ahead of me, so I decide to keep up. I can't let him get away.

The path is soggy and rocky, twisty and up and down. It is impossible to get any rhythm.

After about two miles, Govinda makes a mistake and runs wide, following the wrong path. I pounce, racing by him. He is soon back on my heels. I don't need to look behind, I can hear him splash, splashing along. His presence, so close behind, forces me on. I feel good, so I push hard up the hills, through the woods. His splashes begin to drop further and further behind. And each time I dare to glance back – I don't want to give him too much encouragement – he is further back.

By about five miles I am flying. Racing through the brooding landscape. 'Boring', it turns out, is a relative term. The scenery is wild and beautiful. Though it is hard to look at it. Most of the time it is imperative to keep my eyes on the ground as the path is relentlessly boggy and uneven. One misplaced step could be disastrous.

I begin to relax. In some ways, it is a shame Govinda hasn't put up more of a fight. I'm glad he hasn't, of course, but it is almost too easy. We're reaching the halfway point already. This is a breeze.

Down the steep section to the turning around point, a few people catch me. Watching the ground I'm not aware who they are, but I can tell they are itching to get past. Rather than hold them up, I run up on the grass beside the path to let them by. One, two, three, they go by.

'Go on, Dhar,' says the last one.

Huh? It's Govinda.

They make the turn and start coming back, and he runs past without looking at me. As I turn and begin to clamber back up the way we came, my legs feel suddenly heavy. I can't find the strength to even try to stay with him. I can only watch as he starts to pull away, looking strong, like a man making his move. I am done. I have nothing.

I struggle on gamely. I have vague thoughts that he might blow up and come back to me, although I know it's unlikely. And also, in my charitable moments, I think it would be a shame if he did. I resign myself to running my own race, but it is a long nine miles back to the finish.

By the time I get there, Govinda is already changed, cheering me over the line. He says afterwards that he kept thinking I was going to come back past him, so he kept pushing hard. In the end he beat me by over 15 minutes. It was an annihilation.

Later, on the way home, he phones his wife. 'How did it go?' I hear her ask. 'I won,' he says. 'You won the race?' she asks. No, he didn't win the actual race. But he won the race that mattered. He beat his big brother.

So, well done to Govinda, but it isn't a great start for me. I realise that I need to get out on the trails more often, to learn to run up and down wet, muddy hills. To run with a pack on my back. Even though this race was only 19 miles, it was a long way from a road marathon.

Luckily, living in south Devon, I have the moor and 100-odd miles of coast path to train on. I just have to get out there. Embrace the early mornings.

By the time my ultra race rolls around a few weeks later, I'm feeling a little fitter, a little sharper, but I have still never run more than a marathon in one go. Even in Oman, no single stage was longer than 26.2 miles, so this is, in some ways, my first bona fide ultra marathon. Will my body hold out? There is only one way to find out.

The day before the coastal ultra, there's a knock at my door. I open it on a striking-looking man: 5ft 10in tall, a big, rust-orange beard, long hair plaited at the front across his forehead, and a huge grin.

It's Tom Payn, a good friend of mine.[1] He has travelled down from Essex to join me for the race. He's also planning to run the UTMB and is in the hunt for points. We can be a team.

Tom is a serious runner and I already know that he's likely to win the race tomorrow. In fact he tells me that he has never lost an ultra race in the UK.

I first met Tom in Kenya when he was the fourth-fastest marathon runner in the UK. It was 2011 and he had given up a desk job at a water filtration company in Portsmouth to pursue his dream of qualifying for the London Olympics. He spent six months living in a Kenyan training camp in the small town of Iten, coping with cold showers, a hole in the ground for a loo, a tiny shared room, and beans and rice for lunch every day. He didn't quite cut the striking figure he does today, but he had a friendly face and a chirpy, generous nature, always willing to see the bright side of situations.

---

[1] See *Running with the Kenyans* and *The Way of the Runner*.

Which was just as well because when he returned from his six months in the Rift Valley, he ran a full ten minutes slower than his best time and missed out on the Olympics.

'I actually ran my slowest ever marathon right after Kenya,' he says. Obviously disappointed, it left him feeling lost with his running. 'I wasn't really sure what to do next.'

But a page had been turned in his life and there was no way he was going to give up and return to his nine-to-five office job. Using his Kenyan contacts, he got a job with an athlete management company, taking elite Kenyans to races around the world, looking after them, training with them, pacing them in the big races. He even lived in a flat in London that acted as a lodging house for the Kenyan athletes when they came to Europe to race. But it still didn't quite work out for him on the roads, and by the time he comes to stay with me in Devon, his best marathon time is still the 2hrs 17mins he ran back in his days as an office worker in Portsmouth.

Yet here is a man brimming with vitality. A lot has happened since those post-Kenya days. In particular, he has taken up ultra running, and has met Rachel, his fiancée. Both things have had a huge impact on him.

'Ultimately, the life I was living, where running and training had become something I had to do rather than something I wanted to do, led to an early, and short-lived, retirement,' he tells me as I cook up a pasta surprise in our small cottage kitchen. 'So when I started running again, and took up ultra running, I vowed I would only run because I loved it, and that love of running has been there ever since.'

The switch to ultra running began almost by accident. 'Not long after my "retirement",' he says, 'I had the idea of trying to run from where I lived in London back to my mum and dad's house in Tiptree, in Essex. I had no idea how far it was but I knew it was longer than a marathon. For the first time since I joined my local athletics club as a nine-year-old, I wasn't following a training plan, and so I realised I could run as far, and as fast – or slow – as I wanted.'

So he woke up one morning, put on his shoes and a back-pack containing a few energy bars and a bottle of water, and set off. 'I felt free, no pressure, took it easy when I wanted and pushed a little if I felt good. I soon hit marathon distance, then 30 miles. Feeling good but with slightly sore feet, I arrived at Chelmsford, where the sight of the train was too tempting, so I hopped on for the final 15 miles.'

As soon as he did this, however, he regretted it, so the next week he packed his bag again and ran the full 56 miles to Tiptree in around seven hours. 'It was such a great feeling to travel that sort of distance by foot, and it wasn't long before I signed up for my first ultra, the Ring O' Fire, a 135-mile race around the island of Anglesey.' He won the race by over three hours.

Tom was still mainly focused on road marathons, however, when he turned up at a trendy Adidas-sponsored event in south London a year later.

Before the run, Tom says he saw a woman he recognised from the track where he trained. 'We had a quick chat, and I thought "I'd better run fast tonight".' Keen to impress, Tom made sure he won. 'I went up to her after and said: "I won!" But she didn't seem very impressed.'

Things went better the next time he saw Rachel at an elimination-style race called Wings for Life. In this the runners set off and are followed thirty minutes later by a car moving at 15km/h and slowly getting faster. Once runners get overtaken by the car, they are pulled out and taken back to the start, where everyone watches the rest of the race on a big screen. Tom, of course, won.

'Because I was the last one running, everyone was watching me,' he explains. He was the hero of the day. Rachel sat looking on with growing admiration. 'She put something up on Facebook saying "Cheering Tom Payn" and tagged me. After the race she came over and gave me a big hug. So I asked her out.'

Rachel and Tom have since inspired each other to give up their jobs, buy a yellow VW Beetle, move to France and take up ultra running full time. Oh, and they're now both vegan. And engaged. It's been quite a few years. I've seen it play out largely on social media, watching on as Tom's hair grew longer, his grin wider and the backdrops to his life bigger, more colourful and more epic. Tom and Rachel have even bought a flat in Chamonix, the ultra running capital of Europe, the base for the UTMB, where they live during the summer when the running is good, and rent the flat out during the ski season – when they head off to Kenya and Morocco to run.

'Why Morocco?' I ask him.

'We're quite impulsive,' he says. 'We just tend to go with our heart. We wanted somewhere warm to go in February and March and thought, where would be good? When we got there it was freezing.'

Despite the unexpected coldness, the following-the-heart business has worked out pretty well. A few months before he turns up at my house, Tom was selected to run for Great Britain in the World Trail Championships. Pulling on a British vest was something he had been striving for since he was a child, and finally, when perhaps he thought his moment had passed, he had achieved it. His mum and Rachel travelled out to Portugal to watch him race.

'It was the happiest day of my life,' he says, his voice quivering a little. 'I cried at the finish.'

The next morning we leave the house at 6 a.m., driving through the narrow lanes to the start of the race. I'm supposed to be navigating, but I keep getting us lost as I'm more preoccupied with selecting the right pre-race music.

The official parking is a large residential area on the edge of a village a few miles from the coast. It's like a silent dawn invasion as the usually undisturbed streets fill up with cars, doors opening, one after the other, men and women in tights and running jackets stepping out. Any uninformed resident peeking through the curtains must be wondering what on Earth is happening. At the end of the road a queue of people wait for the buses to ferry us to the start.

A few people try to start conversations. 'Did you see the rain yesterday?' But no one has the stomach for much chatting. The task ahead of us looms. Tom is munching on a fruit bar. Six days earlier he ran the Marrakech Marathon, pacing the elite women to 30km before 'jogging in' to finish in 2hrs 35mins. He says he's quite tired and doesn't have a plan for the race.

'Sometimes I go off really hard for the first few miles and then relax,' he says.

'To scare everyone?'

He laughs. 'I guess so.'

All around you can see people clocking him. He just looks fast, even at a casual glance. He is skinny, of course, and wiry, but it is more than that. He almost seems to be from a different world. The grey drabness that can settle over busy, working lives, that can make our skin pasty, our eyes tired, doesn't seem to touch him. He looks like a cartoon super-hero, with his flaming hair and general brightness.

Inside the registration tent a person with a clipboard asks Tom his surname. 'Payn,' he says. He even has a superhero name – though admittedly it does sound a little sinister.

'That's a good name for an ultra runner,' says the man with the clipboard.

With all the wrong turns driving to the race, we don't have any time for a warm-up, and before we know it we're being called to the start. I follow Tom right to the front and stand next to him in the middle under the starting arch. I'm enjoying piggy-backing on his aura for a few moments, aware of the nervous glances coming our way. I slap him fondly on the shoulder.

'Let's do this!'

The countdown is already on. Three, two, one . . . and like that the ball is set rolling. The journey to Chamonix and the UTMB has begun.

Tom races off across the field like he left the gas on at home. Everyone lets him go, watching him dart through the gap in the hedge at the top of the field, never to be seen again.

I take my time, making sure I'm not pushing myself already, jogging slowly up the first hill.

We come out along a cliff top, the sea big and bristling, the waves rolling in and crashing on the rocks somewhere below us. It's a fairly still day but the ground is soggy and slippery. All week the wind and rain has been pounding the coast, soaking the trails. A few days earlier, the forecast had been for heavy rain and dangerously high winds. Luckily the storm has blown itself out, but its ravages are marked underfoot.

My trail shoes, unfortunately, are designed for dry, hard-packed trails, not mud. I use them because most of my training runs include some roads too, and on hard surfaces the heavy-duty trail shoes clack along uncomfortably like football boots. So I thought these would be a good half-way measure, but I'm slipping and sliding all over the place. Already I decide that my primary goal is to make it through the race without gashing my knees on some jagged rock along the way.

Running at a relatively slow pace means that for much of the first 10 miles, when I'm not watching the ground to make sure I stay on my feet, I can enjoy the scenery, the sharp cliffs and sandy coves, the churning sea that fills your nose with its smell, the spray from the waves almost like a mist at times drifting across the trail.

At around 10 miles the first serious pang of tiredness hits me. I grab a protein ball from my bag and take a few bites. One of the most common things I've heard in my nascent investigation into ultra running is that it is basically 'an eating competition with some running thrown in'. In an ultra marathon you are going to run out of energy and you are going to have to replace it with food. It is possible to get through some of the shorter ultras on energy gels, but too many gels can make you feel sick after a while. It's better to eat some real food. Of course, this is not as simple as it may sound. Not only is running and eating at the same time a test of dexterity, it can also upset your stomach. So you need to practise, and find out which foods work for you. Then, as I find out later in some of my longer races, it can become difficult, after ten, twenty or thirty hours of running, to even move your jaw to chew, or to generate enough saliva to actually swallow food.

For now, however, eating is no problem. My biggest worry as I chug along is that one of my recent niggles will flare up at some point. I rarely go for a run without feeling some little twinge, and I have visions of ending up sitting by the side of the trail, much like in Oman, as yet another person runs by saying: 'Come on, you can do it.'

But the legs are fine so far, and I find myself starting to overtake people. Maybe I've been running too slowly? I work out that I'm in about eighth position and decide for some reason that my goal is to finish in the top ten. It just pops into my head unsolicited, but once it's there it becomes chiselled in stone. Race goal: top ten.

And so I start racing. When I stop to relieve myself in

the bushes at one point, and two runners pass me, I quickly get running again and pass them back. At a water station, while other runners stop to refill their bottles, or grab a few biscuits, I keep moving, making ground.

After about 14 miles, the course heads inland, crossing muddy farm fields, ancient unused cart tracks and some regular paved roads. At times I find myself running with someone and we get chatting. It's strange to be in a race but still have the energy to chat. The tiredness is in the legs, the body, from the cumulative grind of the hills, the mud, the time on your feet. But there isn't the gasping breathlessness of shorter races.

And so we talk, until someone takes a downhill quicker, or stops for a drink, and then I'm alone again, with just the grass, the trees and the cows. At one point I run by a hunt, the riders in their red jackets looking down disdainfully as I struggle by, the dogs milling around excitedly. I hope they don't mistake me for a wounded animal.

I reach 24 miles in just over four hours and for some reason decide that my goal is no longer to finish in the top ten, but to beat six hours. I'm beginning to suffer now, my legs taking shorter and shorter strides, as though some invisible band is tightening around them, and I don't want to be worrying about people passing me, as I'm sure they will. But I need something to focus me.

A few weeks before, I noticed that the women's course record was 6hrs 6mins, and someone on Twitter saw me posting about the race and told me I should try to beat that. I didn't even know the person, but his tweet pops into my head. So I push out the top ten target and replace it with a new goal to finish in under six hours. It's a nice round number. All I have to do is cover the last 10 miles in two hours. Surely I can do that. People can pass me if they want.

Why do I need a goal at all? Why not just keep running? Isn't just finishing enough? I don't quite know, but just to finish, well, I could do that by walking. But something in me knows I'll be disappointed in myself if I just amble in. I need to push myself, that's why I'm here. I need to force myself to fight, to compete. Otherwise it is just a long walk, a day out. And that wouldn't feel right. This is a race and I need to race it.

The next few miles are completely flat, along an exposed stretch of beach. The village at the end doesn't seem to get any closer as I grind on. My legs are aching, my form hunched, shuffling. I must look terrible. It is now becoming as much a mental challenge as a physical one. I have to keep chasing away negative thoughts, like some scullery keeper with his broom, chasing away pesky mice.

'Maybe I'm just not cut out for this sort of thing' . . . 'I'm just not a tough guy, why pretend?' . . . 'Think how great it would be to stop.'

Go! Go! Shoo! Shoo! The fact that my body is holding together gives me strength. Nothing has broken or snapped. And so does the fact that, after four and a half hours, I'm still actually running and not walking.

After the long beach it is back up on the cliffs, up and down. The ups are really taking their toll on me now, most of them forcing me into a walk/run tango.

The race cruelly passes the finish point at around 27 miles before heading out for another seven-mile loop. A wave of emotion hits me as I run through the small seaside village of Beesands by the finish. I want to see Marietta, who said she was coming to watch the end of the race. I suddenly want a hug, to be told that I can do it. But I can't see her. I almost get tearful when I see our car parked up, but no sign of Marietta. To make matters worse, no one else offers any encouragement. People are gathering for the finish of the race, parking their cars, buying fish and chips, fixing leads on their dogs. I seem to be invisible. I feel I could cry.

'It's too early for that,' I tell myself, pulling myself together. As we head out on the final loop, one runner overtakes me, and then another. I really don't want swarms of people to pass me now, not after all this. So I grit my teeth and run on. A few desperately slow miles up big humping cliffs start putting my six-hour target in jeopardy. But on I grind. God, will this never end? Somehow no one else passes me. Where are they? I begin to fear the sight of a figure in the distance behind me. I'm like a convict on the run, hoping no one is closing in. But each time I look back, thankfully the path is empty.

My feet are soaked to a pulp, I've run out of water to drink, my legs are no longer legs but two iron stilts attached to my hips, with a useless moving mechanism that has got itself stuck. My arms pump the levers but they barely move.

And then, at the top of yet another muddy track, I see a beautiful sign. It reads: 'One mile to go.' I look back. Still no one. I have sweet visions of collapsing across the line and lying in the grass.

On I go. It's all downhill from here. As I enter the final field where it all started hours before, I find myself surrounded by runners finishing the marathon and half-marathon, which have all been taking place at the same time. I want a clear run at the finish, so I start sprinting down the hill, chasing a gap in the crowd. Make way for the ultra runner! I do it, flying across the line, collapsing in the soft grass. Marietta is there. 'Well done, well done.' She's taking pictures and smiling. It's over. 'Tom is about to get his prize,' she says.

I glance over at the man with the flame-red hair and bright yellow jacket.

'And our winner,' says the voice on the PA system, 'by a huge distance, 23 minutes ahead of second place, is Tom Payn.'

A polite ripple of applause. I sit up. We did it. We bloody well did it.

And so, with that, I become, officially, an ultra runner. In the end I achieved both arbitrary goals: I finish in tenth place in 5hrs 51mins. It is a great start. My body, though aching, is still in one piece. We hobble down to the seafront and get some chips, before clambering into the car to drive home. As we're pulling out of the car park, I spot an ultra runner coming through. I remember passing here, with no one cheering, and seven miles still to go.

'Go on,' I shout from the car window. 'You can do it.'

The man glances up, and perhaps guesses, from the tired look on my face, the medal around my neck, the bag of chips, that I've finished and I'm going home. He smiles.

'Bastard,' he says.

4

A few weeks after my coastal ultra I meet up again with Elisabet Barnes, this time for a training run. I need to see how an ultra runner does a 'long' run. The plan is to recce a section of an upcoming ultra marathon called Country to Capital, a 45-mile race from the Chiltern Hills in Buckinghamshire to Little Venice in central London.

Right from the moment we landed in Oman, Elisabet stood out among the excited scurry of runners. She was clearly there to win. Rather than looking around with tourist eyes, taking it all in, joking nervously about her lack of training, like the rest of us, she was business-like in everything, asking the race officials questions, nodding attentively to the answers.

During the race, while the rest of us shook our heads in disbelief at the end of each stage, collapsing in heaps on the ground, the serious athletes like Elisabet crossed the line with a steely look and immediately started preparing post-run drinks, food, already focused on recovering, ready for the next day.

By accident Elisabet found herself in a tent with mostly young Omani men. She had just plonked herself in the corner of a tent with no care for who else would join her. The rest of us looked for a tent with our buddies, or the people we had already connected with in the first hours. We then kept these tent partners for the full six days of the race. I had zoned in on the only other English guy in the race and had jumped in with his tent. It turned out to be a good choice. In the afternoons we sat around joking and telling stories. In her tent, Elisabet sat alone, preparing her food, sleeping, staring out at the desert, while the men in her tent chatted together.

She wasn't completely antisocial and was happy to chat if you stopped by, but she rarely ventured out around the camp in search of company. She seemed to like her space. And, of course, she was conserving energy.

I found out before the race that we had both run the London Marathon that year in exactly the same time – 2hrs 50mins. So I thought she would be a good person to run with. Partly I was thinking about stopping myself going too fast. A number of studies have established that women are better at pacing themselves in races than men. Most of these studies only speculate about why this is, and suppose that it is men overestimating their abilities and going off too fast, while women tend to underplay their abilities. One study of finishers at the Houston Marathon confirmed this theory by comparing the final data with the runners' own predicted finishing times. It concluded that poor pacing by men was 'in part explained by [their] overconfidence'.

I'm regularly guilty of this. As soon as a race begins, I seem to think I'm Superman, that I can take this, just try holding me back. My recent crash in the Great Wilderness Challenge, where I even thought I might win the race outright, was just the latest case in point.

So each day in Oman I'd start off running beside Elisabet, to slow myself down. I would last a few minutes, before I'd start falling behind, the sand sucking my legs down, siphoning off any pretence at running, while Elisabet powered away from me, relentless, her quick, shuffling step ploughing through the sand like some small traction engine. Each day she beat me by huge margins, sometimes hours. Our similar marathon-running abilities had no bearing in the desert.

It is many months later when we meet for our training run, in Marylebone Station in London. She isn't hard to spot, standing out among all the black and grey suits and jackets in a bright orange running top and headband. We take a train out of London to the start of the route for the Country to Capital race, which is due to take place a week later. A few years ago Elisabet ran it and broke the course record, but this year she's just using the race as a hard workout, as she builds up to bigger challenges ahead. Despite being a desert specialist, and professing to a hatred of hills and mud, Elisabet is also targeting the Mont Blanc race, the UTMB. It is a hard race to avoid when you start becoming a serious ultra runner. It sits there like the grand final at the top of the season, the race of champions. To help her prepare, she has lined up a little 100-mile stage race later in the year in Nepal, called the Everest Trail Race.

One of her first ultras, she tells me, spotting my surprise that she is planning some mountain races, was the Petite Trotte à Léon (PTL), the longest race at the UTMB festival – a more technical, 300km loop of Mont Blanc. She says it is more of a mountaineering race than a running race. It's also a team competition, and she entered it with her husband, more for the experience than with any thoughts of being competitive.

'We shouldn't really even have attempted it,' she says. They didn't make it to the end. 'In hindsight we could have finished, but we made some irrational decisions after four days with only two hours' sleep and hallucinating.'

Listening to her account of the race, it sounds like they were lucky to get out alive. In the dark one night, a group of people above them on a scree slope set a rock tumbling down the mountain. 'We couldn't do anything as if you move fast on that terrain you slide and fall and most likely die,' she says. 'We were standing only a few feet apart and the rock went between the two of us.'

It has been a long time since she raced in the mountains, but she's excited by the idea of the UTMB. 'It's always interesting to push your boundaries,' she says. 'If you always succeed you don't know where your limits are.'

Since I last saw Elisabet, she has run the Marathon des Sables again, but this time she only finished fourth. She says she had concerns about one of the other athletes, that her bag was too light, that someone else was acting as a 'mule' and carrying stuff for her – such as extra food – in their bags. She says it is annoying and, to her, unethical, but that as long as a runner is carrying the required kit they're not technically breaking any rules.

I had this suspicion in Oman. Not that it mattered to me, of course, but every day the leaders in the men's race lined up with tiny rucksacks a quarter the size of mine. Yet they sat together with their friends each evening to share food and they seemed to eat well. Of course, they weren't carrying unnecessary protein bars and a pillow – but still, their packs seemed incredibly small.

Elisabet's life was changed by winning the MdS in 2015. Suddenly she had a sponsor, she was invited to races across the world, she became a name, a personality. And as the rewards for success in this nascent sport grow year on year, so do the incentives to bend or break the rules.

One of the most infamous examples was the downfall of Londoner Rob Young. After watching Mo Farah run the London Marathon in 2014, he bet his wife 20p that he could run fifty marathons. She retorted that he was too lazy to run one, and he freely admits, in the book he wrote about it, that he was untrained and had always been a terrible runner. But the next morning he went to his local park at dawn and ran a marathon. Then, that same afternoon, after a full day in the office, he completed another marathon around the same park, this time even faster. The next morning, less than twenty-fours hours after his first run, he says he ran his third marathon, this one in an impressive time of 3hrs 19mins.

Discovering an unexpected running prowess, he was off. He ended up running 370 marathons in a year. He then broke Dean Karnazes's world record for running without sleep, completing 373 miles non-stop. TV news channels lined up to interview him. His book, *Marathon Man*, was well received, with *The Times* calling it 'an astonishing story'.

Keen to do more crazy running, Young announced in 2016 that his next goal was to break the TransAmerica record for running across the US, which had stood since 1980. After all his incredible feats, people were excited to see what he could do. However, early on in his run, suspicions started being voiced online about the validity of his progress. Poring over screen grabs from his GPS watch posted on Facebook, critics said he was running implausibly fast and far each day, especially when he looked so fresh in his photographs.

Things got really stirred up when, late one night, a man called Asher Delmott, who was following Young's live tracker online, spotted that Young was passing close to his small hometown of Lebo in Kansas. According to Delmott's account, which was posted on the website letsrun.com, he thought Young might be lonely, so he headed out in his car intending to run a few miles with him. What he found, however, was Young's support vehicle moving along the road at running pace, but no sign of Young. He says he passed back and forth, and drove up and down the road, without seeing any sign of anyone running.

After Delmott's story was posted online, things started to turn nasty. In his book, Young told of the extreme abuse he had suffered as a child at the hands of his father, including having a nail hammered through his foot. It was this, he said, that had taught him to block out pain, and that had got him through his incredible ultra-running feats. Also, everything he did was to raise money for a children's charity. To many people, he was a hero and an inspiration and they wanted to believe in him.

To try to get to the bottom of it all, a posse of ultra runners calling themselves The Geezers decided to track Young in person, following him in a car as he continued, despite the allegations, on his run across America. Led by legendary race director Gary 'Lazarus Lake' Cantrell, they found Young out on the road moving, running, walking, but in a state of rapid deterioration, his pace much slower than in his incredible early days when the suspicions began to arise. After five days, Cantrell said he had a lot of respect for Young's efforts, but he didn't believe he was capable of the feats he claimed in the early days of the run. At one point, The Geezers saw Young fall face-down on a road, cutting his forehead. When his crew reached him, his face was covered in blood and he was asleep. But he got up and carried on running.

In the end, Young had to abandon his contentious record attempt after 34 days, not because of the allegations but because of a fractured toe, as well as cellulitis – a painful and potentially serious skin infection.

And that might have been that, but with all the accusations flying around, the sponsors of Young's record attempt, the compression-wear company Skins, decided to investigate. They employed two respected sports scientists, Roger Pielke Jr, of the University of Colorado Boulder, and Ross Tucker, of the University of the Free State in South Africa, to assess Young's GPS data. The pair pored over the data and interviewed key witnesses to produce a 110-page report. Its findings were damning, saying there was little doubt that Young had cheated by receiving 'unauthorised assistance – most likely in the form of riding in or on a vehicle for large parts of the attempt'.

The smoking gun, they said, was his cadence data, which measured how many steps he took per minute. At times in those first days, before Delmott's posting on letsrun. com, Young's watches were recording impossible times and numbers, such as a stride length at times over 40 metres long. After the letsrun.com posting and all the attention that followed, his pace and stride length returned to normal. This change, and the fact it coincided with the sudden scrutiny, they said, ruled out the possibility that the watches were simply faulty.

Young continued to maintain his innocence, but he could offer no explanation for the cadence data. Skins fully accepted Pielke and Tucker's report, severing all ties with Young and saying they were 'extremely disappointed'.

It's a sorry tale, but Young is far from alone in boasting of unlikely and ultimately unbelievable feats of ultra running. In 2018, a former beauty queen, Maude Gorman from Massachusetts, even managed to cheat her way on to the US team for the Skyrunning World Championships. It was again online sleuths who detected discrepancies in her results, showing she had taken shortcuts in some of her races. She was forced to hand back a number of prizes and she was removed from the national team.

Another recent case is that of Kelly Agnew, who raised suspicions with strong results in a string of ultra marathons in the US, including winning a 48-hour race by 55 miles despite stopping before the end.

Suspicious of his amazing results, at another 48-hour race in Arizona, which was run in laps of a one-mile loop, the officials decided to pay close attention to his movements. One of them witnessed Agnew in the dead of the night crossing the timing mat at the end of a lap, before heading into a portaloo beside the track, waiting there for seven minutes, and then re-emerging and crossing the timing mat again – and so registering another lap despite not having gone anywhere.

The question everyone has when they hear stories like this is: why would anyone do that? The feeling among the ultra running community is one of incredulity. Ultra running likes to think of itself as a sport full of good guys, people willing to push themselves into a pulp for hours and days on end for no reward. They do it because they want to find their limits, to discover something about themselves, to experience a life fully lived. Why would anyone cheat at that? You would only be cheating yourself. How could you live with yourself? There is no prize money, in most cases, no TV coverage, no adulating fans. It doesn't make sense.

'It sounds like something Mr Bean would do,' says Marietta when I tell her about Agnew's stunt in the portaloo. Yes, I can imagine Mr Bean doing something like that. Perhaps in some people, that inner Mr Bean, that devious urge to cut corners, to come out on top even in the most trivial and minor of circumstances, even if it's only to impress the one man and his dog who have turned up to watch, is strong enough to make them cheat.

These days, of course, we don't really do anything for the people around us. We do it for the virtual audience we imagine are sitting at their laptops waiting patiently for our next trick, to clap and give us the thumbs up when we impress them with our feats. Running an ultra marathon is a sure-fire way to make an impression on social media. Win one, or place highly, or record a fast time, and things can really start to escalate.

Run 370 marathons in a year, race across America, and you start to find the rewards multiplying pretty rapidly as people log on to post messages telling you that you're an inspiration, that you have changed their lives.

To try to understand why someone would cheat in a low-key running race, *Runner's World* journalist Duncan Craig decided to cheat in a 5km parkrun by cutting out a section of the course. It was the smallest of small-scale cheating, and he soon owned up to it and got his result annulled. In his article, he neatly captures his feelings before the race, as he thinks about the new fast time he will soon be able to claim: 'My social media network is full of runners, quick runners. Wait until they get a load of this.'

The science behind cheating is fascinating and numerous studies across the years have found that most of us will cheat given the right circumstances and if the opportunity to get away with it presents itself. Many of the circumstances that scientists say make us more likely to cheat, such as being in the dark, being tired and sleep deprived, are familiar to ultra runners. In many smaller ultras, the lack of markings, marshals and strict race controls also means that getting away with it is easier than in most other sports.

Dr Dan Ariely, of Duke University in North Carolina, says we will cheat if we can justify it to ourselves. In his book *The Truth About Dishonesty*, he says humans are storytelling creatures by nature, and that we will tell ourselves story after story until we come up with an explanation that sounds reasonable and believable.

Cheating, psychologists say, is especially easy to justify when you frame situations to cast yourself as a victim of some kind of unfairness. Then it becomes a matter of evening the score; you're not cheating, you're restoring fairness.

Elite track coach Steve Magness, on his blog 'The Science of Running', writes: 'We all cheat. But only how much we can get away with while still telling ourselves we are good, decent people. There are very few people walking around thinking in their head that they are a horrible person.

'Think about the cheats like Lance Armstrong. To the end, he didn't truly feel like he was cheating. He rationalized it by stating that everyone was doing it so the line was shifted. This is what happens with every person.'

I contacted Dr Ariely to ask him why people would cheat in ultra running, when there seems so little to gain since the sport, even at a high level, is primarily about personal achievement and finding your own limits rather than any material rewards.

'In general people don't cheat for material gain,' he said. 'We cheat to think about ourselves differently, to feel more pride in ourselves . . . it's about wanting to see reality in a certain way, seeing ourselves as more successful, faster, or whatever.'

He says most people who are caught will truly believe that they haven't cheated. 'People will find a way to rationalise it so they can say they didn't cheat. "I lost two minutes here, so I just gained two minutes there" or "it was hard to find the way in the dark".'

Dr Ariely didn't know anything about Rob Young's case, but it is interesting to note that even after the damning Skins report, Young continued to stress that whatever else went wrong, he wasn't a cheat. 'I certainly made mistakes,' he said, in his last statement on the affair before he disappeared from public view. 'But I did not cheat.'

It is easy to mock and ridicule low-level cheats, but

perhaps we should be more understanding. Like Rob Young, Maude Gorman says she suffered abuse as a child. Perhaps at the bottom of all this is simply the need for love and attention. People may say they would never cheat, but perhaps they have enough stability and loving support in their life. Perhaps they were raised in a loving family. Skins were keen to point this fact out when they cut their contract with Young. 'The findings are clear and we absolutely accept them,' said Jamie Fuller, the chief executive of Skins. 'But we must remember that beyond being a runner [Young] is a human being. In my view his background means there are special circumstances.'

He is a human being, and he is fallible and in that he is not alone. The Comrades Marathon in South Africa, which bills itself as 'the ultimate human race', puts undisclosed timing mats out on its course each year to catch the multitude of people who try to claim that they completed the famous race when instead they hopped in a car or on a motorbike and rejoined the race further along the course.

Of course, the most prevalent method of winning by foul means in sport is doping. Until recently, the ugly shadow of drugs hadn't reared its head over the happily low-key and niche world of ultra running, but it was only a matter of time. The idea that ultra running only attracted people competing with the purest of intentions, all done in a spirit of respect and close camaraderie with their fellow runners, was shattered when British ultra runner Robbie Britton noticed that a competitor who had recently finished fifth at the UTMB, the Ecuadorian Gonzalo Calisto, appeared on the IAAF's list of banned athletes.

It was only when Britton put this information on social media that the UTMB even found out about it and subsequently disqualified Calisto and amended the race results. In what can only be described as a shambles, even though the test was actually carried out at the UTMB, the race was never informed that Calisto had been found with Erythropoietin (EPO) in his sample.

'The whole Calisto story is a bit ridiculous,' says Britton when I ask him about it, 'as testing positive for EPO actually in the race is pretty stupid. If there's someone getting caught for it on race day, then there will certainly be more who are a bit smarter.'

Britton is a world 24-hour running bronze medallist, he lives in Chamonix and is a coach as well as an athlete. He's one of the most outspoken anti-doping voices in the sport. I ask him how much of a problem he thinks it is in ultra running.

'All sports most likely have some cheats, ultra running included. We've had people taking shortcuts, not carrying the mandatory kit, all sorts. It doesn't just have to be doping. There were even two twins at Comrades who swapped their timing chips halfway.

'People who say there's no money in ultra running, so why would anyone cheat, aren't thinking about it enough. A lot of people in our sport come from a decent background anyway. It's ego and a form of laziness and impatience.'

He says the problem will only get worse in the future. 'More money, more "fame", that Instagram lifestyle, more pressure from sponsors. All that is growing. And people in the sport are getting faster, so weak people will make excuses.

We have people who have been banned previously but it seems to have been forgotten.'

But even Britton, who is never afraid to call someone out, says he still doesn't think doping has become endemic in ultra running.

'I put that down to the personalities and the openness of the athletes,' he says. 'You can really believe in a lot of them. Some people might see that as naive, but we just don't have the anti-doping infrastructure to look at it any other way.'

I ask Elisabet about doping, as we travel on the train to the start of our run. Does she think it's a big problem in the sport?

'I'm sure better testing would reveal more cases,' she says. 'Why wouldn't there be? It exists in every sport, it's not like ultra runners are a different breed of people. Sure, there's not big money in the sport yet, but there are sponsors, fame, glory . . . If you get a taste of it, you want more, and there will always be those willing to go to extremes to get it.'

Has she ever been tempted, knowing she is unlikely to get caught?

'I like to think I have strong ethics,' she says. 'That's how I was raised. Cheating has never interested me in anything. Be a good person and good things will come to you. It's simple.'

It's a damp squib of a morning as we arrive in the small town of Denton for the start of our run. A grey drizzle hangs in the air, draining all the colour from the world.

The drab suburban streets surrounding the station do little to brighten the mood, but we're soon running beyond the houses and heading into the woods.

Elisabet is an unusual ultra runner in that she doesn't often run on the trails. 'I hate mud,' she says, as we squidge and squelch our way along the trail. 'But it's lovely to be out in the woods for a change.' She lives in Westcliff-on-Sea in Essex and her usual stomping ground is the town's promenade. If she's going to make a mark in the UTMB she's going to have to get used to this sort of thing.

This run is a useful recce for her upcoming race as runners are required to navigate the route themselves. She has an app on her watch that points out the general direction. However, despite that we still manage to go the wrong way numerous times. 'Some people like finding the way and using a map,' she says. 'I hate it.'

Ultra running is a wide and broad church. It is running, sure, but it can also be hiking, mountaineering and map reading. But I agree with Elisabet, I'm happiest when the route is marked – which luckily is the case at the UTMB and most of the other races I'm lining up.

We trundle along at a leisurely pace for over three hours, chatting and stopping now and then for a bite to eat. Today I'm experimenting with chocolate-covered hazelnuts and dried mango. They both taste delicious after a few hours' running. After we finish, covering 21 miles back towards London to another train station, we stop off in a mini supermarket. I feel like I could eat everything in the shop, but limit myself to a fizzy drink and a flapjack. It tastes heavenly. Perhaps part of the appeal of ultra running is simply getting ravenously hungry and then stepping into a shop full of brightly packaged food with a five-pound note in your pocket. Elisabet can't resist a Pepsi Max. 'Don't tell anyone,' she says. Clearly it isn't an integral part of her ultra running diet, but at the end of a 21-mile run, anything goes. Pick your worst, guiltiest secret and tuck in joyously. I decide to go wild, indulging my dark side and reaching for a Wispa chocolate bar. Don't tell anyone, OK?

Over the next few months, I edge up my training volume. I get myself a coach, Tom Craggs, who sets me a schedule. However, despite the best intentions, I struggle to follow it very closely. Tom is understanding, constantly tweaking things whenever I write to him telling him I haven't quite managed to keep up with all the running he has set me. I seem to be constantly making excuses and promising to catch up, when before I know it my next race is upon me.

It's a 100km (62-mile) race in California, called the Miwok 100K, and it's worth four UTMB points – to qualify I need to accumulate fifteen points over three races.

By the time I board my flight to America, my longest training run is still the 21 miles with Elisabet, with my longest ever run the 34-mile ultra in Devon. So this race will be a journey into the unknown, almost twice as far as I have ever run before. And all in the coastal mountain range north of San Francisco Bay.

But before I get to California, I have an invite to visit a top ultra runner in Colorado. I contacted him on Facebook, when I was looking for people to interview during my trip to the US.

'Come and stay,' he wrote back, offering to put me up for a few days and inviting me to train with him. I said I'd be delighted to, and so I asked him where he lived.

'I live in an off-grid cabin halfway up Pikes Peak mountain,' he replied. 'There aren't any roads, so you have to run or hike six miles up the trail to get to us.' It sounds wild. I tell him I'll see him there.

5

I close the boot of the hire car and stand looking up at the mountains. Beyond the raised wooden houses of Manitou Springs, with their postcard verandas, the peaks rise in jagged points. Pine trees cover the lower slopes, while in the far distance the tops are white with snow. On the drive here from Denver, the radio has been warning of a big storm moving in, dumping four feet of snow up on the mountains. That's where I'm headed – six miles up, to a small wooden hut in the woods and home to one of the world's top ultra runners, Zach Miller.

In elite ultra trail running there are, broadly speaking, two main domains: Europe and the USA. In Europe, the trails are considered rough and technical, and are dominated by mountain men, Alpinists such as Kilian Jornet and François D'Haene. In the US, the trails tend to be smoother, more runnable, and the scene here is slowly being taken over by a bunch of young stars with a background in track or road running, guys like Jim Walmsley and women like former US Olympic marathon runner Magda Boulet.

Zach, at twenty-nine, is young for an ultra runner, and he was a track athlete at college. He has an unusual story of how he got into the sport, but before he can tell me about that I first have to find him.

Through a car park behind the railway station I find the trail-head right where he said it would be. A sign points the way with a warning: 'Expect winter on top. Dress for it.' Right now, after walking through the town in the May sunshine, I'm taking off my jumper and tying it around my waist. It's hard to imagine feeling cold in a few hours. The trail is dry and dusty as I start the long hike up.

It's almost dusk by the time the rickety wooden entrance-way to Barr Camp appears three hours later. It's just above the snowline, but fresh snow hasn't fallen for a while and the path is well trodden.

Barr Camp is a hiker's lodge halfway up Pikes Peak, a 'fourteener', Zach tells me, meaning the summit sits at over 14,000ft. Zach lives here in the lodge, at 10,200ft (3,100m), with his sister, Ashley, and her husband, Nathan. The three of them share duties as the camp's caretakers, cooking breakfast and an evening meal each day, keeping the fire stoked and generally making sure visitors have what they need. They're also the mountain rescue team, the first responders in case anyone gets lost or hurt up here.

I arrive to find Zach alone inside the cabin, pottering around in the small kitchenette at the back. The cabin is a warm, cosy room with a table, and some armchairs around a log burner. The kitchen sits tucked behind a wooden bar with a couple of bar stools. Along the wall are snacks you can buy, M&Ms, energy bars and the like, and T-shirts and hats bearing the retro Barr Camp logo. At the back, a sign over the door to the bunk room reads *Karibu*, which means welcome in Swahili.

'Oh, hi,' Zach says as I introduce myself. 'Good to meet you.'

I first heard about Zach when I was logging on to watch the UTMB live feed the year before. For most of the race, whenever I checked in, this young American guy was out alone, tearing away at the front. He eventually finished sixth, but for me, and many other people, Zach's swashbuckling attempt to destroy the field right from the start was one of the most memorable things about the race.

Every time I tuned in, there he was, his backwards cap bobbing away as he scurried on, taking no time to rest at the aid stations, glancing back like a man running for his life. The accepted wisdom in ultra running, of course, is that it's generally a good idea to start off steady and conserve energy. Play the long game. It's an ultra marathon, not a sprint. But Zach ran without fear, without holding anything back, constantly pushing, and only buckling at mile 92, when he finally surrendered the lead for the first time.

Then, later in the year, Zach popped up again on my Facebook feed in a video that went viral in the running world. It's the last mile of another fiercely competitive race, the North Face 50 (miles) near San Francisco, and Zach is leading. He's well clear of his rivals, but again he's turning conventional wisdom on its head with his guts-out approach.

In ultra running, most people, even the winners, usually finish at a jog, enjoying the last section of the race, waving to friends, the crowd, often embracing their family just before the finish line and crossing it together with them. What's the rush, after such a long race?

But here is Zach in the North Face 50, well clear of everyone else, heading for an impressive victory, but still running like his life is in danger, his arms pumping, his breathing hard, guttural. He keeps it up right to the line before collapsing into the arms of his girlfriend.

It's this all-or-nothing approach he brings to his racing as much as his victories that has made Zach such an admired figure in the sport, and I'm expecting to meet a brash, high-energy jock with a Superman handshake. Someone who can't stop talking and moving around. Instead he speaks with a slow, easy drawl and seems a little shy if anything. He says he is cooking burritos if I want some.

While he cooks, I settle myself at the bar with a cup of tea and he tells me the story of how he got into this crazy sport.

After graduating from college, where he had run track and cross-country, he says he got a job working in the print shop on a huge cruise ship, the *Queen Mary II*. Most runners would probably consider their training days over if they got a job like that, but Zach was not so easily put off.

'By the time I left, I had it dialled in,' he says. 'I could write the book on how to stay in shape on a cruise ship.'

Whenever the ship was docked, he would go out and run. 'So, we'd go to, like, Chile, Patagonia, and I'd just go and run in the mountains. Wherever we were, I would look around for the tallest thing or the coolest mountain I could see and try to run to the top and back before the ship left.

'Sometimes I had to run really fast to get back in time. If you miss the ship you have to get yourself to the next port, and then when you get there you may or may not have your job any more.' He never missed it.

On sea days, he found the best place to run was up and down the crew stairwells. 'Not the nice ones, but the ones they used to cart supplies up and down,' he explains. After an hour or so running up and down the stairs, he would go straight to the gym to run on the treadmill.

'My last sea day, I did 70 minutes up and down the stairs and then 20 miles on the treadmill. My co-workers thought I was half crazy. They'd be in the bar, poking their heads around the corner, usually drunk, yelling at me to stop running.'

It was during a break from the ship that he decided to enter his first ultra marathon, a 50-mile race in Maryland called the JFK50. His old high school coach had been telling him for a long time he should try to run something long, that he'd be good at it, but Zach wasn't sure.

'My family thought I was crazy running that far,' he says, grinning at the memory. I guess 50 miles doesn't seem such a long way to him these days. 'My grandmother thought I was going to die or something. And I didn't know what I was doing, I just turned up and bought some water bottles in the store the day before.'

About halfway through the race he found himself running at the front with another guy.

'We were running together stride for stride, so after a while I figured I should try to find out who he was. I said: "My name is Zach, what's your name?" And he said: "Rob." I said: "Rob who?" He said: "Rob Krar."'

Rob Krar was one of the biggest names in ultra running at the time, having just won the most important ultra race in the US, the Western States 100. Zach says he felt like an idiot. 'I mean, I didn't know much about ultra running, but I knew who Rob Krar was.' They ran together until about mile 38, when Zach started to pull ahead.

'At the next aid station, when I arrived ahead of Rob, apparently everybody just kinda went crazy. Everybody started pulling out their phones trying to figure out who I was, but there wasn't really anything to figure out. I had been a college runner, but I wasn't that good. I mean, I ran for a division three school, I ran 31:23 for 10K, which in the elite world is pretty mediocre, so they started asking my friend, "What's his marathon PR?" And he told them I hadn't run a marathon.'

Zach won, running the third-fastest time in the race's history, and this was the oldest ultra race in the US. His victory was a big shock in the ultra running world, with lots of coverage in the specialist media. 'It was pretty fast considering I didn't really know what I was doing,' he says. That's when he got signed by Nike.

'I was going to go back to the ship, and I did, but Nike got in touch with me, and so I actually signed my Nike contract while I was working on the ship. Like I signed it and mailed it from Bermuda or something. I worked on the ship for another three months, then I got off it.'

'I'd always dreamed of being a pro runner,' he says. 'And then it happened. Just not how I expected it to.'

The burritos are ready. Zach eats them without a wrap, so I do the same – just a big plate full of beans, rice and vegetables – he sticks mayonnaise and mustard on his. It reminds me of the food of the Kenyan marathon runners, who eat a lot of beans and rice. Interestingly, Zach was born in Nairobi in Kenya to missionary parents. He lived there until he was three or four years old before moving to Pennsylvania. Perhaps being born and living at altitude as a baby had some effect on him, making his lungs bigger and stronger for distance running. Perhaps he ate some of the magic ugali – a maize dish which Kenyans often say helps them run so fast.

I ask Zach about his sponsorship deals. Just before I arrived in the US, he announced on his social media pages that he had switched from Nike to North Face. How did that happen? Does he have an agent?

'Yeah,' he says, almost hesitant to admit it. 'It's funny, five years ago, if you told someone you were a trail runner with an agent, they would have laughed at you.' But this sport is growing, and so are the financial rewards for those who know how to tap into them.

'My agent said your value is whatever you can get a company to pay you. That's how it works. In other jobs or even in other sports you usually know what your worth is. If you win a certain tournament or something, that's worth so much. But in ultra running there are no set parameters, there's no set list that says that since you won this and that race we'll pay you this much.'

Value to a sponsor is not easily defined in this evolving sport, but being a viral sensation known for your gutsy running style certainly helps. Zach says that for the first time, with this new contract, he doesn't really need to work outside running. Although, as he loves Barr Camp so much, he plans to stay on as caretaker for the foreseeable future.

Everything about life up here, he says, is conducive to being an ultra runner. When he's not training, he is mostly hauling logs, chopping wood or clearing snow.

'I spend a lot of time up here doing manual labour,' he says. 'I love it. The North Face 50 race in the video [that went viral] was at the end of the fall, and I'd spent all fall splitting wood and hauling it into the store. I was pretty strong.'

The next morning dawns bright and clear, with no sign of any snowstorm. Zach is up early preparing a hearty oatmeal mix on the wood burner. He chops banana, dates and walnuts into it, before ladling in two giant spoonfuls of peanut butter. It tastes like cement, but I'm sure it's what you need when you spend the day running around up on a 14,000ft mountain.

I'm halfway through the job of eating it, sitting opposite Zach, when the door opens and a red-faced man in his fifties steps into the room. He stands looking at us, grinning.

'Good morning,' says Zach after a moment. 'Can I get you anything?'

'I can't believe you're here,' says the man, beaming at him. 'You inspired me to run, man.'

Zach just smiles back. 'You made it up here pretty early,' he says.

'Yeah,' the man replies, clearly awestruck to be standing here talking to his hero. 'Man! When I told my wife I was coming up here – last night I showed her some of the You-Tube clips – she just raised her eyebrows.' He's looking at me now. 'My friends laugh at me, tell me I have a man crush. They don't get it. This guy has a God-given gift to connect with people. He's so damn inspiring.'

Zach takes it all in his stride, asking the man about his own running, calming him down. But the man is not for calming. He pulls off his gloves, walking around the room. Zach gets him a cup of water.

'You know, I quit drinking. I don't smoke. So I run. It's

sad, I know, but I sit up at night watching YouTube films of races. And you know what, there's something different about this guy. Right from the gate he's just gone, no excuses, he just gives it everything.'

Suddenly he looks at his watch. 'I gotta go,' he says. He told his wife he would be back by 8 a.m. And so, after a quick selfie with his hero, he's gone. Zach starts clearing the bowls.

'Does that happen often?' I ask.

Zach is non-committal, sort of shaking and nodding his head at the same time. 'I don't know. Sometimes, I guess.'

His sister, when she gets back from a visit off the mountain later that day, tells me it happens all the time.

Shortly after breakfast, Zach reappears from his bedroom, which is simply a raised platform over the kitchen, in his running shorts and jacket. The sun has gone and a grey coldness has blown in across the mountain. That snow they promised is coming. Zach is wearing a Buff headscarf. Still the short shorts, though. He starts lacing up his shoes. He had mentioned before I came that I could run with him if I wanted, but perhaps he had been joking.

'You going for a run?' I ask.

'Sure. You coming?' I nod. OK, sure.

Luckily for me, Zach is just returning from an injury. He says it was nothing much, but one day out on the trail he slipped and twisted his back, so he had to take a few weeks off running. He is only now getting back into it. So he's not planning anything too insane. I tell him I'll try to keep up.

Five minutes later, we're ready to go. We set off heading down into the pine forests. Zach chats easily as we go, and as it's all downhill, I trip along happily behind him, catching glimpses of the surrounding peaks through the trees. Zach tells me about an annual marathon from Manitou Springs up to the summit of Pikes Peak and back down again. It's a big race attracting some of the world's best mountain runners.

As the sport of ultra running has grown, with younger and faster athletes taking part, in most races around the world course records are regularly being broken. Times people once thought were untouchable are being smashed by the likes of Kilian Jornet and Jim Walmsley. But the Pikes Peak record remains a rare exception. In 1993, local runner Matt Carpenter raced up and down the mountain in 3hrs 16mins. It was the third of his twelve wins, and it remains the course record.

'He's the king of this mountain,' says Zach. Last year, the world mountain running champion Joseph Gray ran just the ascent and got as close as anyone ever has to one of Carpenter's Pikes Peak records. But he was still four minutes off. In 2012, Jornet had a go at the marathon, but was almost 25 minutes off Carpenter's time.

'He [Carpenter] now lives down in Manitou Springs and owns an ice-cream shop,' Zach tells me. 'It's called the Colorado Custard Company. If you go in, he's the small guy behind the counter.'

I ask Zach if he ever stops by to see him. 'Ah, I don't

know,' says Zach. 'I don't want to bother him.'

Zach is clearly in awe of Carpenter, and I can't help smiling at the idea of one of the greatest mountain runners that ever lived – he also still holds the course record at the famous Leadville 100 ultra marathon – serving ice cream in a little shop in Colorado.

We're still descending gently through the trees. The more we go down, however, the more worried I get. It's going to be a long slog back up.

Sure enough, up the first small incline, Zach is gone. He waits for me at the top, no more than 100 metres ahead, but by the time I get there my lungs feel like they're being squeezed to nothing. Zach doesn't seem to hear how much I'm gasping, because he turns and runs on as soon as I catch up to him. Eventually, after much stopping and starting, I have to cut him free.

'You go on,' I say. 'I'll follow the trail straight back up from here.' Keen to run at his usual pace, he doesn't argue, and with a quick nod he's gone, scarpering off into the trees, leaving me to walk, relieved, the last few miles back to the camp.

Later that afternoon, the snow comes in. Big, heavy flakes landing in a silent riot outside. Throughout the afternoon the door swings open and snow-covered hikers step in from the cold. It's Saturday, so the mountain is busy, and around fifteen people come in during the day. Most of them plan to stay the night. One group of men are on a stag weekend, though they all fall asleep before 9 p.m.

I get to talk more to Zach, between his forays outside to fetch firewood. Despite some shyness, he says he's happy meeting the people who come up here and chatting with them.

'People think it's lonely up here,' he says, as he stokes the fire. 'But I interact with people more than if I'm in town. People don't just burst in through the door like today if you're in your home.'

I ask him if he has a girlfriend and he gives me a wry smile. 'I'm single,' he says. 'It's not easy to go on a date living up here.'

For a while Zach dated the ultra runner Hillary Allen. It's her arms he falls into at the end of the North Face 50 video. He doesn't say why the relationship ended or whether it had anything to do with living six miles up a mountain.

'On my first date with Hillary,' he says, 'I was halfway down when I came across a hiker who had hurt her back. I helped her get off the mountain, but it made me late for the date. I mean, hopefully it sounded heroic, but I don't know.'

If Hillary wanted to visit him, she had to make the hike up to Barr's Camp. 'Luckily I always seem to date runners,' he says. 'Other people are concerned for me. They say, "Man, you're single, you live in a cabin in the woods up a mountain." But I love it up here. I figure I'll work it out somehow.'

It's getting dark now and Zach's sister and brother-in-law have cooked up a large pasta dish for the guests. A few of them decided to pitch their tents and cook outside in the snow, but have come in to sit by the fire for a while to get warm. They look freezing. I'm not sure they had much success cooking out in the blizzard. They just pull a pained smile when I ask them.

At nine o'clock on the dot, everyone is kicked out of the main cabin, either to their tents outside, or to the bunk room. As this is Zach and his sister's home, this is their private time. Not that they do much with it, other than go to bed. Zach keeps stepping out to check on the snow, excited about going for a big run in the morning. I get to bed down on the floor next to the log burner, which is lucky for me, because the unheated bunkhouse where the other guests are staying is a fair few degrees below zero. Zach has also given me a warm jacket – one of his now obsolete Nike puffer ones – and lent me a decent sleeping bag. Winter really has come up here, as the sign at the bottom of the trail warned. But tucked up in my cosy bed I settle down for a good night's sleep.

We wake to a fresh four feet of snow. Zach is already bustling around screwing his trainers on to special running snowshoes. They're like two mini skateboards without the wheels, and let him run on top of the snow, rather than sinking waist deep at every step. He asks me if I want to join him again, but it was hard enough trying to keep up on firm ground, I don't fancy my chances in the snow.

Zach's brother-in-law suggests I try going for a hike up

the trail. Walking is hard enough in these conditions, he says. He gets me a pair of regular snowshoes.

And so I zip up and leave them, and head out alone into the silent forest. It's hard to walk, and I make it about two miles, to the tree line, where the forest ends and the open mountain begins, before I decide to turn back. It's meditative out among the trees, the snow still falling gently, each step the same. It's like walking through a dream.

When I get back Zach is still out running. He'll be gone for another couple of hours. It seems like his serious training has begun again. In a few months he plans another crack at the UTMB. No American man has ever won it, so it's a big goal for him. It would mean a lot in the US ultra running world. Big sponsorship bonuses, no doubt, as well as the unofficial title of the world's best mountain ultra trail runner. It's hard to imagine many of his rivals are living a life as focused on training.

He tells me about the time when the camp was so busy that he didn't manage to get his run in, so he decided to run to the Pikes Peak summit at two o'clock in the morning. He says he enjoyed it so much, he went up again the next night. And the next.

'I ended up doing it seven nights in a row,' he says. 'I don't know why, I just felt like it.'

Before I leave, later that day, back to civilisation, I ask Zach what it is that motivates him to run. It can be a difficult question for any runner. 'It's the closest we can get to flying,' he says. 'I didn't say that, someone else did, but I like it. I love the feeling of running.'

But it's not only that. I sense something more altruistic

in Zach, as though his running is part of something bigger. 'Right,' he says. 'I believe people identify with watching someone who's really trying their best, someone who's struggling but is still trying to push as hard as they can.'

Ultra running can be a metaphor for life, with all its ups and downs, its struggles and revivals. And when someone is good at it, and they run with their heart, with the sweat and the effort written across their face, the rest of us can connect with that. It stirs something in us.

'There's a lot to be said in life for just giving your all,' says Zach. 'I think a display of that in sport is really cool, because people can be inspired, and whether it motivates them to run or go out and work their office job really hard, it's a human thing that people connect with. It's doing your best.'

Zach is the embodiment of the honest toil of ultra running. He lives in a hut in the woods and chops wood instead of going to the gym. He doesn't use Strava or wear a fancy GPS, but runs with a five-dollar Casio watch he bought in a market in Portugal. Before that he used to run using the clock on the wall at Barr Camp. He would go out and run, and only look at the time when he got back. If the clock on the wall said only two hours had gone by, he would go back out and run some more. When he races, he eschews tactics and strategy, pushing himself as hard as he can for as long as he can. It's reckless and it can leave him broken, even when he wins. But it is inspiring. It is the heart triumphing over the mind. And for that, everyone who has seen him run, in all those YouTube videos, finds themselves rooting for him.

Feeling all inspired, once the snow has stopped, I head off back down the mountain, through the thick snow, down past the icicles hanging off the rocks like dinosaur teeth, back into the warmth of homespun Manitou Springs and back to my hire car.

Before catching my flight to San Francisco for the Miwok 100K race, I have time for a quick afternoon stop in Colorado's running town: Boulder. This bright, quirky university town is home to dozens of the world's top distance runners; not just ultra runners, but also track and marathon stars.

My first port of call is a quiet suburban street about twenty blocks from the city centre, the sort of place kids wheel around on their bikes after school or shoot hoops in the front yard. At the ends of the long, tree-lined roads, the Rocky Mountains rise up like an Athena poster in the mid-day sun.

I'm at the house of a prosthetist who is perfecting a new leg for local ultra runner Dave Mackay. I find them together in the garage, which has been turned into a workshop.

'Come in,' says the prosthetist, pulling out a chair from among the racks of spare limbs. 'You want to sit down?' They're both standing, so I decline. 'I'm OK.'

Dave is forty-seven and has been a giant in the US ultra running scene for twenty years, winning a truckload of the top races. In 2004 and 2005 he was USA Track & Field's Ultrarunner of the Year, while in 2011 *Ultrarunning* magazine named him the North American Ultrarunner of the

Year. But then in 2015, while out on a run in those mountains at the end of the road, the ground collapsed under him and he fell off a ridge.

After a year and a half of surgeries, recurring infections and constant pain, he had his left leg amputated below the knee.

He says it was his decision to amputate. He had already undergone thirteen different surgeries on his lower leg, and had suffered infections, as well as bone and muscle grafts not taking. A scan showed that a rod inserted into his shinbone was moving around, and he still needed a cane to walk.

'Amputation wouldn't be an osteopath's first option,' he says, with a pained half-smile. 'But as a physician's assistant, I knew what the other options entailed: basically years of painful rehabilitation that was unlikely to work.'

Dave was desperate to get back out on the trails, and saw amputation as the quickest and most certain way of making that happen. 'I knew there were amputees out there climbing Everest,' he says. 'So I knew there was a high chance of being active.'

As Dave tries out a new, tighter-fitting prosthetic, jogging gingerly up and down the road outside the house, his prosthetist tells me her main job is to slow him down.

'Most people in his situation would be more reticent, more cautious,' she says. 'It's only a few months since the operation and he's already out running on the trails. There must be something about the mindset of an ultra runner that they can override pain.'

'There is,' says Dave as he goes by. His determination is unnerving. He seems frustrated that it is taking as long as it is to adjust.

'It has been harder than I thought,' he says. 'I had pictured being out jogging after a couple of weeks, but it has taken longer to heal, and I've had to get my muscle memory back . . . I wasn't even weight bearing for six weeks.'

'I'm still figuring out downhill skiing,' he says, like it's a surprise to him that he isn't already flying down black runs. 'But it shouldn't be a problem.'

As for running, Dave still has goals. He says he wants to run the Leadville series – a six-race series that culminates in the famous Leadville 100 (miles) race. 'Not to win,' he adds, wistfully, as though this needs saying. He's still readjusting.

I ask him what drives him on to continue running, even now after his accident.

'I love being outdoors, in the hills,' he says. 'It gives me a lot of energy and fulfilment.' The pull to be out there running must be strong for someone to keep doing it even after they lose a leg. Someone who was once driven by competition, trying to win. But for Dave, like Zach, running clearly transcends simply the act of moving, racing, being in a state of flow. 'Adventure is a big part of it,' he adds. 'Exploring, and experiencing the everyday changes in the mountains. Being out with friends, too. I guess the rewards are still too great to stop.'

In the days before getting to Boulder, I shot off messages to all the ultra runners I could find online who were based in the city. A few of them, drawn by my offer of a free coffee, agreed to meet me. So after he's done with the prosthetist, Dave and I make our way to The Laughing Goat coffee shop, which is full of young people with laptops making a single coffee last the entire morning.

The first runner we're meeting is a guy I've heard a lot about. When people tell me how the biggest change in ultra running recently is all these young, fast, ex-college runners coming into the sport, they always refer to 'young guys like Sage Canaday'.

'I'm not that young,' says Sage laughing as he sits down. He's thirty-one. Maybe it's his Japanese heritage and vegan diet, but he looks younger. He's fresh from winning the Lake Sonoma 50, a big 50-mile trail ultra in this part of the world.

Sage became a professional runner straight out of college and for three years ran on the roads, setting his personal best time in the marathon of 2hrs 16mins in 2011. But he says he grew up running on trails and was always intrigued by the idea of running further than a marathon.

'My coaches in the post-collegiate programme wouldn't let me run more than 20 miles,' he says. 'I used to read the magazines, seeing articles about the North Face 50-mile championships, reading about Western States 100-mile races, seeing pictures of Kilian [Jornet] on the cover of *Running Times* magazine, and I was like, what is this part of running?

'It seemed like more fun to be in the mountains than always in a big city on pavement. And I wasn't going to make the Olympic team in the marathon. It's fun to do the road marathons, but it's harder to make a career out of it.'

Young, fast and good-looking, Sage is a hit on social media, with a huge following for his video blog in which he talks about his training, his races, his diet, and shares tips and advice. This is all a big draw for sponsors, and Sage, along with his coaching, has managed to make ultra running his career.

Despite winning races, he says prize money doesn't really count for much, unlike in marathons. 'There's no prize money at Western States,' he says. 'But a win could be worth thousands of dollars in bonus money and a new sponsorship that could change your whole career.' It's the same for the UTMB, he says. 'The first American man to win at UTMB, well it would be worth a nice contract extension, extra salary, maybe a $10,000 bonus.'

The conversation winds its way around to the uneasy subject of doping. Sage is well known in the sport as a vociferous anti-doping campaigner.

'In ultra running, we never get tested,' he says. 'It's too easy to hide in the mountains and train and never get tested.'

He says he has only ever been tested once, at the UTMB, but he says it wasn't a surprise, as they test all the elite runners. 'Mike Wardian [a fellow ultra runner] told me, "they're going to draw your blood the day before UTMB, just so you know",' he explains. 'Everyone knows it's coming. But EPO is something you would take in the months leading into the race when you're doing the big training, and then a week before, you just taper off and you don't get caught. Only an idiot would come into the race glowing with EPO.'

As well as the lack of testing, says Sage, there's plenty of incentive to dope. 'For the top runners, there's tens of thousands of dollars at stake. You get a budget to travel the world, you get to make running a career, it could be very lucrative for a top runner.

'The average US ultra trail runner, mid-pack runner, thinks no one ever dopes in ultra running because there's not enough money involved, but they don't know, there's a lot of money involved.'

Dave has been listening in, quietly nodding along. 'It's addictive too . . . to do well, have the social media attention, the fame, especially now, maybe that's as powerful as anything.'

Sage agrees. 'It goes back to your ego. There's the greed for the money, but then there's the ego, the social media following, the articles . . . and it would be very easy to dope.'

It's interesting the number of times social media comes up when talking about ultra running. It seems incongruous. Here is a sport that can lead you to such profound depths of struggle that you need to summon a huge amount of mental strength and conviction to push on, to keep going to the end. Surely if you were just doing it for the online kudos, you would give up at the first sign of trouble. Or perhaps that's why so many ultras have such a high drop-out rate, with close to half the field regularly failing to finish in a lot of races.

To find out how important social media is, I decide the most appropriate thing to do is post a message in one of the big ultra running communities on Facebook. I immediately find myself buried under a barrage of responses, with many people saying that while social media and Strava – the app for publicly sharing GPS files of your training – play a role, the real reason they run ultras is to challenge themselves and to find their limits. Others say they post online not to show off, but to encourage others, to show them what is possible.

One person from New Mexico says: 'If I can go from a fat alcoholic to a fit endurance runner, anyone can do it. But I won't lie, though, the *attaboys* from my friends and family certainly are encouraging.'

Race director Steve Diederich says he sees the role of social media in the sport as a positive thing, saying it fires people's imaginations. 'People see their friends' pictures and they go "Wow, I want to do that,"' he says. He believes that the way people spread the word like this, inspiring each other, is at least in part responsible for the rise of ultra running over the last ten years, a growth that has corresponded with the huge rise in the influence of social media over the same period.

Many of the replies to my Facebook post are from people telling the story of how they were first inspired to run an ultra marathon after hearing about it on social media. One typical post says: 'It's what got me into this whole palaver in the first place. I did my first ultra because I saw things about it on Facebook and thought that sounds fun.'

For some people, social media has even helped them to keep running during a race. Helen James from the UK says that while she wouldn't do a race simply to brag about it online, a few times she has been in a race and considered stopping, but the thought 'How will it look on Facebook?' made her continue.

Ultra running coach Ryan Knapp believes online bragging plays a 'massive' role in the popularity of the sport. 'Ultra is the new marathon,' he says. 'People like to be a martyr. They want to go out and talk about how "epic" it was, or how they finished with four broken legs, a fractured spine. It makes for a better story than "I ran well and finished pretty good".'

For some people, it can go too far. One person, from

Cornwall, says: 'I've put so much pressure on myself via social media in the past. I thought posting stuff would make people think "Wow, look at what she's doing", but instead most people I aspire to be like couldn't give a shit. I've stepped away from posting in social media pre-race or in training and I'm already seeing the benefits. I did a race on Sunday and loved every minute of it. No pressure, no social media posts.'

For all its pitfalls, social media has helped some of the top runners such as Sage Canaday to forge a career out of the sport. 'When I switched over from road running to ultras,' he says, 'my social media channels just grew exponentially. You get way more interest when you do ultras. If you're just another 2:16 road runner in the US, no one really cares.'

Even Zach, for all his low-tech approach to the sport, regularly posts on Instagram.

'Ultra running fans love those big mountain shots,' says Sage. 'If I go up on top of a mountain and take a selfie, that's going to get more likes than some picture of me running on a track, even though the track workout may be just as hard or just as important.'

Sage is planning another crack at the UTMB in a few months. I ask him what his goal is.

'First is to finish. Last time I was in the lead pack when I fell and needed stitches. I tried taking an antibiotic powder, but it was excruciating trying to go downhill.' There were no roads out, so they had to get a helicopter to rescue him. 'It was really embarrassing,' he says.

'So the first goal is don't fall, don't get stitches. But then, to win. That's the ultimate goal. It's going to be the most competitive ultra trail race in world history ever, and no American has ever won. It's such a spectacle, it's the biggest race . . . I mean you go to a 100-mile race over here like Western States, but at the UTMB there are just so many more spectators, media, runners – it just blows it out of the water.'

Here in Boulder I have one last interviewee before I fly out for the first qualifying race in my quest to toe the line at the famous UTMB. Her name is Hillary Allen. I'm getting a little jittery with all the coffee, but Hillary is so energised and full of beans, constantly smiling and amazed at everything, that I don't think she notices.

Hillary was US Skyrunning Ultra Champion in 2015 and is currently leading the Skyrunner World Series. She also happens to be the former girlfriend of Zach Miller. I don't pry into why they stopped going out and whether it was anything to do with the fact he lives halfway up a mountain. Instead, I start by asking her how she got started in ultra running.

A former tennis player, she was just running to keep in shape when a top ultra runner she got to know began noticing how strong she was in the hills and took her under her wing. 'I just had a knack for it,' she says.

After my conversations with Zach and Sage about how they make a good living from ultra running, I'm keen to know if Hillary thinks it's as easy for female ultra runners. Despite her high world ranking, Hillary has a job teaching at a small college in Boulder.

'Oh, that's a good one,' she says, her eyes narrowing. 'I was in an interesting position this year – and it's a sensitive subject as athletes are not allowed to disclose how much they get – but I was out of contract for the first three months of the year so I was able to talk to different sponsors and talk to different people to get a feel for what's going on, and so this isn't my imagination but this is an actual fact: if you compare strictly results, if you compare my results versus a guy who has the same results, nine times out of ten he will get paid a huge percentage more – and this is even coming from the same sponsors.'

She says this is partly because there are more men running ultras, but she points out that if there are fewer women then there's more potential for growth in that market. I also find it a strange idea that a man can't be inspired by a female ultra runner. Hillary nods, almost spluttering and putting down her coffee.

'Here's another interesting fact: when I run a race I'm placing in the top twenty, sometimes the top ten, I've placed as high as third overall in an ultra. I mean Stephanie Howe, she's on the North Face team, she just won a race outright. Then there is . . . oh I forget her name, but she was winning Hardrock outright, one of the hardest ultra marathons in the world.' I think she means the women's Hardrock 100 course record holder Diana Finkel, who finished second overall in 2010. There are plenty of other examples of women winning big ultras outright, though. Pam Reed, for instance, twice won the 135-mile Badwater ultra, run through Death Valley in California, in 2002 and 2003. More recently, Denver-based Courtney Dauwalter won the Moab 240 ultra race outright, beating the first male finisher by over 10 hours. And in January 2019, Jasmin Paris became front-page news in the UK when she broke the men's course record in the 268-mile Spine Race – one of Britain's most brutal ultras – by over twelve hours, while stopping along the route to express breastmilk for her fourteen-month-old daughter. Over twenty-five hours after she had finished the race, and had been home, slept, and done interviews on BBC television, the third male finisher – out of 126 starters – crossed the line.

Ultra running is certainly one of the sports where women come closest to competing equally with men at the sharp end – which only makes it all the more baffling that their efforts are not equally rewarded.

Just weeks before my US trip began, the ultra running website irunfar.com published a survey on this very subject. The author, Gina Lucrezi, sent a questionnaire to over one hundred of the top male and female ultra runners in the US and western Europe, making sure to balance out those in both genders with similar results, social media profiles and types of races. The runners responded anonymously.

The results were stark, if not surprising. It turned out that 30 per cent of the women surveyed earned over $10,000 a year from their running, compared with 70 per cent of the male athletes.

Another top ultra runner from Boulder, Clare Gallagher, a former winner of the famous Leadville 100, is out of town the day I'm in The Laughing Goat drinking too much coffee, but she sends me her thoughts on all this via email. She doesn't mince her words: 'The whole pay gap is BS because it's perpetuating discrimination in an industry that has the intelligence and lack of precedent to not make a stupid and sexist precedent. It's embarrassing for the sport.'

She's right. Ultra running doesn't have a history of inequality to overcome. As a young sport – young in terms of having any commercial value at least – it had the opportunity to start off on the right foot. But that opportunity hasn't been taken.

Interestingly, the survey also asked the athletes how much they would like to be paid, and only 51 per cent of the women said they would like over $10,000 a year, compared with 85 per cent of the men. This goes back to Zach's point, that in this new frontier that is ultra running, where no one seems to be in charge and the rules on earnings are not clear, you are simply worth what you can get a sponsor to pay you. Are men just more aggressive in the negotiations? Do they simply value themselves more highly?

Hillary is nodding. She has to get back to teach a lecture, but she answers quickly. 'It goes back to gender roles and how people are raised; guys are taught to be aggressive and ask for this . . . I mean the reason I got more money in my contract was because I asked for it, and I got a lawyer to talk me through it, and I think fewer women are willing to do that.'

And with that, one of the world's top ultra runners has to rush off to her job. Meanwhile, I pack up my bag, pay the bill and wander off through the sunny streets of downtown Boulder, past the family of buskers in dungarees singing country and western songs, and the vegan falafel shacks, back to my hire car. My next stop is another ultra running mecca: the San Francisco Bay area and my first 100km race.

6

I land in San Francisco where I'm met at the airport by a man with thick, dark hair and glasses, his T-shirt tucked into his jeans, and a firm handshake. This is Gary Gellin, a top ultra runner in the California scene and a former winner of the Miwok 100K. He is with his wife, Holly, who speaks softly and seems to find him quietly amusing. They've agreed to put me up while I'm here and Gary seems keen to help me out with my book research.

Holly lets me sit in the front as we drive back to Marin County and into the foothills of California's northern coastal range. Gary and Holly live in Mill Valley, where wooden houses with epic verandas perch on the hills among the redwood trees.

This, again, is running country. The oldest trail race in the US, the Dipsea Trail race, begins in the main square in Mill Valley. It's a 7.5-mile handicap race, with the slowest runners getting to start first, and although it follows a set route along a steep, rugged trail, shortcuts are allowed, making for a chaotic but exciting spectacle. First run in 1905, the race finishes at the nearby Stinson Beach, which is where in a few days the Miwok 100K will begin.

From the back window of their house, where Gary and

Holly eat their meals at a small table for two, you can see the Golden Gate Bridge in the far distance. It's quite a view, and Gary is rightly proud of it, pointing it out to me most days.

As soon as we get home, Gary dons his apron and starts rustling up some supper. He's quite the chef and prides himself on his meticulous systems for everything.

As well as a huge bowl of kale and quinoa with nuts and feta cheese and a million other things – which we end up eating for the next three days – he concocts a batch of his Gary's Famous Energy Bars ™. It's his own elaborate recipe with precise measurements of everything from pumpkin seeds and sliced almonds to dried cherries, dark chocolate chips and peanut butter.

'The peanut butter has to be oily,' he says, opening a fresh king-sized jar with a theatrical twist of his wrists. 'Sometimes, if it's not, I have to add some extra peanut oil.'

Over the next few days, anyone who comes by the house goes home with a few of these jet-fuelled bricks of energy food.

As he cooks, Gary tells me about all the runners in the area he thinks I should talk to. 'Gediminas Grinius,' he says. 'Now that guy is gnarly. He came second at the UTMB last year. A former Iraq vet who took up ultra running to get over PTSD. I'm going to help him go for the Tahoe Rim FKT next year. I have his email.'

'Grinius?' asks Holly, looking up from the paper. 'Yeah, you should talk to him.'

'And talking of people with demons, Holly, I gotta take him to see Catra. She's a former drug dealer, got arrested and everything, covered in tattoos, blue hair, fruitarian, millions of followers on Instagram. She runs 100-mile races like every second week. She doesn't win, she's not fast, but she inspires a lot of people.'

He's getting more excited by the minute.

'And then you got to talk to Adam Campbell,' he says, a big grin on his face as he remembers the story. 'This guy got struck by lightning at Hardrock and still came second behind Kilian. Gnarly. I have his email, I'll drop him a line.'

It seems like everyone in this sport has a crazy backstory. Sometimes I wonder if a traumatic past is a prerequisite for ultra running. Perhaps the pain of running helps numb the pain of the past. In all those hours pushing yourself on the trail, perhaps the feelings of despair, loss, rejection, whatever they are, start to soften, and things get put into perspective. There are examples of ultra runners with a difficult past everywhere. The fastest ultra runner in the US right now, Jim Walmsley, started running after being discharged from the army, where he had been working 24-hour shifts as a nuclear missileer in an underground bunker. Although he had been a strong runner in college, he only took the sport up again to help him deal with the depression that followed his discharge. When I finally catch up with him, at the UTMB, he smiles thinking back on it. He's now a champion ultra runner, with sponsors and fans, and a cool, relaxed manner. 'Looking back, getting discharged was the best thing that ever happened to me,' he says.

The story of Gary's friend Gediminas Grinius, who is originally from Lithuania, is well known. In one interview with the *South China Morning Post*, he says he had a choice after his time in Iraq: 'Either vodka or drugs, or something else. So I started to run. I never counted the kilometres. It just felt good. You put your running shoes on, and after a while everything is OK.'

Perhaps I don't have enough demons in my past, enough issues to work through, to be a good ultra runner. Perhaps, when the crunch comes, I won't have a strong enough desire to drive myself into the fire in the hope of resolving my past, of re-emerging on the other side with a clean slate and a fresh perspective.

The San Franscico Bay area turns out to be a hive of ultra runners, and over the next few days Gary dedicates himself to taking me around to meet as many as he can pin down, starting with former drug addict Catra Corbet.

Gary is constantly dictating text messages to his phone while he's driving. It's supposed to recognise his voice, but like a badly trained dog, it never does what it's supposed to. He's always pulling his glasses down and peering at it instead of the road, trying to work out what garbled message he has just sent.

A lot of his texts involve defending his new electric bike against a barrage of abuse he seems to be getting from his cycling buddies. Gary is an all-action hero. As well as being a champion ultra runner, he organises an annual 1,000-mile bike trip across the western US and Canada for around forty people. His latest toy is an electric bike, which, he is at pains to explain, is not a replacement for his bike, but for his car. He is now going to cycle twice as much. But no one seems to get this.

'Oh man, listen to this,' he says, reading out another message of abuse on Strava, telling him he has sold out or that he's cheating on the Strava segments.

'Man. Full stop. Space. I labelled that ride as e-bike. Full stop.' He looks at me, shaking his head. 'You're going to love Catra,' he says. 'She's wild.'

We pull in at a nondescript roadside Starbucks somewhere near San Francisco, and stride across the car park. She's not hard to spot. Sitting outside by the roadside is a woman in a striking blue mini skirt, shiny green tracksuit top and red hair in two bunches. Her blue sunglasses match her skirt and the jacket on the little dog perched on her lap. Her powerful legs are a cascade of tattoos, and she has piercings all over her face. She looks about twenty-eight, though Gary assures me she's fifty-two.

Gary tells her what I'm doing, that I'm interviewing ultra runners, but she seems almost shy and talks to Gary for a while about his running before I get to ask her any questions. She tells me she used to be a goth, and liked to party. A lot. She took up ultra running after she got arrested for drug dealing.

'Running saved my life, for sure,' she says. 'People go to AA or whatever, but I don't. My recovery is out on the trail.'

Catra has run 100 miles (in one go) over 130 times. 'I like to do one or two 100-milers a month,' she says, as though they're trips to the beach. And it's not like she even finds them easy. She has been pulled out of races for being in a dangerous way, dehydrated, barely able to stand up. She got a stomach ulcer from taking anti-inflammatory pain-killers during races.

'I'm just stubborn,' she says. 'When I set my mind to do something, I do it. Like quitting drugs.'

She says her boyfriend at the time took the blame for the dealing. She escaped jail because she had a job and a car. The next day she went to the gym and started walking on the treadmill. That was where it all began.

'I always feel high when I'm out on the trails,' she says. 'I prefer to run by myself. I like the solitude.'

She carries a knife in case she comes across a mountain lion. 'The knife is mainly for Truman [her dog], in case he gets attacked.' Truman is a miniature dachshund who sometimes runs along beside her, but mostly gets carried in her pack. Since she has been running, she says she has seen eleven mountain lions. 'But we've never been attacked.'

Sitting at this unremarkable roadside Starbucks some-where in the city's suburbs, she seems like someone from another world. She has extreme written all over her, in her style, in her stories, in the worldly look in her eyes. In fact, it is literally written on her in the form of her favourite quote, which is tattooed among the skulls and butterfly wings on her thigh. It reads: 'Only those who will risk going too far can possibly find out how far one can go.'

Gary is looking at his watch. We have a tight schedule, criss-crossing the county, meeting ultra runners and at the same time carrying out Gary's charity work. He has it all intricately planned. We're like two Japanese trains, leaving and arriving exactly on time. But as we bid goodbye to Catra and continue on our way, I'm again left wondering if I have what it takes to be an ultra runner.

'Here we are,' says Gary, as we pull in to the staff car park of a large supermarket. It's about midday and the sun is glaring down at full blast, painting everything California white. We hop out and head into the store through the back trade entrance. Gary bustles past boxes and trays of cakes, nodding to people and weaving through the aisles. I try to keep up.

We find the manager, a tired woman in a white lab coat.

'Hi,' she says. 'You're here for the out-of-date stuff?'

Gary takes food past its sell-by date and delivers it to charities, who then hand it out to the needy and the homeless. It's worthy but tiring work two days before an ultra marathon.

The store has an unusually large offering today, so we wheel it out by the trolley-full and Gary stashes it in his car. Soft rolls, cakes, cheese. More cakes. Melting in the sun.

Gary chucks in the last items and squeezes the boot closed. Next up we have a meeting with a guy called Scott Dunlap. We find him sitting outside a coffee shop in what feels like a hipster part of the city.

By now I'm getting used to ultra runners having crazy stories, particularly in this part of the world. So when he starts telling me about the time he found himself, the day before a race, backstage at a Jay-Z concert in Los Angeles handing out marijuana to Justin Bieber and Katy Perry, I just nod along. Apparently marijuana, which is legal in California, is a good recovery tool for ultra runners, and Dunlap used to have a business supplying it.

'The best way to get over an ultra is to kick back on the couch, take a few edibles and stick on all six *Star Wars* movies,' he says, grinning so much I can't tell if he's messing with me. I don't think he is.

'Isn't that technically doping?'

'It would show up in a test, sure. But I know some of those top guys are taking Ibuprofen in races every two hours. That's doping. Do I have any ethical qualms about using pot? The next race I'm doing, they hand out marijuana from mile 50. So it's up to the race director, that's how I see it. If it's a Wada compliant race, then I'll abide by the rules.'

He sits back and sips on his coffee – which was also considered a performance enhancing drug until 2004, when Wada's caffeine restriction was lifted. 'You know, the runner's high feels like a good marijuana high, except with the runner's high you feel great the next day. But it's the same chemical system you're stimulating.'

Perhaps that's really all we're after when we run: the high. Some people take drugs, some people compete in ultra marathons. Some people do both.

Every question I ask leads to another wild story. Even the simple question of how he got into ultra running ends up with a story about 9/11 and a gruesome murder.

'I first got into trail running in 2001,' he says. 'I'd been working crazy hours in Silicon Valley when by some lucky chance I narrowly missed the attacks on the Twin Towers. Usually I went to the World Trade Center for an investors meeting, but just the week before, I quit my job. I would have been in that office. All our investors died. I was shaken up by that, so I took some time out, some time for reflection. That's when I began trail running, to regain my health and get into something a bit more fulfilling for the soul.'

Dunlap only started training properly when he was forty, after his first child was born. A few years later he was named US Masters Ultrarunner of the Year. He recently won the national 50-mile championships in his age group. He says he prefers the shorter ultra distances and still regularly runs road marathons. 'I hate 100 miles,' he says. 'But I do one every year. For the journey.'

He sits back, the late afternoon sun bathing the street in a pale yellow light.

'Tell him about the Brit,' says Gary. Scott nods, like he's just getting to it.

'I ended up being sponsored by Inov-8 shoes. I was introduced to them by a Brit, Robert Brown, who was a talented fell runner and also a pilot for British Airways. He was doing the London–San Francisco route, and would often come to the local trail races and kick our butts. I invited him to sleep on my couch. He had these crazy shoes, and so he brought me a pair, and I loved them. Later when Inov-8 came to the US, they saw I was already in their shoes and added me to their elite team. Robert Brown, it turns out, was later convicted of killing his wife and burying her in the backyard.'

Two days later . . .

I'm sitting outside on Gary's front porch. The street is as still as a photograph. It's 3.30 a.m. A car rolls slowly into view and pulls to a stop in front of where I'm sitting. I walk over and open the door. Inside, Hal, another of Gary's running friends, is slung low in his seat listening to Metallica at low volume. He nods nervously, not making any jokes. I get in.

We cruise up and over the headland to the start of the race at Stinson Beach. Once we're there Hal gets out and walks off, making his own way to the race. I follow the general bustle through the darkness to the starting area outside a wooden community centre.

Half an hour later, after retying my laces about six times, we gather under the arch that marks the official start of the Miwok 100K. There are about four hundred of us huddled together, head torches zipping around, waiting to go. The race director stands up on a chair to lots of half-hearted yelps and cheers. We're not quite in the mood for this yet.

'OK, twenty seconds to go,' she says. 'Have a good time out there. Ready for the countdown? Ten, nine, eight . . . two, one, go!'

I shuffle off. My main mission, particularly at the start, is to preserve my body. This is almost twice as far as I have ever run, so I don't know what will happen. Something may snap, or cramp up, or I may just grind to a halt. Preservation is the key, so right from the start anything even slightly steep gets walked. We follow mostly in single file up the famous Dipsea Trail, our head torches making a long row of lights strung up across the mountain. Around me people are talking. 'Jack? Is that you? How's it going, man?' I keep focused. This is a lot of going up already. Mostly steps cut into the hill.

It's almost light by the time we get to the top. A man stands there heralding the day on his bagpipes as we skulk by one after the other, cranking ourselves back up through the gears as the trail begins to roll downwards.

We get to the first aid station quicker than I was expecting. Watermelon, that tastes good. I take a few chunks and head on. Up we go again, zig-zagging to the top of a headland overlooking the Golden Gate Bridge and the skyscrapers of San Francisco. In the early morning mist it's quite a sight, but I barely glance at it. These stony descents require all my focus.

The second aid station is at 18 miles. I get there in one piece, taking on some more food, stopping for a moment this time. I'm feeling OK. Tired, sure, but still fairly strong. My stomach is a little funny and I'm hoping it doesn't get any worse. I really need to practise eating on the run.

I'm also really feeling the stones and the hard-baked earth on the descents. My shoes are pretty thin, and those padded Hokas other people are wearing look enviably comfy. Maybe it will be my feet that go. The wrong choice of footwear.

I find myself yo-yoing up and down the field, passing people on the gradual ups and downs, but seemingly the slowest person in the race through any walking sections. I chat for a while with a guy from Canada, also running his first 100K. 'I know my body can do it,' he says. 'I just hope my head can.'

At about 30 miles, we start one of the longest climbs in the race, the aptly named Cardiac Hill, rising to 1,355ft (413m) above the Pacific Ocean. I start off running one minute and then walking one minute, but about halfway up all the life drains out of me. At first I don't notice, I just decide to walk the rest. That seems reasonable, to preserve my body. In my mind it's a precautionary measure.

A while later a guy standing by the trail calls out: 'One more corner and this bitch of a hill is over.' I can't help a wry smile. He knows. Around the corner, there it is, the aid station. Oh man, the watermelon tastes incredible. I grab more slices, dipping them in a tray of salt, as Gary had suggested. Hey, there is Gary.

'Finn!' He looks suitably impressed and unimpressed at the same time. 'How's it going?'

I shake my head. 'Bloody tiring,' I say.

Thirty-two miles on the clock. Considering that, I'm OK. Always keen to link me up with other ultra runners in the area, Gary calls over a man helping hand out the food. His name is Paddy O'Leary.

'Paddy, this is Finn, he's British, you guys will get along.'

'Ah, I don't know,' says Paddy, in a thick Irish accent. 'Four hundred years of oppression and all that.'

But he's smiling. I tell him my mum's from Dublin. My dad's from Galway. He just smiles, friendly – everyone's Irish around here.

Right, I had better get on. But as the course opens into rolling hills, alive with wild flowers, I'm hit with the full extent of my demise. Everything feels tough now, even the flat bits. The downhills hurt my feet and I feel like I'm going to fall over. Even a brisk walk is exhausting. I've felt like this before, at the end of a marathon. It's not nice. Your whole body is pleading with you to stop. Your legs, your feet, your back . . . everything complains. Even my arms are aching.

But I've never felt like this with 28 miles still to go. And it's now around midday and getting hot. The grassy hillsides are thick with pollen, the sunlight as sharp as a blade.

Ultra runners often talk about how they love this part, how they long for the moment the pain kicks in, when the storm comes to challenge them. They're all mad, I think. How can you want to feel like this? I'm swaying now as my thoughts cut and thrust, moving in for the kill: *I'm not made out for this, why am I doing it? I should just stop. The whole thing is pointless.* The problem is, the thoughts make sense. Right now, it does feel pointless. I try to remember why I care.

Ultra runners also like to talk about conquering the mountains. It's you versus the mountain, they say. I look at it. But the mountain is unmoved. As I struggle along its grassy trail, it stands there serene, impassive. The mountain isn't fighting me back, and I have no truck with the mountain. We could just as easily lie down together and be friends.

If anything, it is me versus the race organisers. Why did they make us run up this steep path? Goddam them, it's like they picked the hardest route on purpose just so they could go on about how tough their race is. Just for their bragging rights, I'm up here killing myself.

Of course, it was me who chose to run the race in the first place. The night before, I'd sent a WhatsApp message to my family with a picture of my race number and the simple caption: 'Help!' Lila, my eldest daughter, responded: 'Haha, it's your own fault.' It wasn't what I was hoping to hear, but she was right. It isn't me versus anyone except myself. But now I am here, for some reason that I forget, I have to finish.

Slowly, painfully slowly, the miles tick by, a steady stream of people passing me the whole time. I try to hang on to each person for a few minutes if I can, before I grind to a crawl again. Some people seem dead to the world, passing me like zombies, grunting replies to my attempts at friendly one-liners. Some are calm and running within themselves, offering me encouragement. Others run along together chatting as though they are out for a Sunday stroll, discussing mortgages or holidays. In my state of almost total deterioration, it's a little disconcerting to get passed by two women discussing the cost of hotels in Venice.

At 46 miles, the course drops down a huge hill, which we then have to come straight back up again. It's painful going down, but at least it's relatively quick. The people coming back up are mostly walking and I decide already I will be doing the same.

'Good job, good job,' they say, as they come by. Everyone says it. I know I'm being a grouchy curmudgeon, but it's starting to annoy me. Can't they think of something else to say? 'Good job, good job.' I was not doing a good job. I was hanging on by the worn-down ends of my fingernails.

At the bottom of the hill is another aid station. The Miwok 100K is a race, like many ultras, that asks you to bring your own cup. It's to reduce waste, so you re-use your cup at aid stations rather than grabbing a disposable one. My racing backpack came with a neat, folding plastic cup, so I was sorted – or so I thought. It turned out to be fiddly to use and a little too small, but I pulled it out at each aid station and patiently took on a cup of water, a cup of energy drink and a cup of Coke. But here, at the aid station at the bottom of the hill, one of the volunteers sees me struggling to get water into my flimsy cup.

'That's not a cup,' he says. 'This is a cup!' He grabs a steel vessel about the size of a pint glass, fills it up with Tailwind (an energy drink) and hands it to me.

'Thanks,' I say, guzzling it down.

I walk back up the hill as I planned. Shortly before the top my GPS watch turns over to 50 miles. It seems crazy. I rarely run that far in a week. I stand there and actually clasp my head in my hands. 'Fuck-ing-hell,' I slow curse, taking a deep breath, and walking on.

After the long climb we are back in the forest, the trail rolling up and down along the top of the mountains. Since I saw Gary at around 30 miles, I've been walking every little uphill section and painfully running the flat and downhill ones. But now I'm struggling to run even on the flat bits. I start calculating how long it will take me to walk the rest of the way to the finish. The thing is, even that feels like torture – four hours, I calculate. I can't take that, I have to keep grinding on as best as I can.

Then, as I hobble along, a thought pops into my head; among the thick, suffocating foliage, a small shaft of light on a single flower. My eye just catches sight of it. I look at the hill looming before me – like one of the hundreds I have walked up already, and the thought is this: *it really isn't that much of a hill, why not try to run up it?* I have just over 10 miles to go. Although I feel more broken and tired than ever in my life, nothing has snapped. I'm not injured or sick. I could throw a bit of caution to the wind for one small hill, just to try it. Go wild.

And so I start to run. One step, two . . . yes, it feels OK, I could do a few more steps, to the next rock. Hey, I'm at the top, starting to roll down the other side.

I run down and immediately there is another up, but I keep running. One more hill, go on! I'm up it like a breeze, rolling off the top, striding down the other side. Hey, this is fun. Up again . . .

My legs, my feet, everything has stopped hurting. This is insane. I feel like I have just started. I power up the next hill, sprightly. I feel like my sixteen-year-old self, when I would run at full pelt through the local woods. Except these are Californian redwoods at the end of a 100km race. I can't help but laugh out loud. I'm flying past people now. People who passed me earlier, offering me encouragement but probably thinking, man, that guy is suffering. Deep in the pain cave.

'Good job!' they call as I pass, but this time with feeling. 'You're crushing it!' they shout. 'You're slaughtering it!'

I get to the final aid station in no time. What I had estimated would take me eighty minutes at best has taken only forty.

'Six miles to go, you're looking great,' says one of the volunteers.

'I feel like I've been spiked with EPO,' I joke.

'What can we get you?'

With only six miles to go and feeling this good, who needs aid? Six miles, at this pace I could run that in forty minutes, especially with the downhill finish. I'm fine, thank you. So I run on, without eating or drinking anything.

That, it turns out, is a mistake. With about two miles to go, I crash again. The last mile is all down through a steep, tangled wood and is my slowest mile of the entire race, as I clamber over fallen trees, my quad muscles whimpering down every step. But no one passes me, so I guess everyone is feeling pretty smashed by now.

And so I make it, emerging out of the forest to see the finish just a little way along the road. A small gaggle of people are there, and start cheering as soon as they see me. I manage a laboured run over the line. I've done it. One hundred kilometres. My body rebelled, my mind almost gave up the ghost, but step by step we pulled together. And for eight crazy miles near the end I was flying. What the hell was that about?

I spend a sweet few hours in the early evening warmth sitting by the finish, cheering other runners over the line and chatting happily with anyone who happens to sit down next to me, like a tipsy guest at a wedding. I'm flooded with warm feelings of happiness. In the end I finished seventy-seventh out of 375 starters, in just over twelve hours.

Gary is nowhere to be seen, but he has organised for his friend Magda Boulet, a former US Olympian turned ultra runner, to give me a lift home when I'm ready. In the car on the way back I tell her the story of my incredible recovery.

'After a 20-mile bad patch, I felt as fresh as a daisy. It was so strange.' She smiles back, but she doesn't look that surprised, especially when I tell her about the giant flagon of Tailwind I downed at the bottom of the hill.

But I didn't just recover, I went from broken to blitzing, from dead to a jumped-up racehorse after an adrenaline injection. Looking at the Strava segments of all those people who uploaded them after the race, I'm the second fastest of everyone over that section.

Was it really all down to the big drink? It happened once I got in sight of the finish. Once I got to ten miles to go, I was in territory I could understand. I knew what it was like to run ten miles. Did my mind, at that point, simply decide to relent and take the brakes off?

I remember the Canadian runner saying he hoped his mind could do it. I knew the mind could put you off, cause you problems with its negative thoughts, but could that physical pain, that intense struggle, actually have been partly my mind shutting me down? Was it that powerful? Or was it simply that I was dehydrated and running low on fuel, until I guzzled the huge cup of Tailwind? One thing for sure is that not a single ultra runner I tell about it shows the least bit of surprise. This, it seems, is just something that happens in these races.

The day after the race I get a call from Scott Dunlap, checking in to see how I got on. I tell him the story of my miraculous resurrection with ten miles to go. I start telling him about the Tailwind, the big cup, but he just laughs. 'It's all in the mind,' he says. 'All in the mind.'

Whatever it was, I now have four UTMB points in the bag. Eleven more to go. The game is on. My next stop on the

UTMB points trail is a 135-mile race around Anglesey in Wales. But before I take on that challenge, which will again push me into new territory beyond my known limits, I'm putting my pursuit of points on pause while I take a trip to a country where ultra running is not considered extreme or crazy, but completely normal. A place where ultra running is, well, just running.

7

'The race comes up here, along this road.' Craig is pointing out of the front window of his car, as we rise up along a three-lane motorway out of the hazy sprawl of downtown Durban. It doesn't look like the most inspiring place for a run. It's early evening and the rush-hour traffic has died down, so we make swift time up to the leafy suburb of Kloof, where Craig pulls his car up to the front of a gated driveway. He talks into the intercom and the gate begins to slide open. Inside is a large, colonial house, shaded by large trees. As we drive through, two dogs bound out of the house, barking and yapping.

I'm in South Africa to take part in the Comrades Marathon, the biggest and the oldest ultra marathon in the world. Billing itself as The Greatest Human Race, Comrades fails to fit into any of ultra running's main boxes. Despite being a 56-mile road race, its appeal, at least in this corner of the world, far outstrips any other ultra race. Even the UTMB can't match the history, the scale and the sense of occasion of the Comrades Marathon.

Craig is on the Comrades Marathon Association board and tells me he has run the race twenty-seven times, though he is not running this year in protest over some issue he has with the entry process. He takes me up some steps into his immaculately tidy house and switches on the television, turning it to the sports channel before handing me the controls. 'If you want to change it,' he says.

He then walks into the kitchen. I follow him, doing my best to be a good house guest. Craig has agreed to host me for a few days while I'm here. He opens the fridge, peering in.

'Are you hungry?'

'A little,' I say, wondering if he has remembered that I'm vegetarian. I don't want to cause any trouble. He pulls out a few bowls of food his wife has left for him, covered in cling film.

'You like pasta?' he asks.

The Comrades Marathon was first run in 1921 and was the brainchild of First World War veteran Vic Clapham. Struggling to readjust to life after returning from the war, and missing the camaraderie of his fellow troops, Clapham came up with the idea of a race between his home town of Pieter-maritzburg and the city of Durban on the coast, a distance of around 56 miles.

The idea was initially met with considerable resistance, with his detractors saying people might die if they attempted to race over such a distance. But Clapham reasoned that 56 miles was nothing compared to the marches his troops had covered in East Africa during the war, and he felt that such a test of endurance and willpower would be a fitting way to remember the fallen comrades.

Eventually he got his way and in 1921, thirty-four men set off at dawn from the city hall in Pietermaritzburg. The first to arrive at the finish line in Durban just under nine hours later was a man called Bill Rowan. It was a name I would soon become a lot more familiar with.

Although it has been run almost every year since 1921, with the exception of the years during the Second World War, Comrades grew exponentially during South Africa's late apartheid era, when the country was excluded from international events. With no Olympic teams to cheer or international competitions to witness during the country's period in the sporting wilderness, this annual stampede along the Natal valley took on greater importance.

The first black runner, Robert Mtshali, completed the race way back in 1935, but the official admittance of black competitors, and their inclusion in the official results, didn't begin until 1975. While some had called for wider inclusiveness before then, this still far predated the end of apartheid in the early 1990s.

'Even in 1975, we had to go against the law of the country to allow blacks to run,' says Mick Winn, who was chair of the Comrades organising committee at the time, and who has himself run the race twelve times. 'One region the race went through refused to give us permission, blaming it on a traffic issue. We got around some of the issues by calling the black runners international runners.'

I'm sitting in a shopping mall café with Mick and his wife, Cheryl, a former winner of the race and the current chair of the Comrades board. Craig has organised the meeting, keen for me to understand and fully appreciate the race's history. Also sitting with us is Dave Rogers, a wiry, energetic man in his seventies, who has finished the race a record forty-five times.

'Comrades always showed the country in its best light, what it could be,' Cheryl says. The year 1975 also marked the first time women were officially allowed to enter the race, even though the first woman to complete it was Frances Hayward in 1923. Cheryl won the race in 1982.

Throughout the years, despite the official ban, black and female competitors received enthusiastic support from the majority of their fellow runners and from the spectators lining the route. Bob de la Motte, who finished second in Comrades three times and was a vocal critic of apartheid, recalls the story of Vincent Rakabaele, who in 1975 became the first ever black runner to officially finish the race. Yet, de la Motte tells me, it may have been his unofficial run in 1974 that had a bigger significance.

That year, after training with white students from Wits University, who also drove him to the race and acted as his crew throughout, Rakabaele was at one point leading the race. 'This was quite a profound moment in South African sport and the history of apartheid,' de la Motte says. 'He was running illegally and had no race number, yet he was leading and had a legitimate chance of winning.' Although he faded to finish forty-second, de la Motte says: 'He was encouraged and applauded throughout and absolutely no attempt was made to interfere with his participation. The official history of the race confirms that the three biggest cheers that day were for the winner, Derek Preiss, for the oldest finisher, Leighe Boulle, and for Rakabaele.'

In his book *Runaway Comrade*, de la Motte describes the role Comrades played in 1980s South Africa: 'At the end of the day the black competitors had to return to township life and the indignity of apartheid but, for 11 glorious hours, everyone was treated the same and left the finish with dignity and the same sense of camaraderie, regardless of race, age or gender. It ameliorated racial tensions during a volatile time and inadvertently became a glue and a catalyst for social and political change.'

De la Motte tells me that the mass participation of black runners at races overwhelmed many of the other apartheid rules like segregated washing facilities, restaurants and beaches. 'There were no black members of golf clubs, rugby clubs, cricket clubs, tennis clubs,' he says. 'Yet running became a trailblazing success story. At Comrades and other weekend road races the running community showed how South African society could function peacefully. It did not go unnoticed.'

One of de la Motte's training partners and rivals at the time, the black runner Thulani Sibisi, says his community appreciated the help from the white runners. 'Whites were always giving us support and giving us lifts to races because we didn't have transport,' he tells me. 'We were welcomed by runners, although not by all, especially some of the Afrikaners who treated us badly.'

And despite the breakthrough of being officially allowed to race, life for South Africa's black runners continued to be complicated by apartheid long after 1975. Sibisi says he was arrested nine times in 1980 while out running or after running, simply because he wasn't carrying his identity papers. 'Imagine, how can you carry papers while running? It was very traumatic, I still think about it now.'

In 1985 Sibisi was arrested again one evening for being in a white area after the prize-giving ceremony of a race in which he had finished second behind de la Motte. He was waiting for a lift with his girlfriend, but had to leave her in the street when he was taken away by the police. The incident sparked a media furore as Sibisi was by now a well-known runner, with de la Motte scathing of the police's heavy-handedness in an article in the *Star* newspaper, calling the arrest 'absolutely disgusting'. Mick Winn says he remembers the incident. He was chair of the South African Road Runners Association at the time, and says within days of the newspaper reports he received a phone call from a senior Cabinet minister assuring him that an incident like this would not happen again.

De la Motte says this illustrated just how much running was influencing change. 'Running was when the black guys could show the country that they were as good, and mostly better, than the whites. Impeccably dignified in victory, they were doing Mandela's work on the road.'

Craig stands out in the mall's main thoroughfare talking on his phone. All day it hasn't stopped ringing. As the race nears, he seems to be involved in everything, from erecting signposts to ironing out logistics at the race expo. He has to explain to everyone who calls, with a few dramatic pauses and flourishes, why he isn't running this year. Around here, not running Comrades is a bigger deal than running it.

At our corner table in the café, meanwhile, Dave Rogers is telling me about the first time he ran the race in 1961.

'Back then you were part of the loony bin if you ran Comrades,' he says. 'I turned up in a pair of takkies, old tennis shoes. Man, they gave you blisters. The older guys said you had to run with a razor blade wrapped in your hanky. Then when you start getting a blister, you cut away that bit of the shoe.'

What he most remembers above all were the crowds. Although there were only ninety-eight finishers that year, thousands of people came out to support the runners.

'I'd played big soccer games with ten thousand spectators,' he says. 'But coming in to the finish, it was a crowd like I had never seen. I thought there must have been an accident or something. The winners had long been through, but the crowd was still there. I was running through a funnel of people, getting narrower and narrower. I felt like I'd won the World Cup. It was magic.'

After more stories of the old days, and discussions about the number of finishes achieved by people they knew, Craig comes back. He settles the bill and we say goodbye as he whisks me back to his house, where another Comrades legend he has coerced into talking to me is waiting for us in the sun-drenched driveway. At 78, Barry Varty will be the oldest competitor in this year's race. Another former Comrades committee chair, Barry has finished the race twenty-eight times out of thirty-six starts. 'I just need two more for a green DNF,' he says.

'That's the joke,' he adds, when I look a little confused. At Comrades, when you notch up ten finishes, you get given a hallowed green number to wear and are inducted into the Green Number Members Club. It's a highly respected achievement and the green numbers even have their own VIP area at the race expo. The joke is that he is only two non finishes away from having a 'green' number of DNFs (Did Not Finish).

'Barry is Mr Comrades history,' says Craig, setting us up at a table with two glasses of water, placed down on Comrades Marathon coasters. Barry lays a big pile of papers and folders down on the table. He has set up a history display at the expo and has been charged by the current Comrades committee with being the guardian of the race's history, something he clearly relishes.

'Comrades is an act of remembrance,' he says. 'Sometimes the reason for the race is forgotten a little, and we want to remind people of this. People are attracted to it because of its atmosphere, because of the challenge, but we think it is important to remember the fallen comrades. It's the "ultimate human race" to honour the ultimate human sacrifice.'

The huge growth in the race's popularity in the 1980s was in part down to the beginning of television coverage in 1976, as well as the emergence of a young, long-haired, swashbuckling runner named Bruce Fordyce, who won the race a record nine times between 1981 and 1990.

The sight of Fordyce catching the leaders year after year and powering to victory with his trademark finish, his blond hair flowing in the afternoon light, captured the imagination of millions of fans and contributed to a 164 per cent increase in race participation during the period.

Walking around the expo the Friday before the race, I spot the now white-haired Fordyce sitting in the staff area of one of the key sponsors. He's taking a quick break from meeting fans who still queue up for a moment with their hero, and a word of advice or a selfie. He looks exhausted, but he invites me to sit down with him for a moment.

I ask him about his enduring popularity. He must have made quite an impact during his years at the top.

'Everyone loves a winner,' he says. 'It's like Wimbledon. The crowd always cheers the champion and is against the new guy. But I was hated when I first won in 1981.'

That year he wore a black armband in a protest against apartheid. 'That year I was the new guy, a student with long hair, and protesting against segregation. I had tomatoes thrown at me.' It seems not everyone viewed the race as a beacon of racial harmony. That year Comrades had been selected by the white government as part of its celebrations of the twentieth anniversary of the Republic of South Africa. Many other students boycotted the race in protest, but Fordyce thought he could have more impact by winning it.

Out on the sponsor's stand, the queue to meet him is growing. I should leave him. As I get up to go, he gives me the advice he has been handing out all day. 'Start slow, and get slower,' he says. It's what I've been hearing again and again. This is a long race, take your time. But it's not what Fordyce did when he ran. Even today, with all the professional teams and their support crews and pre-race training camps, the international field of thousands, Fordyce would have been a contender.

'Last year, just comparing the times, I would have come second,' he says.

In any other part of the world, a former ultra running champion would return to anonymity after retiring, like Matt Carpenter in his ice-cream shop in Colorado. Ultra running, despite its huge global growth, is still a niche sport. Except here in South Africa, where this road ultra marathon is quite simply the biggest sporting event of the year. The peak in the race's numbers came in a special millennium edition in 2000, when the final cut-off time was extended from eleven to twelve hours and over twenty thousand runners took part. Today, South Africa's main television channel dedicates thirteen hours of wall-to-wall coverage to the race, with an audience of around six million.

One of its quirky traditions is that each year the route alternates between the 'up run' and the 'down run', traversing the road in opposite directions between Durban on the coast and Pietermaritzburg, 56 miles inland and 600m (2,000ft) higher in elevation. This year it's an up run.

I should go and rest my legs, but I'm finding the buzz around the expo too compelling. I've moved out of Craig's house for the last night before the race and into a hotel near the start. I'll go back and have a nap soon. I've been struggling ever since I arrived with a cold I picked up on the flight from London. An afternoon sleep would be sensible. But first I have to stop by the first-time runners area, which, among everything else he's doing, has been set up by Craig. I find him there, happily swanning around in his Comrades blazer.

'Finn,' he says, shaking my hand, pleased I've stopped by. He's introducing me to everyone, to some older men who have run the race forty-odd times, to the women handing out goody bags full of corporate bumf, drinks and energy bars. I realise I haven't eaten since breakfast. I try one of the sticky oat bars.

'By the way,' says Craig, a gentle hand on my shoulder, directing me. 'I want to introduce you to a compatriot of yours.' He gives a tap on the back to a seated figure, who turns around with a huge grin on his face. It's Steve Way.

'Hi,' he says.

Steve is well known in British running circles for his incredible mid-life transformation from overweight office worker and twenty-a-day smoker to international elite athlete. In 2006, Steve was thirty-three and a tad overweight at 16.5 stone when he started entering some local races to lose weight. Then, with only three weeks' training, he ran the London Marathon in 3hrs 7mins.

'Even when I was smoking, drinking and eating badly, I found I could still run,' he says. 'I looked around and I was this fat bloke bouncing along next to club runners.'

It was eighteen months after his first marathon that he decided to actually start training properly, following a schedule he found in a book. Two years later he ran London again, and this time finished in 2hrs 35mins. Two years later his time was down to 2:19. It was a startling rate of progression and articles about him were beginning to appear in the running press. Then in the 2014 London Marathon, now aged forty and still starting in the mass field behind the elite runners, and after sleeping in his camper van the night before the race, Steve finished as the third British runner in a new best time of 2:16.

Even more incredibly, he says he wasn't expecting to run fast that year as he had recently taken up ultra running and was actually using the marathon as a training run for his attempt a few months later to break the British 100km record – which he went on to beat at that year's British Championships.

Before he knew it, he was running for England in the Commonwealth Games and finishing tenth in another marathon best, this time 2:15.

'It was ridiculous really,' he says. 'I was the guy at school who hid in the bushes with my mates during the cross-country.' He has his 'fat bloke' story, as he calls it, well rehearsed, having told it countless times over the years, most famously on the night of his Commonwealth Games run when he was interviewed on BBC television by both Gary Lineker and then later by Clare Balding, where he sat on the studio sofa grinning from ear to ear like a guy who had just won the lottery.

Fast forward a few years, however, and after a few injuries and setbacks, Steve hasn't quite recaptured his form from those heady days of 2014. But with his strength in ultra running and his preference for the roads rather than the mountains, Comrades seemed like the perfect fit. So here he is, taking part for the first time as part of the famous and dominating Nedbank professional team.

Unfortunately, like me, Steve picked up a cold on the flight to South Africa, and he is nervously necking Strepsils as we talk. He says his training has gone well and his goal is to run the race in under six hours. He hopes that will be good enough for a place in the top ten.

'If I can make the top ten here it will be the biggest achievement of my career,' he says.

'Bigger than the Commonwealth Games?'

'Yes, definitely.'

Despite the high stakes, Steve is planning to tackle the race in a novel and experimental way. Rather than worry about time or pace, he is going to run strictly according to his heart rate.

'My watch won't even show the time,' he says. 'Only my heart rate. The plan is to keep it under 145 the whole way.' He says he has never done this before, but feels it will stop him going too fast early on.

Start slow, start slow, that's the message I keep getting. It's not my strong point, but maybe this time I can do it. After all, I don't really mind how fast I run. I just want to enjoy the experience and get to the finish. At least, that's what I thought as I bade good luck to Steve and made my way back to my hotel.

That night, in the unfamiliar hotel bed, I struggle to get to sleep. My cold seems to have got worse and I'm now coughing and spluttering like an old man. I try lying on one side, then the other. Then on my back with two pillows. Nothing helps.

I'm eventually put out of my misery by my watch buzzing on the bedside table. I sit up and turn the alarm off. 3.30 a.m. Feeling fully ill now, I lumber into the bathroom and click on the light. It's not a pretty sight that greets me in the glare of the wall-to-wall mirror. My eyes are bloodshot. I look exhausted. *Maybe this isn't a good idea. Perhaps I shouldn't run.* But the thought is fleeting. I can't give up already.

On the floor next to my bed I've laid out my race kit. I get dressed slowly. The number on my vest also has my name printed on it, though I'm not expecting many people to attempt to pronounce it. Under my name is the number '0', to indicate that this is my first Comrades. Out there waiting for me are 56 miles of road. Mostly uphill.

The hotel is putting on an early breakfast buffet, so once I'm dressed I head out into the corridor to make my way down to the restaurant. I've only gone a short way when a woman steps out of her room in a panic and starts talking to me in a language I don't recognise. She's about fifty years old and wearing running kit. She beckons me into her room, clearly upset about something.

I pause at the door. It's dark in the room. 'I'm sorry,' I say. 'I don't know what you're saying.'

'Oh, sorry,' she says, in English. 'I can't get the name tag on my bag.'

That's it? She's still flustered, so I go in and clip the tag. It fixes on easily.

'It's done?' she asks, as though I've just performed some miracle. I nod.

'Sorry,' she says. 'I guess I'm just nervous.'

I can't help smiling to myself as I carry on to breakfast. I'm not the only one facing little demons already this morning.

The race starts on one of the main thoroughfares in central Durban. It's still dark and the streets feel grimy, but the atmosphere is charged. People in running clothes zig-zag back and forth trying to find their starting zones, following the rumble of the crowd. People recognise each other, joking, back slapping. Most of them have been here before.

I make my way to Zone B, the second-fastest zone, for people who ran a qualifying marathon between three hours and 3hrs 20mins.

Comrades is a statistician's dream, with every element measured, quantified and analysed, from the ages of the starters to the professions most represented, and so on. The expo before the race is full of boards listing all this data. But the two key numbers are how many Comrades Marathons you have finished and your finishing time on the day. The time is important because it determines which type of medal you get, and this, I soon find out, is a big deal.

Craig had proudly laid out on his kitchen counter what he said was probably one of the only full sets of medals in existence. As I stood looking at them, trying to get my head around the significance – to me they were just a row of smaller-than-normal sized medals – he asked me about three times if I wanted to take a picture. Finally, realising he was getting offended at the tepidness of my reaction, I pulled out my phone.

This is how it works: the first ten finishers in the race get a gold medal. These are obviously coveted by the elite runners – not least because the top ten places also come with a fairly decent-sized packet of prize money. Anyone with one of these medals is a mighty serious runner.

However, these are not the rarest medals. That accolade goes to the Wally Hayward medal, which is for anyone who runs the race in under six hours, but finishes outside the top ten. Often this is no one, as under six hours is usually fast enough for a top ten placing. That's what makes it so rare.

Wally Hayward is a legend in Comrades folklore, considered by many the greatest Comrades runner ever. He won the race five times, the first time in 1930 at the bright age of twenty-one, making him the youngest ever winner. He went on to break the course records for both the up and the down run, becoming in the process the first person to finish the race in under six hours. Then in 1954, age forty-five, he became the oldest ever winner. And then he was banned.

Despite being an Olympic marathon runner, he was ruled to be a professional sportsman after he accepted a donation towards his travelling costs to get to a race in the UK. Comrades, as with most athletic events in those days, was strictly for amateur runners only.

The ban was eventually lifted in 1974, and then in 1988 Wally Hayward returned to the race at the age of 79 and beat half the field to finish in 9hrs 44mins. Craig says he finished just ahead of Hayward that year but has always regretted that he didn't slow down and finish together with the great man.

'Ten years later he agreed to hand me my green number,' Craig says, 'as long as I finished before teatime, as he said he would be going for a nap. One of my proudest running memories is my photo with Wally presenting me my green number.'

In 1989, Hayward became the oldest ever finisher, although he only crossed the line with less than two minutes to spare before the final cut-off.

Clearly, with a history like that, Wally Hayward warranted a medal named after him, and a rare one at that.

The next medal is the silver medal, awarded to anyone finishing between six hours and 7hrs 30mins. At the race expo, experts and veterans are on hand to help you assess your target and decide which medal you should be aiming for. I asked a few of them about my hopes for the race, and each time the conversation went basically like this:

> **Race expert:** What's your best marathon time?
> **Me:** 2hrs 50mins.
> **Expert (looking quite impressed):** This year?
> **Me:** No. This year 3hrs 8mins.
> **Expert (looking slightly less impressed):** You should be a comfortable silver. How many kilometres have you been running in training?
> **Me:** About 70km a week since January.
> **Expert (looking quite unimpressed):** Hmmm, I'd want a bit more for a silver. It all depends on the day.

So, it seemed I was a borderline silver, for what it was worth. Not that it really mattered to me, I was just here to run as well as I could.

After silver, the next medal is called the Bill Rowan, awarded to those running under nine hours. Bill Rowan was the winner of the first ever Comrades Marathon. His winning time was 8hrs 59mins.

Those running under 11 hours are awarded a bronze medal, while anyone finishing between 11 and 12 hours is awarded a Vic Clapham medal, named after the founder of the race.

And after that? Well, there is no after that. On the stroke of the twelfth hour they close the finish and the race is over. Anyone still running is disqualified and declared a non-finisher, even if they are only a few steps from the end at that point.

It may seem cruel, to be ruled out after 12 hours of running, but debate rages among the old timers I meet about whether even that cut-off is too generous. Each year, over half the field finishes in that last hour, with a huge proportion finishing in the last 10 minutes. But for most of the race's history, the final cut off was 11 hours. It was only in 2000, in an effort to increase the number of entries and to celebrate the new millennium, that they changed it.

Craig for one is not happy. He points to people in the past who had to retire once 11 hours became too difficult – this is roughly the equivalent of running two 4:45 marathons back to back and then a 5K in 30 minutes, all without stopping, and over a hilly route.

'It's not really fair,' Craig says. 'Now you get guys racking up thirty and forty finishes, but they wouldn't have been able to do that before 2000.'

I can see what he's saying, but I'm struggling to get worked up about it. The number of races you can accumulate is impressive, sure, but it seems unique to Comrades that it matters quite so much. At his first-time runners area at the expo, Craig had arranged for some of the race veterans with the most finishes to their name to come to talk to the newbies. I asked a few of them why they kept coming back to do the race again and again.

Barry Holland, who had run the race forty-four times, put it simply: 'I'm from Durban. Comrades is in the DNA.'

Dave Williams, meanwhile, who had run the race a mere forty-one times, said: 'I treat it like a guy playing a round of golf. I take my time.' I wonder if there is anywhere else in the world where people would consider an ultra marathon similar to a round of golf.

Another new runner I meet at the expo, a woman from Cape Town, tells me that sixty-seven runners from her club have done it, so she thought it was time she did it too. It's funny that she knows the exact number.

The consensus for running Comrades seems to be: if you're a runner in South Africa, then it's just what you do. Comrades is the foundation on which South African running is built. It was the starting point, and everything else has worked backwards from there. Most of the other iconic races in the country, such as the Two Oceans marathon, began as warm-up races for Comrades. This is why they are all slightly shorter ultra marathons. And because of Comrades, in South Africa ultra running is considered normal and mainstream in a way it isn't in any other part of the world. In the same way people elsewhere may talk of one day running a marathon, in South Africa, the equivalent challenge is Comrades. Unfortunately for them, their Everest is over twice the size of everyone else's. Or perhaps fortunately, because as I'm about to discover, Comrades puts just about every other mass participation race in the world in the cold shade.

8

The start area is a heaving mass of people by the time I get there. I have to push through bodies like I'm in a football crowd to get into my starting zone. A sound system is blaring out tub-thumping 1980s pop classics, while the announcer, who sounds like he has drunk a gallon of coffee, gees everyone up, constantly telling us how long until the start, getting everyone to shout out how ready they are, while huge projections light up the office blocks and apartment buildings across the city. It's only just after 5 a.m. No one is sleeping in Durban tonight.

And then it starts. I'm worried I've been oversold the Comrades pre-race ritual. Countless people have told me how they stood there in tears with the emotion of it, getting goosebumps in those final moments. I'm expecting too much. Without the spontaneity it won't work, surely. You can't pre-register for emotion, timetable it like that. And sure enough, as act one begins, as they blare out the South African national anthem, I'm watching out for the goosebumps, my cynicism on guard to chase them away. I'm not manipulated that easily. At any rate, the people around me continue chatting, ignoring the music.

But then part two of the Comrades opening sequence

kicks in, and despite myself I start to get swept up in it. It's a traditional song sung by a mass choir, full of deep, soulful voices. Runners begin singing along, swaying . . . '*Shosholoza*' . . . it means go forward, and it bleeds with the pain of generations of struggle. As the song rises it seems to bring everyone together in a huge mass of noise and energy, as though the country's turbulent history is being faced down by seventeen thousand voices all at once.

But this is not the time to dwell on the past; what is happening here is a movement of emotions, a surging and falling, a coming together. The first strains of 'Chariots of Fire' induce cheers from the crowd. This should feel clichéd, but we're drenched in it now and the famous Vangelis music has us soaring like Olympians about to embark on our greatest challenge. I'm smiling and clenching my fists, ready to roll.

The final send-off is a cockerel's crow. Comrades is buttered thick in traditions and this is yet another. In 1948, local runner Max Trimborn couldn't contain his nervous energy on the start line, so he cupped his hands and gave a hearty rooster crow. It was a spontaneous gesture, but the other runners demanded repeat performances in subsequent years. Trimborn obliged for the next thirty-two years, sometimes even turning up wearing feathers and a rooster vest. By his death in 1985, Trimborn's crowing had been preserved on tape and is now played out at the start each year. It's followed by a bang. And we're off running.

I'm drifting back in the rush to cross the start line and I soon find myself mostly surrounded by runners from Zone C – I know because our starting pen is included along with all the other information on our numbers, which we all wear on the back and front. A slow start is fine. This is what I was told to do. Start slowly.

Despite the chill in the air at this early hour, the streets are lined with people watching, clapping and whooping. Along the edges of the road, runners are rushing by, zig-zagging through everyone like it's a 10K race. Patience, patience, I tell myself. The first mile clicks by in 9mins 36secs. Slow, but it's too early to worry about the time.

We wind through the concrete outskirts of the city, past shuttered-down shops, following the biggest roads, three lanes wide, swooping bridges over markets being set up for the day. The runners around me are mostly quiet. A few, spotting that I'm a first-timer, offer advice or ask me where I'm from. My number also points out that I'm a foreigner, but doesn't specify my country.

'I read your book,' one person says, recognising my name. Another just says 'Go, Adharanand', somehow pronouncing it perfectly.

As the road sweeps up into the hills and out of the city, all I can see ahead of me are thousands of bobbing heads, a sea of moving life in an otherwise concrete landscape. I started a mere 30 metres or so from the front but I seem to be way back now. I glance behind, where the faintest paling of the sky has begun. The road behind is another swarm of humanity, stretching as far back as I can see.

At one point we pass under a road bridge and I catch a

glimpse of a group of people in white hooded robes standing around a fire with their arms out, their eyes closed. It's an eerie sight. Who are they? Are they praying for our wellbeing, or perhaps our eternal damnation?

I don't notice it get light, but by the time I'm struggling up Cowies, the first of the 'big five' hills – even the hills have their own folklore at Comrades – the day has begun to bloom. I decide on a pattern of walking one minute and then running five minutes until I get to the top. I'm managing my body, saving energy for the struggles ahead.

It feels nice to walk, to take the strain away for a few moments, to look around and take it in. We're still on a major road, going up, but the concrete city has given way to roadside scrub, scrawny trees, tough-looking grass.

Along the road are big signs counting down the distance left to run. The numbers are still huge, 73km, 72km, but the fact they get smaller each time helps. It's a little boost whenever we reach one.

The crowds lining the route grow bigger as the day awakens, with music and people dancing. It's one big party. While they close the roads for us, and we get to be cheered on like heroes, I realise we're also providing the day's entertainment. People are not only supporting us out of the kindness of their hearts, but because it's a fun thing to do, to witness all these people attempting this ridiculous distance. You get to stand there by the road eating a burger, or sit on your deck chair with a beer, and watch the pain, the effort, the madness, all for free.

Another runner, who lives in Canada, recognises me from my books and we run together for a while chatting. The kilometres click by unnoticed, which is how it should be at this stage. He tells me he ran the race the year before but didn't finish. He started too fast, he says, so this year he's being careful. We're on pace for around 8hrs 15mins, he tells me. It's the first time I've tried to work it out. The silver medal, I realise, is already gone. I would have to run so hard from here to even attempt it, and I feel right now that any faster would be dangerous. So I settle in my mind for a sub-nine-hour finish and a Bill Rowan medal. That should be comfortable.

We run on, mostly up, through open countryside, cliff faces jutting above the road, and on through built-up areas where people sit in their gardens stoking barbecues and drinking.

I start to get ahead of my Canadian friend at some point. 'Are you pushing on?' he asks, looking a little concerned.

I feel like I'm going the same pace. 'Maybe a little,' I reply. 'I'm sure we'll pass each other again later.' But we never do.

About 30km into the race I start feeling the first signs of fatigue. My legs are finding it heavy going up some of the bigger hills, it's getting gradually hotter and I find myself looking out for the aid stations with more urgency. I start hearing talk of 'the bus' from people on the sides of the road.

'The first bus is coming,' they say, excited. We pass an Elvis impersonator up on a stage.

'I was looking for a big bus on wheels,' he says, to a tiny ripple of laughter.

I feel it, hear it, before I see it. A surge of feet on the road. I hear a South African voice: 'We're now passing a lot of people who went out too fast, but we need to stay in control. Pick your seat on the bus and stay there, we'll get you to the finish.'

And with that I'm swallowed by the bus, a huge group of runners following a man with powerful, determined shoulders and carrying a flag on his back that reads '8 hrs 30'.

The Comrades pacemakers are yet another race tradition, and the groups that follow them are known as buses. They're often full of songs and chanting as the runners work together to reach their goal time. At first I'm a bit shocked to have slipped back to 8 hrs 30 pace, but now I'm here I decide I'll ride the bus for a while.

The 'driver' is an impressive guy, talking, cajoling, encouraging us constantly as he runs. Occasionally he gets us to walk a little, for twenty or thirty seconds, as we raise our arms above our heads and stretch out our hamstrings.

When we get to an aid station, we swarm all over it like a band of marauding Vikings, grabbing water, Coke, potatoes dipped in salt. As we approach, we hear the aid station captain warning his team to prepare. 'The first bus is coming,' he yells. 'All hands on deck.'

The further we get through the race, the bigger these aid stations get, lining the road on both sides for 100 metres or so. It's chaos as we hit them, those slowing runners ahead of us looking over their shoulders in panic as we bludgeon our way through.

On the other side we regroup and find our rhythm again. It really feels like we're a unit on a long march. It brings to mind Vic Clapham's experiences with his comrades during the First World War, over a hundred years earlier, and how he wanted this race to live on as a tribute to their strength and sacrifice. At the end, of course, we will reach not a battlefield, but the finish line, a shower and a hotel bed, yet for a moment we get to catch a glimpse of greater struggles and the camaraderie that can help to overcome them.

As we reach halfway, I'm finding it hard to maintain the pace, but I can feel the power of the bus, carrying me along. In the middle of the group, I can switch off and just run. Here with my comrades, I feel like I can make it.

'Run the kilometre you're in. Don't worry about how many you have left, just run this one,' our leader tells us. It's good advice. The signs are still declaring 46km to go. I'm too tired, surely, to keep this up for that long. But for one kilometre, I can do it. Hang in there.

'You all came here today for your Bill Rowan,' he says. 'Stay on the bus and you'll all do it. We'll get you there.'

As we catch and pass people, many of them, as I did, join the bus, and so it keeps growing. At times it's hard not to bump into other runners. Two men beside me are getting irritated with each other, each blaming the other for the constant knocks. Then one of them receives one knock too many.

'You want to fuck with me?' he yells. The bus driver glances over his shoulder and spots the source of the animosity straight away. He holds up his hand. 'Hey,' he yells, screeching to a halt. 'Stop the bus!' We all concertina to a juddering halt.

'If you're going to fight, get off my bus.' He's not messing around, glaring at the two men.

'This is the love bus,' someone shouts.

'We're all comrades, in this together,' the driver goes on.

'We need to help each other. We're all Africans here, I don't care your colour.'

The two men are shaking hands, saying sorry. Tails between their legs.

The driver turns back to the front, gives the command, and we run on, giving each other space, but somehow now closer than ever. 'We are the Rainbow Nation,' he says, his shoulders powering on ahead of me. 'This is our day. Be proud.' I feel an emotional stirring. We really are a unit, a force. And the kilometres are passing relentlessly.

I last in the bus for about an hour, thriving on its energy and momentum, but eventually I lose contact as I begin to hit a bad patch. Left on my own, my deterioration is rapid. Suddenly I'm struggling to run at all, my form has shrunk to a shuffle and everything is aching, my feet, my calves, my hips. It's bearable until I think about how far I still have to run: almost a marathon, like this, already in pain. It's not possible.

I'm at my lowest point, walking as much as running, when someone, another runner, calls me by my name. It's strange how we can be so exhausted but still have a conversation. The runner is a friend of a friend of mine. He has 'Stretch', his nickname, written on his number.

'There's another bus behind us,' he says. 'We're not going to get that Bill Rowan.'

'We're not?' The thought sends me into a mild panic. My ego is stung. The guy who was shooting for a silver, surely he didn't slip to a bronze. Suddenly I need that Bill Rowan.

'It depends how you're feeling,' says Stretch. 'But I don't think so.'

I'm off, picking up the pace. I realise I can still run if I have to, that I've been giving in to my aches and pains, dwelling on them, on the slight sick feeling in my stomach, on the beginnings of a blister on one toe. I've been focusing in on them, feeling sorry for myself. The thought of losing the Bill Rowan is like a slap in the face. 'Come on, get going!'

It lasts a few miles. I'm passing people again. The road is full of people walking, dejected, hunched over. But then, like the wind dying in my sails, the energy at my back fades. I decide to walk a little. Then I can't start running again.

Stretch passes me again. I grab a drink and some food from an aid station. I think of that bloody Bill Rowan slipping away, and I'm back up on my toes and running. It's funny, a few days ago I had never heard of Bill Rowan or his medal, but now it is my sole focus; my entire existence right at this moment is filled with the effort to attain it.

It goes on like this, my energy ebbing and flowing. Then with 30km still to go, my hamstring seems to tear. It hurts like hell going down the hills, so I stop at one of the many massage stations, where two people, one on each leg, rub like crazy, pressing ice into my legs. 'OK, go, go,' they say, and I lumber off again.

I keep trying to calculate whether I'm going to make it. But my brain is losing its ability to compute even the simplest numbers. One guy, wearing Union Jacks all over, says we have plenty of time. 'Come on, mate, we'll do it,' he says, sounding as fresh and chirpy as a London market trader setting up for the day.

And then, with 5km to go, it happens again. Just like at

Miwok, the cloud lifts. It's like I've been injected with something strong. With the realisation that I'm in sight of the finish, perhaps. That this is a distance I can cope with. My legs suddenly start to run, really run, with bounce, energy. I'm racing past people, cruising, the road seemingly now permanently tilted downwards. The fear, the panic of being passed by the nine-hour bus subsides. I'm going to make it.

I turn into the racecourse where the crowds have gathered for the finish. Someone calls my name and I wave, happily. Bill Rowan, you are mine. I cross the line with 15 minutes to spare, in 8hrs 44mins.

Inside the finishing area a woman hands me my medal. I have an urge to cry, or to put my head on someone's shoulder. Instead I hold her hand. She holds me firm, looking at me. I notice all along beside me other runners are hugging the men and women handing out the medals. This is their job, to be there as we crash against the finish. She looks at me.

'You OK?' she asks. I nod, afraid to speak in case I blubber. I let go of her hand and make my way back out into the world, and she prepares for the next emotional wreck to come her way.

As I make my way to the baggage collection point, taking my time in the late afternoon sun, I see the nine-hour bus finishing a few minutes ahead of the Bill Rowan cut-off, a surge of people, each one completing their goal, each one making it, after all those hours out there on the road. It's too much, I'm crying, tears running down my face. I let them come, it feels sweet, a relief, to shed tears at such an immense effort by so many.

Later, after I'm recovered, having eaten and had a cele-bratory beer, I head back to the finish to watch the final 12-hour cut-off. It's dark now. These people finishing have been out there since before dawn, pushing themselves along the punishing road. I climb up into the grandstand beside the finish and despite my tired legs I stand swaying to the music blaring out across the sky. We have just minutes left. People are arriving now like the gates of heaven are about to close, their arms spread wide, their heads back in exultation, the weak and weary being carried across the line by other runners. I'm an emotional wreck watching it and I'm glad I'm alone so I can let myself go.

We're down to the last 30 seconds. People are just round-ing the last corner, in view of the finish, 100 metres still to run, sprinting, killing it, ten, nine . . . the announcer is counting down . . . three, two, one.

And with that the noise stops, the lights go out and the finish is cut off by a row of officials with their backs to the runners. Those who don't make it collapse to the floor, or stand in the dark, stunned – so close. Mournfully, a trumpet starts playing the Last Post, as the non-finishers – people who have spent the last twelve hours in hope, fear, straining everything, pushing their bodies to get there in time – are led out through a side gate. They are not even allowed the satisfaction of crossing the finish line.

To complete this race is not something that comes easy. I reach in and feel the Bill Rowan in my pocket. It's the smallest medal I've ever won, but somehow one of the most meaningful.

I'm flying home the next day, but before I do, Craig has pulled some strings to get me into the prize-giving breakfast in Durban. I arrive hobbling, my hamstring really gone, to a room full of round tables, athletes in team tracksuits, the officials in their blazers. I nod to some of the people I've met over the last few days, trying to find somewhere to sit. At the Nedbank table – the top elite team – I spot a seat next to Steve Way.

I walk over and sit down next to him. It turns out he had an amazing race. He shows me his gold medal, grinning. He says he stuck to his plan to run according to his heart rate, and at the first checkpoint, at mile 12, he was back in around 120th position. Twenty miles into the race he was still back in ninety-fourth. As people began to falter and drop their pace later in the race, though, he began his charge. 'I was passing people for 70km,' he says. 'It was great.' Up Polly Shortts, the last of the big hills, he moved from nineteenth place into ninth, which is where he finished. 'Running up that hill, people were tired. It was exciting. That's when I realised it might happen.'

The Nedbank table is filling up, so I decide to give Steve some space. He's in high demand after also finishing as the top over-forties runner and the top first-time runner. Both accolades come with sizeable cheques, making it his biggest ever payday. It makes me wonder why more of the world's top ultra runners don't give this race a go.

As I mill around the room, without a designated seat at

any of the tables, I spot the winner of the women's race, an American called Camille Herron. I approach and politely ask if I can have a few words. I'm a journalist, I explain, and I'm writing a book about ultra running.

She smiles, but fixes me with an intense stare. 'Then you have to talk to me,' she says. 'I have a crazy story.'

I'm not sure what to say. What is it about ultra runners and their crazy backstories?

'What is it?' I ask.

'When I was sixteen,' she says. 'My whole family was made homeless by a tornado.'

Before she can say more, the prize giving begins, so it's not until a few months later, on the phone, that Camille gives me the rest of her story. In the meantime, she has been busy, following up her Comrades victory with an insane 100-mile trail world record, breaking the previous women's record by over an hour. Her time of 12 hours 42 minutes is the fastest 100-mile trail run of the year by any man or woman. And it was the first time she had ever run 100 miles.

Not stopping there, a month later she was out breaking the 12-hour world record, which had been set by one of the legends of the sport, Ann Trason, back in 1991.

But I take her back to the tornado she had begun telling me about in Durban. I'm intrigued. Is that what set her on her way to becoming the runner she is today?

She laughs. In fact, she laughs in response to every question. 'My husband can't believe all the problems I've been through,' she says. 'I had seven stress fractures at college, my coach told me I wasn't good enough. But I'm just a positive person. I'm always smiling. I was born on Christmas Day and my mom says I just came into the world smiling.'

She was still in high school when the tornado struck. 'We knew it was coming, but we'd seen them before, so I didn't take anything with me. I'd just got out of the shower when my dad told me we were leaving. I just had the clothes I was wearing.'

The tornado, it turned out, was the strongest ever recorded on Earth, with winds of over 300mph.

'Forty people died where I lived,' she says. 'Afterwards it was like an atomic bomb had hit.'

She says that being homeless – she slept on her grandparents' couch for the summer – motivated her to do well enough to get recruited for a college cross-country team. 'It teaches you the value of life and experiences rather than possessions,' she says. But things didn't go well in her college career and she suffered multiple injuries.

'My coach told me I wasn't cut out for it,' she recalls, her voice wavering just a tiny bit. 'But I really felt there was something inside. I wasn't the fastest, I knew that, but I just never got tired.'

Camille is known for her unorthodox running style – she barely lifts her legs and looks more like she's cross-country skiing than running, or like someone doing the twist on roller skates. 'My gait is different,' she says. 'I was born with my right femur anteverted – twisted inwards. Basically I was born with a not perfect body.'

She says it meant her gait was asymmetrical, so she had to adapt her stride to put less force and stress on the body. 'So I developed this shuffle where I lift off the ground rather than push off it. It's not fast or powerful. I'm probably the slowest 5K runner who can run a sub-2:40 marathon. But for ultras . . . it's like I'm skimming off the ground. Friends who run with me say they can't hear me, I'm like a hovercraft.'

After her injury problems at college, Camille stopped running seriously. It was only when her husband, who was training for the US Olympic trials marathon, noticed that she was running more than he was, that she started to take it seriously again.

'He started coaching me and I went back to grad school to learn all about bones.'

Camille, determined to fix her injury problems, studied physiology and wrote her masters thesis on bone recovery.

'My parents say my greatest strength is my mind, because I apply science to being a better athlete. I read *The Self-Made Olympian* by Ron Daws . . . this guy was not super talented, but he worked very hard and was very methodical.'

The result of her methodical approach is that she has now run over 100 miles every week for eleven consecutive years, with no injuries.

'Now I have legs of steel,' she says.

For a long time she focused on marathons with some success, winning races across the US and regularly finishing in under 2hrs 40mins. It wasn't until 2013 that she tried ultra running. Her first foray was the 56km Two Oceans marathon in South Africa, which she says was not a huge success. Then in 2014 she tried Comrades for the first time.

'I was holding on to fourth place in my first Comrades,' she says. 'But I had a stomach virus and a fever, I had diarrhoea and I was blacking out. I kept thinking of Meb Keflezighi, who had won Boston that year, trying to force myself on.' In the end she collapsed at 83km.

That could have been it for Camille and ultra running, but in 2015 she entered the Mad City 100K in Madison, Wisconsin, which was also the US national championships. She won, finishing in the third-fastest time ever by an American woman.

'I was pretty stoked,' she recalls. 'I'd just won the national title and ran the fastest time in the world in like eight years. On the way home the race director phoned me up and was so excited, and that was when it dawned on me . . . I might be good at this. I was like Billy Elliot doing ballet for the first time, it just felt really good.'

She followed that first national title a few months later by winning the 100km World Championships. Then she broke Ann Trason's 50-mile world record, and then, like an unstoppable ultra-running cyclone, she won the 50km World Championships.

Somewhere between the tornado, the endless smiling, the shuffling gait and the scientific approach to training lies a secret recipe for ultra-running success. Perhaps. 'Maybe it's just genetic,' she says, 'Like maybe I have super mitochondria or something. I'd love to donate myself to science one day to find out why I never get tired.'

It's certainly not what she eats, she says. 'I grew up in

Oklahoma eating meat and potatoes, and that's what I eat. It's funny, because I had my diet analysed and they were surprised by how much meat I ate, but they found that my energy balance was very in tune with what my body needs.'

I can't let Camille go without asking her about the beer. It has become her trademark in recent races to drink a beer or two during the race. Even in her incredible 100-mile world record, there she was, still running and downing bottles of beer. What is that about, I ask her.

'Oh man,' she says, laughing even more than usual. 'That sort of happened by accident. I was running a 100km trail race about a year ago and I caught the leading guy, and he was a bit spooked. It's exciting as a woman that I get to reel in the men. The further I go the more guys I start to pass.

'But soon after I passed this guy, I got a bit dizzy. It was hot and at the next aid station I was slumped on a chair and he overtook me again. They were trying to revive me, and we had this six-pack in the car for after the race, but my husband just said, 'You want a beer?' I chugged it down and suddenly I perked up and got running again. I was flying, and I caught the guy again. I ended up winning and breaking the course record by 27 minutes.'

Is there any science behind that, or was it some sort of miracle performed by the beer gods?

'I don't know,' she says. 'I had taken on all this fuel at the aid station before and I think all the blood had gone to my stomach. The beer sent it back to my brain.'

In Comrades, again, Camille grabbed a beer from her husband with a few miles to go, much to the amazement of the millions in South Africa watching the race on TV.

'My hamstrings had got tight,' she says. 'The beer took my mind off it. It chilled me out and I felt better.'

That old mind again, hey? Of course, people have always known and talked about how important the mind is in running, but I'm beginning to think that in ultra running it plays an even bigger role. Getting on top of it, however, and learning to control it, will continue to prove more challenging than I could possibly imagine.

9

The hamstring I strained during Comrades stops me from running for a couple of weeks, but I'm soon back out training. Which is good, because I have my hardest series of races coming up. When I first planned my year of racing, I posted my schedule online. Reactions ranged from 'Crikey' to 'Christ on a bike' to 'You're the Yuki Kawauchi of ultra running' (in reference to the famous Japanese marathon runner who races almost every weekend).

People usually give themselves two years to accumulate UTMB points, rather than one, and in most cases they don't even contemplate entering the UTMB until they've already been running ultra marathons for a few years. But as well as trying to get the points in a year, there are a couple of other races, such as Comrades, that I felt I had to do to get a fuller experience and understanding of the world of ultra running. So looming ahead of me now, after Comrades, is a crazy five-week spell in which I plan to run the Ring O' Fire, a three-day, 135-mile race around the entire coast of Anglesey in North Wales (worth five UTMB points), a 100-mile race through the Pyrenees in the south of France (six UTMB points), and, sandwiched in between, a little race in south London I just couldn't resist.

The year before, I'd been commissioned to write an article about a 24-hour track race in Tooting for the *Guardian* and I had gone along to watch. What initially seemed rather tedious and pointless, people jogging slowly around and around a track, began, as the hours went by, to turn into something moving and magnificent. In the most uninspiring setting, people were going through life-changing experiences, right there in front of me, as though on stage.

The race started at midday, so I watched the first few hours, before later returning in the dead of the night, at 3 a.m., to see what was going on. And there they were, while most of London was asleep, still lapping the track, each on his own silent journey to nowhere. The air in the arena felt charged, yet somehow peaceful. What was it? I decided there and then that I had to run this race.

I will just have to deal with the fact that it comes two weeks after the Ring O' Fire and three weeks before I run 100 miles through the Pyrenees. My plan is that I will take the Ring O' Fire easy. It is split into three days, so I will just jog around each day to collect the UTMB points. Then I will put everything into the track race. Then, no matter how broken I am, I'll simply drag myself around the 100 miles in the mountains. The fact that I will need the final six points for the UTMB will be enough to get me around, I'm sure. That's the plan.

A few people are so concerned when they see my schedule that they decide to contact me. They're worried about my ability to recover with so little time between the races. My coach, Tom, is also concerned. I'm risking injury, he says. Of course, running ultras and training for them comes with an inherent high risk of injury even without piling the races up like this. I have been lucky so far, but will it last?

Or maybe it hasn't all been luck. Right at the start, as I set out on this ultra running journey, I was already dealing with an injury problem. By then I'd been running regularly for seven years and during that time I had been on a process of discovery regarding running form. Like many people, it began with the 2009 book *Born to Run* by Christopher McDougall. The basic premise of that book is that humans evolved in part through our ability to run long distances. Among the animal kingdom, on a hot day (when we can engage our superior heat reduction system, also known as sweating) we're one of the fastest species at running over a long distance – or at least our ancestors were, before the invention of cars, shoes, chairs, offices, remote control TV and everything else.

In *Born to Run*, McDougall is compelling in his argument that to run without injury all you need to do is run in the way you were designed: without shoes. It was typical running shoes, he said, with all their padding, that were causing everyone to get injured. Without cushioned shoes, your brain would feel the impact of the ground and soon make the necessary adjustments to how you run.

Thousands of people read this, got enthused, but then thought, I can't really run around without shoes on; what about glass, what about dog poo, what about looking like an idiot? In response, a whole movement and industry grew up. Shoe design changed. A running revolution took place. The days of 70 per cent of runners getting injured each year were over. Except they weren't.

A number of studies into the question began to surface with contradictory findings. The biggest and most comprehensive of these, by Allison Altman of the University of Delaware and Irene Davis of Harvard, which was published in the *British Journal of Sports Medicine* in 2016, found almost identical injury rates between regular shod runners and barefoot runners.

In my own case, despite my zeal and willingness to go further than just changing my shoes, but to learn about form, to work on my core strength, to try yoga, muscle activation, to spend hours squatting to improve my mobility, my problem was that as I began my investigation into the world of ultra running, I was injured. Since I first read *Born to Run* and started changing my form, I had been muddling through – including finishing six marathons – with a niggling and persistent pain in both Achilles tendons. But how could I run ultra marathons in this state? Surely I would break at some point. I needed to get them fixed.

Most of my techniques for coping or attempting to fix myself came from my core strength and movement coach, Joe Kelly. Joe is on a lifelong journey to figure out how to get the body to move as it was designed to, smoothly, efficiently, like the pinnacle of evolutionary brilliance it is, rather than the clapped-out vehicle most of us end up riding around in. Just watch the runners in any city at lunchtime, office workers loping by, grimacing in pain. I know they feel better for it afterwards, that after a shower and some food they'll be glowing with endorphins, but it doesn't look like many of them are enjoying the actual process.

I know because I was one of them, jarring along. I loved running, and once I got warmed up and moving, though I was far from perfect, I had got to a place where the sense of movement brought with it a pleasant fluidity, a zip and sensation of strength. But it still felt as though I had all these brakes on, my wheels were rubbing, my tyres were flat and something was clacking in my spokes. And mostly it was my Achilles. They were especially bad on those rushed lunchtime runs in the city. The first mile was the worst. And after the run, when I got up from my desk in the afternoon . . . ouch.

'Are you limping?' someone would say.

'No!' I would deny it flatly. I couldn't bear to admit it. 'It's just my gangster walk.'

Why didn't I simply give up on the barefoot running idea? For a start, I wasn't actually running barefoot or even in extreme minimalist shoes. But I had purposefully transitioned from being a heel striker to being a midfoot striker – supposedly the natural, 'barefoot' way to run – and I usually wore the lightest, least cushioned shoes I could find, even though they were still running shoes made by companies like Nike and Brooks.

Yet I couldn't go back to heel striking. I had injuries in those days too, even though I didn't run nearly as much. Back then I had sore knees, hips, everything. At least now it was mostly just my Achilles. And my new way of running – more upright, landing on my midfoot – felt smoother, faster. It was just that my body wasn't quite able to cope, despite everything I tried.

I decided to go back to my original mentor, the movement coach Lee Saxby. He had first taught me how to change my form to land on my midfoot, but after another few sessions he was close to despair at my lack of mobility.

Saxby has a series of basic tests he says you need to be able to pass before you should even start running. One is a comfortable deep squat. But I was still hopeless at it and I could barely get down below being bent double at the hips.

'I don't know how you run as much as you do,' he said, shaking his head.

I did it by grimacing and pretending I wasn't in pain. In the desert in Oman it niggled but never got unbearable, but maybe that was because we were running on sand. I had managed to run 34 miles along the Devon coast path. But 105 miles around Mont Blanc was going to be too much, surely. I was in denial, but I was a bad injury waiting to happen.

In a panic I finally went to see a physiotherapist. After the Devon race, things had got worse. A lump had appeared on the back of my right heel. It looked really bad and throbbed painfully after each run. The physio examined me and concluded that I had reduced movement in my ankles. It was the same diagnosis as from everyone else, but rather than getting me to fix it by squatting, as Saxby had prescribed, he told me to stop squatting completely. And to stop wearing minimal shoes. I needed support under my heels, he said.

This was a real affront to everything I had learned about feet and running form. The minimal shoes allowed my feet room to move, to expand, to feel the ground and then feed vital information on how to run to my brain. Wrapping them up in cushioned shoes felt wrong. It felt like I was bandaging my feet up, taking them out of the game. But, then, that lump on my heel, it didn't look good.

The physio wasn't actually that concerned about the lump, and was more worried about my Achilles being sore when I ran. I met a few doctors casually and showed them the lump. No one seemed too concerned. A heel spur, they said, as though it was a freckle or something. But it scared me into following the physio's advice, wearing cushioned shoes, stretching my calves three times a day, and doing heel drops off the stairs.

But it was all to no avail. If anything, things got even worse. The only thing that didn't make my Achilles worse was to not do any squats, any stretching or any heel raises. When I did nothing, apart from running, at least it didn't get worse. So for a while I did nothing, putting my trust in a higher power, the god of stubborn injuries, to appear one night and magic away the pain. I wasn't too hopeful.

Circling around me, as I stand in the middle of his tiny gym in a garage in Totnes, in south Devon, Joe Kelly is deep in thought. He's determined to get to the bottom of my problems. Joe is constantly studying, tweaking, adjusting his techniques and treatments, hoovering up all the latest knowledge out there, reading books, attending courses, and then trying it all out on me. I'm like his laboratory rat. I'm often left giggling at what he'll come up with next. He has me in all sorts of ridiculous contortions. One day he has me looking one way with my eyes while jutting my jaw in the opposite direction. Try doing that without laughing. Another time he starts massaging my eyes with a cotton bud. Another time he simply gets me to look at some lines on his phone. That is it; that is the treatment.

We get some small improvement from massaging a scar on my left knee. Joe's basic method is to perform a strength test on me, do the treatment, and then perform the test again. If anything moves or changes, then we might be on to something. Bizarrely, I am clearly stronger after the scar massage. But it doesn't solve the Achilles problem.

'Something else is going on with you,' he says, pondering me, the room, the universe. I'm clearly a complex case. 'All these things are helping, but we need to get right back to the root of the problem.'

We get a breakthrough when he starts asking me about my injury history and I tell him that I've broken my left wrist three times. It's not something I ever thought could be relevant to my Achilles, but Joe is excited by the discovery and starts pressing and prodding my wrist. The results are startling. Just holding my left wrist with my other hand instantly doubles my leg strength. Could this be it? Joe doesn't seem convinced, and sure enough, whenever I run over the next few weeks, the pesky Achilles still hurt.

One day Joe starts talking excitedly about some new thing he has learned. He often does this, moving through techniques, assimilating them and then moving on, like a child opening presents on Christmas Day. His latest new thing is called Anatomy in Motion. He watches me thoughtfully as I walk up and down the room and then gives me 'a movement'. It involves stepping forward on one leg, raising an arm and somehow twisting.

'Do you feel the difference?' he asks. I don't. I feel the same.

'I'm not sure,' I say. But he's so convinced it could help that I give it a go, doing it at home each morning.

Of course, a lot of people will be thinking that this all sounds like mumbo-jumbo and I should stop wasting my time (and the readers' time) with all these unproven techniques. Get yourself some surgery, some people are probably thinking. My coach suggests Shockwave Therapy, which sounds a little scary. But I'm still sold on the idea that humans are by nature designed to run, and that if we can just iron out all the kinks that we've picked up from a lifetime of sitting in offices, in cars, on sofas, everything will fix itself. I'm like a shirt that has been left in a crinkly pile for forty years – Joe is trying to iron me out, but some of the creases are proving stubborn.

One night a few weeks later, I find myself on the train watching a re-run of a TV programme on my laptop. It's a BBC2 series called *Doctor in the House* and Joe has told me to watch it. The basic premise is that a GP goes to live with a family for a few weeks. Rather than only having ten minutes in his surgery with them, he gets to see how they live, and to fix their health issues by treating the source of their problems, rather than just giving them a pill to take away the pain.

In this particular episode it's a family in which the young son has eczema and the father, Ray, has chronic back pain. Ray is a bodybuilder with his own gym, but says he has been on painkillers for 25 years. His back hurts constantly, he hasn't had a proper night's sleep in all that time, and he's permanently grumpy. It's a sorry state of affairs and the doctor suggests a few things that don't make much difference, before he takes Ray to visit a practitioner in London called Gary Ward, who, he explains, has developed a technique called Anatomy in Motion.

In the taxi on the way to the appointment, Ray is sceptical. 'I can't help thinking, I've seen all the doctors, I've seen all the specialists, they've not been able to help me, so what's this other expert got that they haven't got?'

By the end of the session, Ray has some movements just like the one Joe gave me. He seems enthused by the treatment, and goes back to his gym where, rather than lift weights, he does his movements, standing in front of the mirror. It's funny to see Joe's stuff on mainstream TV. And then something amazing happens: Ray gets cured. His back completely stops hurting.

The doctor goes back to see him a few weeks later and Ray is a new man. 'My back pain has gone,' he says. 'I'm on cloud nine.' At the end of the programme, two months later, his back is still pain-free. An emotional Ray says: 'I feel about twenty years younger. I'm not overstating it, this is life-changing for me. It's unreal.'

The ticket inspector on the train stops to check my ticket. When she sees what I'm watching she smiles. 'I saw that the other night,' she says. 'Wasn't it amazing how he got his back fixed?'

I start working harder at my movement and become convinced it is helping. But my Achilles are still hurting. This is about a month before the Miwok 100K and I'm in full training. Before I go any further, I decide I have to see this miracle worker in person.

Gary Ward, the man behind Anatomy in Motion, is clearly a busy man. When I email him I get an automatic reply:

'With all of the recent activity from the Dr in the House programme, it has been unusually busy. If you are seeking some guidance with your body, I have set up the new website so that you can access other professionals that have taken my course.'

Eventually, with a bit of persistence, I get through to him and he agrees to see me. And so, a week later, I'm standing outside his house on a suburban street in north London.

I ring the doorbell. It's a still, grey day. The rows of 1930s semi-detached houses are unassuming, as though even they are bored of nothing ever happening around here. Or at least, that's what they want me to believe, perhaps. The postman nipping in and out through the small, metal gates is the only sign of life.

The door opens and Gary stands there in his tracksuit smiling. 'Come in,' he says.

Before we can start with the treatment we have to make some space in his small living room, pushing the glass coffee table to one side and moving some boxes of children's toys. A huge flat-screen TV hangs on the wall opposite a leather sofa. I tell him as we move things that I'm particularly interested in movement and how it relates to running form.

'I hate the running form question,' he says softly, throwing me slightly.

'Why?' I ask.

'Because it's all bollocks.'

I don't know what to say. Surely good form is a key difference between good runners and bad runners? Good form is my holy grail and I've been chasing it like a toothless prospector for years, sure that my poor form is the only thing holding me back from greatness.

'What about the Kenyans?' I protest. They have great form, born out of growing up living active lives, not slumped on a sofa in front of the TV.

He doesn't know much about Kenyan runners, but says that form is not something you should work on. Form follows function, he says. If everything in your body fires up at the right time, in the right way, if your body isn't broken, if everything is aligned and structurally sound, then you will run with beautiful form. That's how you were designed.

'My question is always: why?' he says. 'Why does a person have bad form in the first place? What is causing that?'

He says a form coach may see someone running with their head bent forward, and they might tell him to hold his head up. In theory, that's right, it makes better use of the elastic energy in the fascia. 'But this person may have his head forward because he can't put his weight in his forefeet,' Gary says. 'Maybe he once had verrucas that were so bad he couldn't put weight in the forefeet, and that was never fixed even after the verrucas went. So his problems are all about not putting the weight in the forefoot. If you move the head you will just shift the problem somewhere else.'

Historical problems are key to Gary's approach. I tell him about the small breakthrough we had with my wrist. This is just the sort of historical issue he loves to hear about. He gets me to place my foot on a piece of paper and measures the range of movement from side to side. Then he asks me to hold my wrist and does it again. The range of movement doubles.

'We're complex beings, but we have this really simple thing called a skeleton that can only move in certain ways,' he says. 'And if you don't move the way the bones want to go, it tends to cause problems, because you're breaking the mould of your own structure.'

But why would I not move the way my bones want to?

'Imagine you sprain your left ankle age fifteen,' he says, 'which is a typical thing we see. So you choose no longer to weight-bear on that left leg. Neuroscience says you can tape two fingers together and within two hours the brain will start to reconfigure it as one finger instead of two. That's in two hours. So imagine wearing a cast, or not putting weight on a foot for six weeks, so you end up putting your weight on the other side. Now your right foot is bearing too much weight, so the foot is likely to pronate more, and the pelvis will take a different shape as you adapt to one leg.

'And when your left leg gets better, you don't necessarily go back to putting your weight on it. You might think you do, but often we get stuck in a shape and adopt it full time.'

The Anatomy in Motion movements show the brain that the pattern it has adopted, the compensation for the old injury, is no longer needed, by gently demonstrating to it the full range of movement. They help the brain to go back to the factory settings. They tell it, in effect, that it no longer needs to operate in safe mode.

After looking at my wrist, Gary films me simply standing or walking up and down the corridor in his house. Looking back at the film, I'm appalled by how crooked I am. Even just standing still, I'm a disaster, leaning to one side, my neck crooked, my right foot turned out.

'We all have this perception of ourselves,' he says, 'which I call our perception of centre. Anybody who stands in front of me in their natural resting position will think they're centred.'

He draws more diagrams and tries out some different movements on me, then he sends me home with a file full of instructions. I'm not sure what to think. We didn't find a magic button that fixed everything instantly, like the way it worked for Ray in the BBC programme. He hasn't healed me with a crank of my foot. I'm going to have to work at this, invest some time into learning his movements, training my body to realign itself. But it sounds less severe than Shockwave Therapy. I hold the file close as I walk to the station, willing it to work. I have a lot of running to do. I need a functioning body.

A week later, the miracle happens. For the first time in years, my Achilles stop hurting. I get up in the morning and the first few steps feel normal. The usual stabbing pain, reminding me of my weakness, is gone. I'm excited to go out and run. And sure enough, nothing hurts. No jabbing and wincing until my Achilles warm up. Right from the start, I'm bouncing along, pain free. The next run is the same. And the next.

The problem with telling this tale is that I have no way

of knowing if it can work for everyone. This is one single anecdote – two if you count Ray's miracle cure in the *Doctor in the House* programme. But Gary is not a highly trained medical practitioner. In fact, he began devising Anatomy in Motion while fitting ski boots in a hire shop where he worked in the French Alps.

The lack of scientific evidence backing up the technique is difficult to ignore. Not for me. For me it works. All the evidence I need is in my Achilles. No research paper could come close to validating it more than the feeling of pain-free running. But when I come to recommend it to others, as I want to, especially when I hear again and again the same story of people who changed their running form and are now struggling with Achilles pain, I find myself hesitating. They'll want to know where the research is on this. Surely you've just drunk the Kool Aid, they'll think. The thing is, if it is just a placebo effect, and he has simply brainwashed me into fixing my injury, I don't really care. Weeks, months (and, jumping ahead, even a year) later, I'm still running pain free. But it does sound a little flaky when I try explaining it to people.

The presenter of *Doctor in the House*, Rangan Chatterjee, now has a book out called *The Four Pillar Plan*. One of those pillars is movement, and his advice in the book is based in part on Anatomy in Motion. Chatterjee is a trained and respected medical professional and still a practising GP. So I contact him to ask whether the lack of evidence to support Anatomy in Motion bothers him.

'It's a good question,' he says. 'But when I look for evidence, first I look at how harmful the treatment is. Something like chemotherapy, for example, I'll need to see pretty good trials evidence before I'll put patients through that.'

It turns out Chatterjee has his own miracle story. 'I had lower back pain for years,' he explains, 'but I hadn't given it much thought. Then one day I was helping a friend move house and I lifted a box, and my back just went.'

Over the next few years he saw a physio, a chiropractor, an osteopath and even a spinal surgeon. 'I couldn't work,' he says. 'I had to give up sports – I had been playing high-level squash up until that point.'

He then came across a video of Gary online and something resonated. 'As doctors we're always suppressing symptoms, rather than dealing with the root cause.' So he went on a weekend course to see if he could incorporate some of Gary's ideas into his GP practice. As part of the weekend, Gary assessed him as an example case. 'He saw that my right foot was stuck. I had an insole in my right shoe because I over-pronated, and I religiously put it in and out whenever I put my shoes on, even though it didn't really make any difference.'

Gary told him his foot was stuck in pronation and gave him some movements similar to the ones he gave me. Within days, Chatterjee's back got better. 'Because my right foot wasn't working, my right glute wasn't firing, so my back was hurting. Now I'm back playing squash, skiing moguls, everything.'

'I went to see lots of people about my back,' Chatterjee says. 'But to change the paradigm, we need fresh ideas. If we have to stop and wait for the evidence, things won't progress. I want to help my patients. Ray, in the TV programme, had been down all the evidence-based treatments. What do you do next? Give up?'

Chatterjee didn't find that it was a particular injury in his past that had caused his problem. 'My lifestyle had untrained my body,' he says. 'The way we live in the modern world, we sit down too much, we stop our feet working, stop them moving by squashing them in shoes.'

Chatterjee is also a fan of 'barefoot' shoes and the theory behind barefoot running. It's all connected, of course. Perhaps this is the final missing piece. For me at least. In any case, I can now run landing on my midfoot, the 'barefoot' way, and not feel any pain.

'Gary's movement re-taught my body how it wants to function,' says Chatterjee. 'My foot muscles have switched back on, and my right glute is firing again.'

The idea that the brain needs to re-learn a movement, so it can switch muscles back on, muscles it previously decommissioned for some reason, is central to Anatomy in Motion. This relates to scientist Tim Noake's famous and widely accepted central governor theory, which in essence states that movement and fatigue and bodily stress are primarily controlled by the brain, and that the brain is like an over-protective mother, shutting things down before they can get too hurt or damaged. It seems that the mother can be forgetful, too, and forget to turn things back on once the danger has passed.

Gary borrowed a lot of his ideas about the way the brain processes movement patterns from a treatment called NeuroKinetic Therapy, or NKT. This was devised over thirty years ago by an American called David Weinstock. It just so happens that Weinstock lives in Marin County, California, near the home of Gary Gellin, my host for the Miwok

100K race. So while I was over there for the race I went to see him, to see if he could shed any more light on how Anatomy in Motion worked, and why my Achilles were suddenly feeling better.

Gary Gellin decides to come along, so we all meet at a sunny salad bar in the nearby town of Corte Madera. Weinstock treats us both to lunch, immediately endearing himself to Gary, who has been telling me the whole way in the car how sceptical he is about NKT. But Weinstock has a wide, Californian smile and a quiet confidence that soon has us both eating out of his hand.

'What we're doing is essentially rebooting the computer in the brain that controls movement,' he says. 'In an NKT session, we interview people, then watch them move. We want to figure out what's over-working and what's under-working. Then you release the over-working muscles, or activate the under-working muscles, which helps re-programme that dysfunctional pattern in the brain.'

'Gary Ward blends his stuff with mine,' he says. 'So what he did with you when he diagnosed you was NKT. It's primarily a diagnostic tool. Anatomy in Motion is then an intelligently designed technique to retrain the motor control system.'

He nods along when I tell him about my wrist. 'When you break something, you create scar tissue that shouldn't be there. We know now through fascial research, that the fascial system is the skeleton of the nervous system, so when you cut it or disturb it, you disrupt motor control.

'People are gobsmacked by the effect when we look at these things. But just because these scars are old, doesn't mean the brain has repaired the damage, it has just learned to cope and compensate.'

Other things that can cause problems, he says, are sports injuries, over-use, bad posture, computer work, mobile phones. 'Soon we're going to have a generation of hunchbacks,' he says.

I tell him I've had five years of Achilles problems. 'Achilles and plantar fasciitis are two of the most common running injuries,' he says. 'Yet they get treated symptomatically. I will tell you, of all the runners I've worked on, 98 per cent of the cause is weak glutes. If you run without glutes – and I'm talking neurologically – the force gets translated down the chain into the hamstrings, then the calves. As they tighten they pull on the plantar fascia or put strain on the Achilles, and you get pain.'

Sitting next to me, Gary is becoming more and more convinced. He starts mentioning his friend Ellie Greenwood. She's a former winner of the Comrades Marathon and has the Western States 100 course record, but she has been injured for over a year. 'We should get her down here for a treatment,' he says, and asks Weinstock where he can find a local NKT practitioner. It shouldn't be too difficult; there are 4,500 of them around the world and the number is growing all the time.

However, like Gary Ward, Weinstock doesn't have any scientific evidence to back up his ideas. What does he say to people who are worried about that, I ask him.

'If I had to rely on evidence for everything I did,' he replies, 'I'd be twenty years behind where I am now. I'm a clinician, not a researcher. People are very fanatic.'

I'm not sure it's fanatical to look for evidence, but if he is getting results – and my own legs suggest he is on to something, however it works – then people will keep coming back. I for one am happy that I came across his treatment.

With that, and one last sunshine smile, he bids us goodbye. Gary is buzzing with excitement on the way home, and as soon as we get there he starts telling his wife, Holly, all about it. Except – and this is exactly how I find it when I try to explain these things to people – she isn't buying it. Where's the evidence? What was that Weinstock said about scars disrupting motor control? Oh shoot, it sounds like nonsense. Holly's looking at us like we've joined a cult and want to get married to each other or something.

But evidence or not, two ultra races later and I'm running with fewer niggles than I have since I was a teenager. I get some more confirmation that it's working when, back in my home town of Northampton, I decide, despite all the ultra training, to jump into a 5km parkrun with my brother Govinda.

We haven't raced since the Great Wilderness Challenge, and so, looking for my revenge, I shoot off at helter-skelter pace, getting a gap on him that he never quite closes. Afterwards he says: 'You know, you've always written a lot about form, in your books and articles. But the truth is, you never looked like you had good form. But today, you looked different. You looked like a runner.'

He's right, I would see pictures of myself running, or see a video, and I would think, god, really, do I look like that? After all I had done to change things, the evidence of good form was hard to spot. But recently, since doing my movements, things have felt different. Not only have the

Achilles stopped hurting, but I feel I can glide along easily at a good pace. Despite all the long, slow ultra training, I run the parkrun in one of my fastest ever times.

And so, with a spring in my step, quite literally, I prepare for the toughest series of races of the entire adventure, starting with my little loop around Anglesey. The Ring O' Fire was Tom Payn's first ever ultra marathon, and, incidentally, it was also Elisabet Barnes's first ultra. They both ran the same year, and they both won. But I'm not planning on trying to emulate those guys. I'm going to be taking it easy, I tell myself. No racing. Just enjoy the scenery, pick up the UTMB points, and leave. Got it?

10

I'm shivering like crazy, as I stand hunched over in the empty showers in a leisure centre somewhere on the north coast of Anglesey. I'm not supposed to be this tired after Day One. I can barely reach down to wash the mud off my legs.

After crossing the finish line, I'd made my way into the Amlwch Leisure Centre, found my bags in the pile in the middle of the main sports hall and laid out my sleeping bag by the wall along one side. I'd had plenty of choice of where to set up as I was one of the first to arrive. Enjoy the scenery, I'd told myself. Then I went and finished the day in eighth place. The thing is, it felt good most of the way, like I was holding back. But now I'm done, I feel broken, fragile, like a baby bird fallen from the nest.

Once I'm reasonably clean I make my way towards the centre's swimming pool. A swim seemed like a good idea, but as I stand by the water, I'm not so sure. There's nobody in the pool, just two teenage lifeguards walking slowly around the outside, a tinny stereo playing Dizzee Rascal. I slide into the water, and just stand there. I can barely move. I sink down and push off, moving my arms in slow motion. It takes me about ten minutes to do one length. The two teenagers look bored as hell. I push off again, doing a second length, a little bit faster this time. When I get to the end I climb out of the water. That's enough, I need to eat.

Back in the sports hall, warm now in my clean clothes, I climb into my sleeping bag and pull out the food I've packed for myself. I sit there eating it slowly, watching as more and more people arrive, looking exhausted, searching for their bags, dragging them to a spot by the wall. One reason people do these races is to get out of their comfort zone, to experience a bit of hardship in their lives, so they can go home and appreciate what they've got. I remember one ultra runner telling me about the joy of a hot shower after a week running through the Gobi desert. The thrill of climbing into a bed with clean sheets. But this here seems to take the discomfort to a new, tragic level. All around me people sit on the floor wrapped in sleeping bags, their hoods up, eating out of Tupperware boxes. And instead of the desert sky to look up at, we have sports hall strip lights.

One man near me suddenly starts writhing around on the ground yelling. He has bad cramp in his legs. He has two supporters with him, but they just stand there watching him, laughing nervously, wondering if he's joking. But he isn't, he's in agony. I sit watching, dazed, but when they still don't do anything, I haul myself up and go over to help him, holding his leg straight until the cramp goes.

He shakes his head, weary, almost gone. 'Sorry,' he says. 'I don't normally do that.' It has been a long first day and nobody here looks like they found it easy. I climb back into my sleeping bag and pull it close around me.

As the time goes by, the hall gets busier and busier. I decide to wander back outside to watch the people still finishing.

I'm feeling a little better now. It seems like everyone except me has a support crew. I didn't think there was much point. They would just have to travel around the island, standing in the cold for hours just to watch me go by for a few seconds. This was my own thing, my own project, it's not really benefiting anyone or achieving anything meaningful. It felt a bit egotistical to expect someone to follow me around like a personal assistant for three days.

But then, in that moment when you finish, when you cross the line, something strange happens. Emotions bubble and rise to the surface. You feel like you've been through something intense out there, like you've survived something. And to just stand there on your own, well it's easy to feel lonely, dejected, in need of someone to tell you that everything will be OK. I guess that's why they have those people to greet you when you finish Comrades. That's the oldest ultra marathon in the world. It has worked out what people need.

But it's a few hours later now, and I'm OK. I'm quite happy, in fact, looking after myself, nothing else to worry about except my own needs. I feel sorry for the people still finishing. It's almost time to sleep, but they still have to get clean, to eat, to make their beds.

Today we ran 36 miles. I hadn't realised we would have to do so much navigating and I wasn't prepared. The race pack told us to bring maps and to mark out the route, and to download GPX files onto our phones, but I kept thinking it couldn't be that hard to follow a coastal path. Just keep the sea to your left. But it wasn't always so straightforward, and I would have gone the wrong way numerous times but for the people around me. In particular I ended up with a guy called Scott and a man from the Netherlands. Scott had done the race before and had a real grasp of where we were going, so I made sure to keep with him. Mostly that was fine. He was going at about the right pace. Perhaps a little fast, but that kept me moving. I probably would have walked a bit more if I had been on my own, but I just got into a rhythm with these two and we ran most of the last 20 miles together.

I had a couple of sticky patches. One was about 20 miles in and I started getting a bit dizzy. I felt like I was wiping out. For a moment I started to think that my race was over already. But I just walked for a minute or so, and remembering my Miwok episode, I drank lots of water, I ate two energy balls and some dates and just took it all on board. After a while I got myself going again, first at crawling speed, but I was moving at least. And then I came through it, and I felt fine again.

I got my second bad moment with just a mile left to go. As we were so close to the finish, I thought I would just walk in from there. It was a nice evening, so I started off, quite happily. But like an ambush from out of the hedges, I was suddenly overwhelmed by negative thoughts, asking what the point of it all was, ultra running, the UTMB and its stupid race points. I actually stepped back, in my head, and watched the comments flooding in over the walls, and I laughed to myself. Am I going to do this in every race? Does there always have to be some sort of existential crisis? 'Come on,' I told myself, brandishing my sword of reason. 'Don't do this a mile from the finish.'

I had dropped off from my two companions at this point, but they had stopped at a junction in the path for a moment, unsure about which way to go, and so I caught up with them again. And although I thought I was going to walk, when they started running again, I went with them, and we ran together to the finish.

Now it's after nine o'clock and we have 66 miles to run tomorrow. I need to mark the route on my map and get some sleep, so I head back in to find my spot in the sports hall.

I don't sleep much that night. They only turn the lights off much later, and only in one half of the hall. Luckily it is my half that's given the partial darkness, and I've brought an eye patch, one of those you get given on an aeroplane. But regardless of the light, my legs ache too much to sleep. As I toss and turn trying to get comfortable, I worry about how they are going to carry me around the next day.

Around 4 a.m., I give up and get up to use the bathroom. I figure that as I'm already awake I'll get in before the rush. As I walk gingerly across the hall, I see people sleeping right under the strip lights, without an eye patch or even a roll mat, just passed out on the hard floor.

After my bathroom trip, I go back and sit up in my sleep-ing bag, waiting, like a condemned man. At exactly 4.50 a.m., as promised, Quentin, one of the race organisers, walks into the hall with a sarcastic grin on his face, and the race song, 'Ring of Fire' by Johnny Cash, blasting out from his phone, which he swings around gaily.

I don't think many people are actually asleep and within minutes everyone is up, shuffling around, packing bags, smearing themselves in Vaseline. My legs don't feel too bad, surprisingly, despite the fact they've been aching all night. My feet also feel fine. For the last 10 miles of the first day they were burning from the impact of running so far in thin-soled shoes.

And so, as the sun rises, we set off on Day Two of our journey around Anglesey. After about 10 miles, I fall into a rhythm running with a man from Yorkshire and a woman from Wales, a TV sports reporter called Lowri Morgan. The Yorkshireman knows who she is and is a little star struck. He keeps asking her about the rally racing, which she covers on Welsh TV.

She has also made some documentaries about ultra running. She tells us she once ran a 350-mile race across the Arctic. It was a race where you have to pull everything you need on a sled behind you. It took her 174 hours and she was the only person to finish the race that year. This race feels like a jog to the bottom of the garden and back compared to that.

The sun is out and it's getting quite warm as we follow the coast path across dry river beds, in and out of isolated coves, past small fishing harbours. The other runner drops off the pace a little and I feel like I'm pushing a little too hard to keep up with Lowri, but she likes to talk and the conversation is helping the time to pass more quickly. I ask her what made her want to do such a crazy race as the one in the Arctic.

'I don't know really,' she says. But we have plenty of time, and so as we go on she ponders the question some more. 'I think ultra running takes us to places we don't go enough,' she says. She's not talking about different countries, but different states of mind. 'They can strip you bare. In the Arctic I was out there on my own for a long time. An experience like that rebuilds the soul.'

She looks at me but I'm just trying to keep up. 'Then you can carry that strength into other areas of life,' she says. 'Say at work, like when I was made redundant, I wasn't worried. I thought, "I've faced far greater demons than this."'

She says she once got asked to talk about her running experiences at a women's shelter. She told them that before she went to the Arctic, she hated the darkness. She said she had feared running in the night, as it was the coldest time, it was lonely, and that was when the mind games would start.

'But the first night of the race I saw the Northern Lights,' she says. 'They were like music in the air. After that, I changed my attitude. I felt the stars were putting on a show just for me, and I started looking forward to the nights.'

She says that after her talk, she told the women she felt bad, because she realised she had chosen to put herself in a difficult situation, whereas they had no choice.

'But afterwards one woman came up to me,' she says, 'and told me not to apologise, that she could relate to what I had said. She said the way I had described the night and the Northern Lights was how she felt the night she left with three small children and two black bin bags.'

The path leads us into the driveway of a large house. A man on a deckchair, reading the newspaper, looks up as we appear. He seems cross. 'Go away,' he shouts suddenly.

'Are you looking for the coast path?' a woman asks, appearing at his side. Lowri's story has been so engrossing, we've missed a turning somewhere. Luckily it's only a few hundred metres back. As we climb over the stile, we can see our Yorkshire friend motoring away further ahead of us. We've only lost a couple of minutes.

As soon as we're back on track, Lowri starts telling me about another race she ran, in the Amazon.

'We were making a film about the race when I got bitten by hornets,' she says. 'My tongue started swelling up and I was thinking, this is bad. I'd been bitten about forty times and I thought, I've got enough footage, I'll stop at the next checkpoint.'

But the person manning the checkpoint looked at her tongue and said it looked normal.

'I realised I'd created the reaction in my head,' she says. 'Because I wanted to give up. I was losing my toenails. Anyway, I decided to get to the next checkpoint at least. We had to get there by 4 p.m. because of the jaguars.'

This story is getting wilder and wilder. I keep suggesting we pause, to make sure we're still on the right path. Really I just need to get my breath back. She has done this race before, however, and keeps telling me it's OK and to carry on running.

'So I was struggling on,' she says, continuing her story, 'when I remembered this card my mother had given me. I mean, to save weight I'd cut the foil off my food bags, trimmed my toothbrush, but I made sure I kept this card with me. I took it out. It was a quote by Confucius: "Our greatest glory is not in never falling, but in rising every time we fall."

'After I read that, the pain disappeared. It was like a spiritual feeling came over me. I had to keep knocking my legs to check them, I was so surprised at how the pain had completely gone.'

It reminds me of my revival in the Miwok 100K race, the sudden, barely believable transformation. In Lowri's case, after she read a quote on a card, it was clearly all in the mind.

Eventually I have to let her go ahead. I need to run at my own pace. The path winds past tiny cottages, perched on the edge of a cliff, then at the bottom of some isolated cove, with a narrow track running down to it and people who look like they've been living there since the 1920s standing in the doorway.

Just before the halfway checkpoint, we reach a small town. My feet are starting to burn as we run on the tarmac, past the harbour and back out along a main road for a short way. When I get to the checkpoint, I find Lowri sitting in a chair with her two-year-old son on her lap. She looks exhausted. I hear her telling the organisers that she is toying with the idea of dropping out. 'Don't be ridiculous,' they say. I suggest she tries walking for a little, remembering how that helped me the day before. But I can see the allure of dropping out, as she sits there with her son. Really, why carry on? There are still over 30 miles to go. And that's just today. She is probably feeling terrible. I know I am, but I need the UTMB points. She has done this race before and finished it. She is already someone who gives talks and makes films about her races. She doesn't need this one.

But I keep all that to myself, and I leave her deliberating as I carry on my way. I find out later that she continued on from there, but that she didn't make it to the end of the day. I contact her a few weeks after the race to find out what happened.

'I got sick at that checkpoint,' she says. 'My dad, he's a doctor, he said it was blood. It played on my mind, so I gave up. I've never done that before. I was playing ping-pong in my head, wondering if I was making it up. After you stop, you think at least the pain will go. And it does. But the disappointment takes over.'

Back out on the coast path, I'm starting to struggle now. Thirty miles still to go. It seems like such a huge distance. I keep looking at my watch, which doesn't help. Every time I look at it, hoping another mile has ticked by, it's not even close. And each time, it's like a blow to the stomach. I try not to look at it, but it's too tempting. It's always there, right on my wrist, the possibility of good news, the promise of progress. But it's a promise that is dashed every time.

I end up running with the Dutch guy from the first day again. He catches me soon after half way, looking strong, so I try to hold on to him for as long as I can. He's not great company, though. When I venture a little conversation, asking 'How are you feeling?' he looks across at me sharply, as though he's surprised to see me there. 'Fine, of course,' he replies.

With the other runners, when we get to a junction and the route's not clear, we compare maps and discuss things before carrying on. But my Dutch friend just seems to know, and heads on without speaking. Initially I follow him, he seems so certain, but after a few wrong turns, I decide to let him go.

One time, after I had been running quite far behind him, he suddenly appears from behind me and strides past. I guess that he must have taken a wrong turn somewhere. 'Did you get lost?' I say.

'No,' is his curt reply.

Later in the race he does something so bizarre, so awkward, that I'm not sure how to react. Perhaps it illustrates the bestial nature of ultra running, the animal state of pure survival it can take you to, where cultural niceties cease to be important. Or perhaps it is just a Dutch thing.

Either way, he's running about 50 metres ahead of me across an isolated, stony beach, when he suddenly stops, pulls down his shorts, squats down and starts to poo, right there on the trail. As I get nearer, he stands up, pulls out some tissue and just starts wiping his bum like it's the most normal thing in the world. There's nothing I can do to avoid him, he's right in the way, so I just run by. A few minutes later he catches me up and runs along beside me. We don't say a word about it.

The warm afternoon has been replaced by the chill of early evening by the time I get to the forest. The race organiser Quentin had delighted in telling me the story of the people who got so lost at night in the forest the year before that they eventually decided to bed down and wait for morning. I've been worrying about it all day, so I'm relieved to be here well before dark. I've got to the point now where I'm having to talk to myself to keep moving. At first it's just a quiet 'Come on' every so often. Then, about 50 miles or so in, I start getting bullish, almost angry. 'You can do it. Only 10 more miles and you're done with this shit.' Everything is aching now.

The pain oozes through my muscles, through my joints, my groin, my hips, my knees. I know that if I stop, it will go away. But I carry on, because I'm in this stupid race.

For a while I find myself singing a long-lost song from my childhood. It was the late 1970s and my parents were followers of an Indian guru. We were at a festival to hear him speak. It was the summer, a baking hot day, when a thunderstorm broke out. I must have been about five years old, but I remember it clearly. My dad took me to shelter in this tent where an Indian man was singing a song. It was a song I knew, my parents played it at home, but here in the storm, it stuck in my memory. The song was called 'Downpour of the Holy Name'. I know it sounds strange, but for some reason this is the song I start singing to myself now, remembering that tent and the feeling of that moment. And for a while it helps. I feel easier, running smoothly, the pain easing away.

I think about that later, why it was that song that came to me, and why it helped. I had also tried chanting a mantra a friend had given me, and repeating my children's names over and over, but neither had the same effect as that song. That may sound cold-hearted, but I wasn't doing this race for my children. They didn't care whether I finished or not. No, I was doing it for that small child buried deep within me. And somehow, making a connection to that child through this song put me in a state, like a dream, where everything else faded away.

Suddenly, just like that, I'm through the forest, arriving at the penultimate checkpoint. Mile 60. Six miles to go. I sit down on a chair and try to eat something. A peanut butter sandwich. I realise I'm still in about eighth position. The competitive side of me is still fighting, still looking around, chattering about finishing in the top ten. But the rest of me doesn't care. Just finish, it says.

I haul myself up, but I'm so stiff. I shouldn't have sat down. An Irish woman, who I remember arriving hours after me the day before, goes by, looking strong. 'Only two parkruns to go,' she says cheerfully. I don't have the energy to reply.

Soon afterwards I get to a crossroads. I'm running alone so I get my map out. According to my hand-drawn lines, it says I should go straight on. But the coast path sign on the road says go left. I look around, but this time I'm on my own. The instructions were to follow the coast path signs 99 per cent of the time. But occasionally, the organisers said, the route went a different way. Is this one of those times? The problem is I don't trust my map. I wasn't precise when I marked it in the sports hall the night before. I was tired. I'm not sure I was paying full attention. So I turn left.

It turns out to be the wrong way. I'm still trying to follow my map, but now it doesn't make sense. Rather than go back, I try to cut across, following a road I think will take me back the right way, but I'm soon completely lost. It's now about 8 p.m. and getting dark.

I'm standing on a lonely country road, when I hear a car coming. A Range Rover. I try to wave it down. The woman driving slows as she approaches. I'm smiling, waving. Then suddenly she speeds up, racing past without looking at me.

I must look like a madman, especially now I'm away from the context of the race. Further down the road I come to a tiny house. The light is on. I need to find the way. I walk up to the door and knock. I can see a man in his sitting room glance up in shock as I approach. Eventually he comes to the door, stepping outside and closing it behind him.

'How can I help?' he asks.

He tells me the way. I'm only a few miles from the finish in the village of Aberffraw. As I walk along the road, I study my map and realise I'm coming from the wrong direction and I'm going to miss the final checkpoint. Missing a checkpoint means a three-hour time penalty. It's only a mile from the town to the checkpoint and the cut-off isn't until 2 a.m., so I have nearly six hours. Even at a slow walk I could do it in an hour. But I'm done. I'll take the time penalty. Just finish.

With a three-hour penalty, my pretence at competing is over. It's actually a relief, like a little annoying voice in my head has been switched off. The last mile into the village is down a long straight road. It's dark now, and my feet are on fire from all the pounding. It's then that strange things start happening.

I go to take a drink from the tube that protrudes from my water bottle and find that it has a lid on it. I didn't even know it had a lid. I've never used a lid, and it's awkward to get it off. Then something starts popping all around me. Pop, pop, pop. I'm looking around. I feel like I'm being surrounded. I'm swiping my arms in the darkness, trying to hit whatever it is away. Maybe it's because the lid is on my drink? I pull it off again, but it doesn't make any difference.

For an age Aberffraw seems to get no closer, like a ghost town in the distance. And then suddenly I'm there. The popping stops as I make my way across a bridge and along the empty, silent street, past grey semi-detached houses, to the village hall. The front doors are open. I walk in.

Hardly anyone is there. It feels surreal. Where is everybody? I sit down on a chair as about three or four people wander around. Quentin comes over to see me. He tells me there's a small room out the back for people who have finished early. It's best to go and get some kip there, he suggests, as runners will be coming in all night, in agony, making a scene. But I can't move. Luckily the organisers have cooked up some pasta for us. My plan had been to get food in the village. I had imagined getting showered, changed, and then walking to the local chip shop. But I can barely reach down to untie my laces. Quentin hands me a bowl of food, but it's a struggle even to eat it. I'm shivering again. And I really, really need a hug.

It sounds ridiculous, I know, but sitting there alone in that desolate hall, I feel traumatised. I can't do anything. I can't think about marking my map for the next day. I can't think about contacting Marietta. She has sent me a message: 'Did you make it?' But I can't reply. I know it only needs a few words. It isn't that my fingers don't have the energy, I simply can't construct the sentence in my mind. I can't get changed. There are no showers, but I have clean clothes, even pyjamas, in my bag. But all I can manage to do is inflate my mattress in the back room, lay out my sleeping bag and, in the clothes I've been running in all day, crawl into it.

I don't sleep. My legs are in so much pain, I have to stop myself whimpering out loud. I have no water. I'm a mess. I'm tossing and turning. We're in the store room of the village hall, lying under stacked tables on rough, worn, carpet tiles. There are only about five of us here. I assume everyone else has either dropped out of the race, or booked in to local hotels for the night, where their support teams can help them to get organised.

For the second night in a row, I don't sleep a wink. Finally, at 4.50 a.m., the strip lights snap on, screaming in my face, and Quentin walks in, smiling, his phone playing 'Ring of Fire'.

Amazingly, when I stand up, I don't feel too bad. I mean, I feel terrible, but somehow my legs are not as bad as I was expecting. It's strange, because normally if you run a marathon, or a 66-mile ultra marathon along a hilly coast path, the next day you would be a wreck, barely able to walk. But it's like my body has gone into some sort of hyper repair mode overnight, even without sleep. It's like it knows it has got to be ready to go again, and has dug into some secret reserve. It's almost like it has been keeping something back.

After packing our bags, we walk outside and into driving, horizontal rain. After all we've been through, it's a miserable start to the last day. It's still dark. The grey houses stand silent and uncaring. It's Sunday morning, their day to lie in, especially on a stinker like this. They roll over and turn their backs on us.

At the word from Quentin, we shuffle off, a mere 33 miles left to go. With my time penalty, my only concern today is not to miss another checkpoint. If I do that I may not make it to the finish in time, and I need those five UTMB points. So I go with care, running near the back of the field, keeping people in sight the whole time to make sure I don't get lost.

Soon after leaving Aberffraw, as it's still getting light, we run past a tiny beach. Big waves are crashing in, and as we run through the car park a man stands by his car pulling on a wetsuit, preparing to go surfing. He looks at us in amazement as silently, one after the other, like ghosts we shuffle by, with our rucksacks and our pained expressions. I catch his eye. 'I thought I was the mad one,' he says.

And at that point, all I can think is that he's right. I can't see the joy, the satisfaction, anything other than insanity in running for a third day around this Welsh island, in this weather, with a bunch of people I don't even know. It doesn't make sense.

But I press on. Running further back in the field, at this slower pace, things are different. Rather than trying to catch people, pass them, stay ahead, rush, rush, rush, I can take my time and experience the journey. If I had done the whole race like this, perhaps I could have enjoyed it. Why do I always have to race the whole time? I could just be taking it in, enjoying the scenery, the atmosphere, the company of my fellow runners. This is my place. I did the first two days too fast. Here, at the back, I'm happy.

But then, after a while, I start thinking that we're walking too much. I'm here to run. I've been sticking close to two men from Liverpool, but after a while I'm itching to go quicker. I'm starting to feel better. So, despite the risk of being left on my own again, the next time they start to walk, instead of walking with them, I carry on, forging ahead. Before I know it I'm racing up the hills. For the last 10 miles, I'm full of running. The magic revival button has been pressed again. A man from Bolton has also been moving quickly through the field ahead of me. I've been watching him, but as we get closer to the finish, I start cranking up through the gears even more, letting loose. I charge up a hill with about a mile to go, passing him like I'm doing hill sprints. He steps aside. 'Go on, Superman!' he yells. 'What a finish!'

I'm at full charge as I round the last corner, waving and yelling as I cross the line. The guy from Bolton finishes soon after. He comes over, grinning at me. 'Bloody hell, lad,' he says, crushing my hand in his. 'Where did that come from?'

Where indeed? The two Liverpool guys come in about 10 minutes later. They're not sprinting or trying to pass anyone. They came here for the experience of running around this island. They want to savour the end of their adventure.

And here he is, my friend the Dutchman. I passed him this time with about two miles to go. He looked surprised to see me. But when he crosses the finish, he gives me a big smile and we shake hands. Perhaps finally I have earned his respect. Though he still doesn't say anything.

I'm buzzing so much that after sitting around for a while soaking up the moment, enjoying the feeling of it all being over, the satisfaction of having run around the entire island of Anglesey, and of bagging myself five juicy UTMB points, I get up and take the short walk to my car. I feel so good I somehow think I'm going to drive straight home, all the way to Devon, over three hundred miles away.

I turn the engine on. It feels strange to be back here, sitting in my car. Like I've just returned to civilisation after months in the wilderness. I pull out of the car park and start driving. But, oh god, my legs can barely press the pedals down. I'm seeing everything in slow motion. People are beeping at me. After five minutes I pull over. I pull out my phone and find the nearest hotel and book myself a room.

11

When I tell people I'm planning to run around a 400-metre track for twenty-four hours, they usually look confused, like they can't quite register what I'm saying. But once they've had a moment to think about it, the most common retort is: 'God, that sounds *really* boring.'

In the event, it was many things, but not once was it boring.

This race holds a bizarre fascination for me. I love the way it merges the mundane with the epic, people attempting mind-boggling feats not out in the Himalayas or the depths of the jungle, but on a running track in Tooting in south London. It shows that you don't have to go to the far corners of the Earth to find adventure, enlightenment, craziness, or whatever it is we're all seeking, but that it exists everywhere if you just open your eyes. In the immortal words of Alabama 3: 'There ain't nothing worse than some fool lying on some third world beach wearing spandex, psychedelic trousers, smoking damn dope and pretending he's getting consciousness expansion. If I want consciousness expansion, I go to my local tabernacle and I sing.' Or I go to my local track and I run.

It reminds me of *Hands on a Hardbody*, the brilliant 1997 TV documentary (later adapted into a Broadway musical) about a competition that takes place each year in Longview, Texas. Organised by a local car dealership, the premise of the competition is simple: people stand with their hand on a brand new Nissan Hardbody pick-up truck and the last one to take their hand off wins the truck. It's banal and boring, yet as these men and women stand in that parking lot with their hand on a truck, a gripping drama begins to play out. With nowhere else to go, nothing else to do, the characters open up to the camera and to each other. As the days go by, friendships and animosities are formed, emotions run high, people reach elevated states of consciousness, and strong individuals – even tough former Marines – break down and run, while the most unlikely people remain unbowed, growing in strength both physically and mentally.

'It's a contest, they say, of stamina,' says contestant Benny Perkins in the documentary. He was the winner of the truck two years earlier. 'But it's who can maintain their sanity the longest. And that's what it comes to, because when you go insane, you lose.'

In that parking lot, human life plays out as though it has been placed on a petri dish and held under a microscope, while the scalpel of time peels back the layers, dissecting it to reveal what lies underneath.

The 24-hour track race in Tooting plays out in a similar way. I saw that when I went to watch it. As the runners and their crews gathered at the pre-race briefing on a chilly, overcast afternoon, there was a frisson of nervous energy in the air.

I stood beside Jamie, a management consultant who lived less than a mile away. He was fresh from completing the legendary 153-mile Spartathlon in Greece. I asked him why he kept doing such long races. 'I suppose I'm trying to find my limit,' he said. 'Maybe when I find it, I'll stop.' Later that night, when I returned at 3 a.m., I found him walking around the track with his leg bandaged up. 'I think I may have found it,' he said, smiling happily.

The race director, Shankara Smith, told me: 'Here, you can't tell yourself it's you versus the mountain, because there is no mountain. It's just you versus you.'

The biggest challenge to overcome, she said, was yourself. 'This race is not mind over matter, but heart over mind. If you can't silence that mind, then you can't do it, because your mind will tell you you can't.'

As in the *Hands on a Hardbody* documentary, the most impressive people were not the ones you might have picked out at the start. Such as 68-year-old Ann Bath. She didn't run fast, she was a little bent over, but she was unrelenting. While others occasionally stopped for a massage, or to eat something, she pressed serenely on, never stopping. And in the end she ran an incredible 115 miles around the track that day.

As I mingled with the runners afterwards, poking my nose into their post-race exultation, I came across 76-year-old Pat sitting in the front seat of her car peeling plasters off her toes. I asked her how it had been.

'I hallucinated, of course. I always do,' she said, chucking the plasters in the footwell of the car. 'Although usually I run with my friend and we take turns to hallucinate.'

Pat was the oldest competitor in the race. She had just run 84 miles, but she was not about to blow her own trumpet. 'It's not that great,' she said. 'Last year I ran 87.'

For Pat, this was all completely run of the mill. As well as countless 24-hour races, she had run 456 marathons, and counting. And she didn't even start running until her late forties.

'It keeps me busy,' she said, when I asked her why she did it. 'What else am I going to do on a Saturday?'

Despite the mundane talk of the runners, something else was going on here. The full name of the race is the Self-Transcendence 24-Hour race, and it was started by followers of the late Indian spiritual teacher Sri Chinmoy, who once said: 'Running means continual transcendence, and that is also the message of our inner life.'

I asked another of the runners after the race that day whether he had experienced self-transcendence? 'At moments, definitely,' he replied, a glint in his eye, as though there was something else he couldn't, or wouldn't, say. 'It's really something. But you can only understand it if you try it.'

And so, here I am, one year later, driving my car on to the track to set up my base for the next 24 hours. We haul out a table and two deck chairs, boxes of energy balls we've made, drinks, strawberries. Marietta has agreed to be my crew. After the Ring O' Fire, I'd rather not face this alone.

I haven't managed to do any training runs on a track, but to help me prepare I did spend a weekend with the British 24-hour running squad. The lowly status of 24-hour running is illustrated by the fact that the national team held their training weekend in a youth hostel in Berkshire. We slept in bunk beds, six men to a room, and each member of the team paid his own way.

As we cooked supper, struggling with the hostel's blunt knives, Robbie Britton, the team captain, who came third in the recent 24-hour world championships, told me that the key to 24-hour running was to stay in the moment. 'I mentally just tell myself to run for one hour,' he said. 'Even when I'm absolutely shattered, I know I can run for an hour, so I just do that. Then I think about the next one.'

Over the training weekend, seminars are given in a little 'classroom' at the back of the hostel by a movement coach and a nutritionist. Despite the setting, this is a serious team of athletes preparing for a world championships. Among them is the European 24-hour champion, Dan Lawson, who after winning that title is now on the World Anti-Doping Agency's list of monitored athletes – which is standard practice for anyone of this level. He says, only half joking, that being added to the Wada list has ruined his life. He lives for half the year in Goa in India and says that before he used to go off on spontaneous adventures, running and sleeping out under the stars, but now he has to tell officials where he is going to be at every moment of the day in case they show up looking to test him.

We go for a couple of steady runs of about 90 minutes and I manage to keep up with everyone easily. This gives me hope. When I ask the other runners about their best marathon times, most of them are actually slower than mine. Although, as I learned in Oman when I tried to run with

Elisabet Barnes, marathon times don't necessarily count for much in this sport.

But still, after my weekend preparing with the British team, it is with some optimism that I lope off on the first lap of the track in Tooting on an overcast Saturday afternoon in mid September.

I pass the first few hours chatting to other runners, and making silly faces to Marietta, and her sister and nephew, who turn up for a while to give some support. I'm sticking to a conservative plan of running for 25 minutes and then walking for five minutes. It seems unnecessary to walk at this stage, and I'm way down the leaderboard, which is updated every hour and posted up beside the track. But this is the plan I hatched with my coach beforehand. I'm playing it clever, I'm playing the long game. I'm sure I'll start moving up the leaderboard as time goes on.

The first time I decide to quit, it's about midnight, 12 hours into the race.

Stay in the moment, Robbie Britton said. In life, like in this race, 'stay in the moment' is great advice. In many ways it is the key to happiness. But in this race, like in life, it is not easy. It's hard not to keep thinking about how long we have left to run. It can short-circuit your brain if you think about it too hard. It's like when someone tells you a star is 100 million light years away and you really try to grasp it.

The first time it happens is about nine hours in. I've been joking with Marietta as I pass on most laps, but this time I look at her hard, as if to tell her, and myself, that something has changed.

'This is getting serious now,' I say. I can feel my body beginning to struggle, an aching oozing through me. My feet are starting to burn. And then the thought hits me: 'I still have 15 hours to go.' Bam! The lights go out. I'm staring into the abyss.

I change my 25 minutes on, five minutes off plan, switching to smaller, more manageable numbers: running three laps and then walking one. My world is starting to shrink. Soon it becomes two laps running and one walking. Then one lap running. And then half a lap running and half a lap walking. Then I just stop.

Marietta tells me to go and see the physio. There is a medical team in a room beside the track, where I get a massage. Afterwards I feel better and get going again. But then, at about 2 a.m., I'm gone again.

'Let me go,' I plead to the night, to the race, to myself. Other people are dropping out, why don't I? I have a big, long list of excuses; real, genuine excuses. It's too soon after the Ring O' Fire. Lots of people told me that. They were right. My legs are mashed. I have to accept that I'm not Superman.

'What about Kilian?' Marietta says. 'What would he do?' God, I'm no Kilian, can't she see that? Why is she insisting I continue? I feel resentful, like she is forcing me to go on. I conjure the voice of my coach, Tom, telling me afterwards that it was sensible to stop, that there would have been no point breaking myself with another race coming up in three weeks, and one I really need to finish to get those precious UTMB points. This race is meaningless. I can't finish every race. Also, I haven't trained on a track. That was stupid. Tom told me to, but I didn't listen. When I went to see the physio, she told me that this was why I was struggling. The bouncy track surface uses different muscles to control and steady the body. This time it isn't my mind. This is simply a tired, unprepared body. I have to accept that.

As the night wears on, I start grinding lower and lower, like a body ageing in fast-forward. I'm now walking two laps and then taking a rest. Then one lap walking and a rest, sitting on the back of the open boot of the car, pulling off my shoes to massage my aching feet.

Earlier, in those first few easy hours, I found myself running next to a man who told me that to complete a race like this, you needed to get your head right. He told me he had dropped out of his first four ultras, but that now his head was right. I asked him what he meant by that.

'You get to a point in an ultra when you want to stop,' he said. 'Your mind will try to convince you to stop, that you can't carry on, so you have to know why you are out there, you need to be strong in your conviction that you need to keep going. If your head is right, you can do it.'

But this is not my head, it's my legs. I try changing my

shoes, but it's the bounce of the track, killing my legs. It's no good. At about 6 a.m. I tell Marietta I'm quitting. The pain is too much. My feet feel the searing of a thousand hot needles with every step. This is not like the Miwok race, or the Ring O' Fire, where I managed to revive near the end. This is a complete wipe-out. She suggests I try the physio again. There's no point, I reply. It might help for a while, but I still have six hours to go. Right now even one lap feels impossible, how can I keep going for six hours?

But I go to the physio. 'My feet are in agony,' I say. 'Please help.'

'These shoes look new,' she says, as I lie down on her bench. 'How long have you had them?'

I'm wearing them today for the first time. I had some dumb idea to treat the race as an extreme kit test for a magazine article. I thought I'd be like the Duracell bunny, seeing which items could last the distance. I didn't think about my body breaking down first.

'Two weeks,' I lie, embarrassed to admit the truth, that I've broken the oldest rule in running, which is never do anything new on race day.

She raises her eyebrows, as though it's painfully obvious. Like I'm a complete idiot. 'Well that's why your feet hurt,' she says with zero sympathy.

I'm mad with myself. Of course I can't do this in new shoes. I've messed up again.

The physio massages my feet and I manage to haul myself around for a few more miles, but by 8 a.m. I'm a broken man. For six hours now I've been walking and resting. I'm barely covering two miles an hour.

Marietta, not sure what else to say, suggests I have a short nap and then try again. I don't take much convincing. I climb into the back of the car and curl up in my sleeping bag. It is blissful to stop, to lie down, to feel the ecstatic relief racing through my veins.

But I can't sleep. It doesn't feel right to be lying here with the race still going on. My head is still out there. I sit up and shuffle around in my sleeping bag, gazing out at the grey morning. Marietta has gone over to the far side of the track to get a cup of tea. I watch the other runners, the last survivors, still moving. How are they doing it? Like clockwork toys they just keep going. Some of them are clearly in trouble, but on they march, or shuffle, or jog. The guy in first place is still bouncing along. Incredible. I feel so useless.

Marietta comes over. 'You'll feel better if you finish,' she says.

'I can't,' is all I can say. My body is broken. It is no longer a choice.

The person with his stuff next to us is a giant of a man named Kartik. He is a Sri Chinmoy follower and has been walking since about seven hours into the race, often with his eyes closed. He sees me sitting in the back of the car and comes over, gentle in his movements. 'It's normal to be in pain at this point,' he says. 'But if you keep going, you never know what is out there waiting for you. Often you can be surprised.'

'I'm broken,' I say.

'Are you injured?' he asks. 'If you've injured yourself, then it is best to stop.'

'I'm not injured, but everything is in pain, especially my feet. I wore new shoes.'

He looks at me straight. 'It would be a shame to give up just as it's getting interesting,' he says. And with that he smiles kindly and hobbles off towards the track, back on his way.

I sit for about ten minutes watching them going round and round. At one point an Indian man who, like Kartik, has been dragging himself along for hours comes by, wrapped in a blanket, staring ahead, barely moving. He looks worse than me. But he's still out there. He's still going.

Marietta tries one last time. 'You don't want to finish this race sitting in here,' she says. 'You want to finish out there on the track. On your feet.'

I look at the Indian man and I want to cry, at the effort, at the effort of them all, each one running, walking, like men and women going through hell, shellshocked, broken, but still moving. One woman runs by singing to herself. I haul myself out of the car. I have to carry on. I don't ask myself why, I just start walking, returning to the fray, hunched over, my hood pulled up over my head.

Each step hurts but as I get to the start of the home straight, I see a line on the track and for some reason I tell myself that from that line, just for one straight of the track, I'll try jogging. Try to be light, bouncy, I tell myself. I start with tiny steps, pit pat, pit pat. I'm running. As I pass the person counting my laps, she looks at me, beaming: 'Adharanand! You're running! Fantastic!'

I had planned to stop right there, but her enthusiasm keeps me going. I'll do another little bit. But I realise that jogging is actually less painful than walking, less impact on my battered feet. Maybe I can run a whole lap. As I come around, back past Marietta, I realise I feel OK. I can go some more. I try walking for a moment, but it hurts more, so I start running again. Marietta gives me an amazed look as I go by.

I'm still running, slowly, barely running, but running, as I pass the lap counters again. They are all genuinely excited to see me again. It has been hours since I was last seen running. 'Yes, Adharanand,' they shout and cheer.

This time as I come around to Marietta, she is grinning. She has her camera out to take a picture, and just for fun, for the picture, I pick up my speed as I go past. I'll pretend I'm flying along, just for the picture. But a strange thing happens. It feels good, great in fact, to run properly. Not a tiny shuffling run, but a real, running run. My legs feel like they've just woken up from a deep stupor, yawned and looked around. *Good morning, boss, what's happening?* Amazed, I decide to keep going. I'm overtaking people now, even some of those at the top of the leaderboard. Maybe I'm overdoing it? The doubts come flooding back, but I banish them. One lap at a time. Stay in the moment.

And so I run on. I manage about twelve laps, three miles, before I give myself a little rest. Each time as I pass Marietta we look at each other in disbelief. I hold my hands out, apologetic, after all my complaining. I've no idea what is going on, how this is happening. I now feel as fresh as I did in the first hour. All the pain is gone.

I sit down for about thirty seconds, massaging my feet. But I'm eager to get on. I have a lot of lost time to make up, and before I know it I'm up and running again.

And then, as though everything is coming alive together, waking up, throwing off the weary yoke, the clouds part and the sun comes out. I feel like I've come through my darkest night and into the light. This is self-transcendence. I've broken through, and on the other side the sun is shining and everything is happy. I blow kisses, offer thanks, and just plain grin as the lap counters cheer and call my name each time I pass.

The last mile I'm really moving, racing along, dodging in and out of the other runners and their supporters like they're pedestrians on a busy pathway. For the last five minutes someone is assigned to run with me, someone who will mark the exact spot where I stop, but he can't keep up. He has to keep cutting across the grass in the middle of the track to try to chase me down. My brother, who has turned up, chases along next to me, whooping and yelling. 'Go Dhar! Go Dhar!' It's incredible, I can't go fast enough. I'm fully sprinting now. When the hooter sounds to end the race, it comes too soon. I don't want to stop, I want to keep flying. I feel better now than when I started.

But of course, I stop. I've done it. I collapse on the ground, but I'm laughing, not crying. Here comes my marker, hot and flustered, shaking his head. Here comes Marietta, my amazing crew. Before the race she had questioned why I needed a crew. Did I really need someone to stay up all night just to hand me drinks? Couldn't I just grab them myself? But now we knew.

Before the race, she didn't plan to stay for the entire thing. She was going to disappear at some point to get some sleep. But she never did. She says it was too moving, watching it all unfold, seeing people being so challenged, but then seeing them carry on. I wasn't the only one dead on my feet, teetering on the brink, but who later broke through the clouds to the blue sky.

'It was like watching a whole life unfold,' she says, as we sit on our deck chairs, hardly believing it's finally over. 'Watching everyone go round and round, going through their highs and lows, being overwhelmed, some staggering, barely able to put one foot in front of the other, others flying around, singing, smiling, crying. Some people were out, lying down, but they got back up and moving again. And all the time there was this incredibly powerful, charged atmosphere.'

Yes, I felt it too as I sat there in the back of the car, in my sleeping bag, watching it all unfold without me, and I decided to plug back in.

'People start out with a plan,' says Shankara Smith, who has watched every race since it was first run in 1989, when her father was the race director. 'They have a goal for how far they are going to run. But for us, watching, the most inspiring thing is to see those people where it has all gone wrong, but to see them carry on, to keep going. That's what inspires us.'

An hour later we all gather together for the awards ceremony. I end up twenty-eighth out of the thirty-two finishers. Thirteen people didn't make it to the end. I ran 89 miles. It's far from impressive written down like that, but the figures are not important. This was a life lesson lived out on a track in Tooting. A bare exposure of what it feels like to struggle, to ache, to feel the passing of time, but also the connection and support of others, to be lifted by it, to reach deep inside yourself and realise that you can do what you thought was impossible.

It still feels like a miracle that I got running again. I reached a deeper point of futility in this race than in any of the others, yet the revival was even bigger. I'll never again be able to tell myself that I can't carry on. After all these revivals, I'll never again be able to say I'm too tired, that I'm broken. Because I now know with certainty that what seems impossible is possible, that however painful it feels, I can revive, I can get it back.

The evidence has been growing with each race. I have been told again and again since I started ultra running that the mind is key, but it is only now, after the Tooting race, that I fully realise what this means. It isn't just the inner monologue of negative comments, or not having enough conviction to finish. The mind can throw seemingly indisputable arguments and reasoning at you. And even more than that, it can create real, actual pain in your legs, or at least the sensation of it. Yet, with a change of perspective, such as realising you are close to the finish, or being moved by the incredible effort of others, or even reading an inspirational quote, the pain can evaporate. It may or may not be real, but it is not debilitating.

From a scientific point of view, this is Tim Noakes's central governor theory again – the idea that during extreme exercise such as endurance running, the brain starts to shut your body down early in order to protect you. We evolved like this in order to keep some energy in reserve in case of an emergency, such as a bear jumping out on you.

In his brilliant book *Endure*, journalist Alex Hutchinson recalls asking Noakes for the single most convincing piece of evidence in favour of this theory. Being South African, Noakes pointed to those finishing the Comrades Marathon just before the 12-hour cut-off. Here we have non-elite athletes summoning huge sprint finishes at the end of a gruelling ultra marathon. They should be at their most fatigued, with damaged muscles and low on fuel, yet they are sprinting. Clearly they were capable of going faster in the preceding miles, he says, so why didn't they?

It fits exactly with my experience in virtually every ultra marathon I've run. Each time, my mind has shut me down early through a combination of clever arguments and the perception of pain. And unlike the top ultra runners, or those with trauma in their lives, who relish the pain, who wait for it and hit it head on, dig into it, I have given in meekly each time, letting myself be dragged into self-pity, my body weakening, my pace grinding almost to a halt. It was only when my mind decided I was close enough to the end, that we were safe, that it released me, and gave me access again to my reserves of strength.

The best way to stop my mind overwhelming me is to try to forget about how far I have left to run and to stay in the moment, as so many ultra runners have told me. In his book, Hutchinson tells the fascinating story of Diane Van Deren, who became a competitive ultra runner in her late thirties after having brain surgery to cure her of epilepsy. A result of the surgery was that she could run for hours and hours and have no idea how much time had passed. While it had many downsides in her day-to-day life, it made her a formidable ultra runner because, according to her clinical neuropsychologist, 'her mind carries little dread for how far she is from the finish'.

'Unable to read maps or keep track of where she is on a course,' Hutchinson writes, 'she doesn't focus on the challenge ahead of her.' And because of her poor short-term memory, she doesn't dwell on the effort she has already expended, either. 'Instead she has no choice but to focus on the immediate task of forward motion, taking one more step, and then another.'

I need to be more like Van Deren. It is always the thought of the challenge ahead that floors me. Once that challenge becomes manageable, I revive. To stop the collapse, I have to stop thinking ahead. One thing that may help is not to look at my watch. Not even turn it on. If I'm trying not to think of the challenge ahead, I don't need a constant, beeping reminder of it right there on my wrist. On the final day at the Ring O' Fire, having given up racing, I didn't start my watch. Of course I was also moving more slowly, but it felt much better. It was a relief, as though I had ditched a particularly annoying friend who kept insisting on telling me every five minutes how far we still had to go. I think about Zach Miller and his five-dollar Casio watch. He's not calculating the miles when he runs. Perhaps that's why he can run with such abandon, unleashed and unhindered.

In three weeks I have my first 100-mile race. In order to

make it to the end without crumbling, the key will be to stay locked in the present, to not think ahead, but to continually accept the moment I am in, like a Zen monk. As the spiritual teacher Eckhart Tolle says: 'As soon as you honour the present moment, all unhappiness and struggle dissolve, and life begins to flow with joy and ease.'

Of course, I'm sure my mind will have a few tricks up its sleeve. But this time, I hope, I'll be ready.

12

While I'd been focused on my own challenges, the rest of the ultra running world had been trundling along. On the same weekend I ran around Anglesey, in the Alps the Ultra-Trail du Mont-Blanc was taking place. Everyone was calling it the greatest, most competitive trail ultra race ever. Zach Miller was returning after his fireworks in 2016; you also had a pair of two-time winners, François D'Haene and Xavier Thévenard, both from France; Gary Gellin's Lithuanian friend Gediminas Grinius, the former Iraq vet who finished second in 2016, was there; and so too were a whole host of exciting Americans, including our friend from Boulder Sage Canaday. Every one of them had hopes of winning, but the real pre-race excitement was largely focused around two men: Kilian Jornet and Jim Walmsley.

Jim Walmsley has been a divisive character in his fledgeling career so far, bursting on to the US scene a few years ago with eye-opening course records in a string of races. He arrived at the Western States 100 in 2016 still an unsponsored athlete, but claiming that he was not only going to win the race but beat the course record. Considering the history behind this race, and the fact that Walmsley had never run a 100-mile race before, his bravado caused some frisson among fans of the sport, exciting some people but riling others.

Right from the start he attacked the race and was soon forty minutes inside the record pace. But then, in what has since become a famous incident, still looking strong at mile 93, Walmsley took a wrong turn. By the time his crew found him, wandering lost along a deserted road, he cut a frustrated and dejected figure. He was so far ahead of the rest of the field, he could have still got back on the course and won the race, but something had switched off in his mind.

'It just turned into this absolutely demoralised deflation immediately,' he said afterwards. He ended up walking the rest of the way, finishing in twentieth place and almost four hours outside the course record.

In 2017, he was back at Western States predicting wild times, but again he came unstuck. Although he raced off at course record speed, by mile 70 he was throwing up constantly, and lying down in the shade for ten minutes every 100 metres or so. In the end he gave up and dropped out.

People started saying he couldn't handle the 100-mile distance, that he was too cocky. But he was still causing excitement in the sport, winning every other race he entered and blazing super fast times. When I was in California, everyone was talking about him. 'This guy Walmsley is unbeatable,' they'd say, before adding the caveat, 'at anything under 100 miles.' But surely he would get one right eventually. So the fact that he was lining up at the 105-mile UTMB for the first time was a big deal, especially given the fact that it would be his first head-to-head with the king himself: Kilian Jornet.

At 29, Jornet has won virtually everything in the sport. His backstory is the stuff of legend. Born in a mountain hut in the Spanish Pyrenees – his dad was a mountain guide – by five years old he had already climbed Aneto, the highest mountain in the Pyrenees.

His first love was ski-mountaineering, a sport involving climbing or skiing up mountains and skiing back down, and he competed internationally, winning some world championship races. When he was just eighteen, he took up mountain running, and in 2008 he claimed the first of his three UTMB wins at the age of twenty-one. He has also won the Western States 100 and just a few months before this year's UTMB he won the Hardrock 100 in the US, despite falling and dislocating his shoulder with 87 miles still to go. Being Superman, he popped it back into place, tied it up in a sling and carried on to win the race.

In 2014 he started looking for fresh challenges and came up with a project, which he called Summits of My Life, to break the speed records up seven of the world's most iconic mountains, from Mont Blanc to Kilimanjaro to Mount Everest.

Shortly after he returned to Europe from his record attempt on Everest, the final summit in his project, I managed to get an interview with him in London. I took him for a drink to a trendy Indian, street-style restaurant in King's Cross. He carried a big bag over his shoulder and looked overawed walking through the city, like a man a long way from his natural habitat.

His press agent told me he hated crowds and spent no more than a few days a year in cities. He used to live in Chamonix in France, the town that hosts the UTMB, but, he said, 'it was too big, too many people'. The town's population is around 10,000. He has since moved with his girlfriend, Swedish ultra runner Emelie Forsberg, to an isolated region of Norway.

Despite all he has achieved, Jornet's latest feat didn't go completely to plan. On 20 May, he attempted to race up Mount Everest. Having already set speed records on Kilimanjaro, Mont Blanc, the Matterhorn, Denali and Aconcagua, it was time for the big one.

Setting off from base camp near the Rongbuk Monastery on a climb that usually takes four days, even with oxygen and fixed ropes – neither of which Jornet was using – he began at a fast pace. However, by 7,700m he was struggling with stomach pains and was stopping every few metres with cramps and vomiting. But he says he pushed on regardless, reaching the summit at midnight. The four-day route had taken him just 26 hours, but it wasn't a record. Rather than give up and come off the mountain, he decided to rest at advance base camp for a few days until he was feeling better, and then went up again, climbing to the top of the world twice in six days, again alone and without oxygen or fixed ropes.

'The record was not important,' he said, puzzling over the menu. 'What I really wanted to see in Everest, to test, is whether it was possible to move light in the Himalayas like we do in the Alps and other places, alone without ropes. Just grab what you need and go, not this big expedition with all this stuff. And it was.'

When I ask him about his preparation for Everest, how much training he had done, he said: 'My preparation began when I was a child.'

'I did my first hike when I was eighteen months old,' he said. 'We hiked for seven hours.' He was scaling summits aged three. This wasn't the case of overbearing parents frog-marching him around the mountains. He said he loved it. And it is a love that has grown and stayed with him his whole life.

'We were just playing, nobody was forcing us. Our parents would let us lead the way and choose the route, so we went as far as we wanted.' From a young age he learned independence in the mountains. His mother used to take him walking outside barefoot at night to feel the earth, to connect with nature.

'Of course, we were always falling over and scratching ourselves, but it was fun,' he said. Incredibly, despite all the thousands of hours he has spent hurtling around in the mountains, before the Hardrock 100 he had only ever had one injury, and that happened when he fell over crossing the street in a small Spanish town when he was eighteen.

In total he said he spends about 1,200 hours a year out training in the mountains (an average of over three hours a day), and climbs in total around 600,000m of ascent, an average of 1,640m every day. For reference, Ben Nevis, the highest peak in the British Isles, sits at 1,345m.

He admitted, however, that it was not only the intense training that made him so good at mountain running.

'I have good running genes,' he said. 'No matter how hard I dreamed, I could never play in the NBA. But I once had a VO2 max test [a measure of a person's oxygen-carrying capacity, a big factor in how fast and far you can run] and it was quite high.' This was an understatement. Jornet's VO2 max test results stunned the researchers carrying them out. At 90 ml/kg/min it was one of the highest ever recorded. His resting heart rate, another measure of fitness, is absurdly low at 34. On top of this, Jornet said he can recover very quickly from exercise, which allows him to train hard day after day.

And what about mental strength? 'I like to feel pain,' he said. 'If I start hurting, I don't worry, I don't mind. Maybe I don't like it, but I don't mind.'

Combine all this with his unusual upbringing, scrambling around in the mountains his entire childhood, and it began to make sense why no one else can keep up with him.

Yet among all his success in races and scaling mountains, Jornet's path has not been completely smooth. He may have turned the world's highest peaks into a playground, but it is a dangerous playground. In 2012, while preparing for a speed attempt on Mont Blanc, during the first stage of his Summits of My Life project, Jornet was with his good friend and three-time world champion ski-mountaineer Stéphane Brosse, when a snow cornice collapsed under them and Brosse fell to his death. The incident hit Jornet hard and made him question why he was doing all this. 'He [Brosse] was my hero, then my friend. We were twenty centimetres apart when he fell, and I thought, why him, why not me? He had children, it would be better if it was me.'

A year later, Jornet and his girlfriend, Emelie Forsberg, who is also a world champion skyrunner, had to be rescued when the weather turned bad out in the mountains near Chamonix. The rescue chief at the time was less than impressed, telling the media: 'I'm very angry when I see the continued rise of running shoes [in the mountains] despite our requests.'

Then, shortly before the Everest attempt, the renowned speed climber Ueli Steck died in an accident in the Himalayas. This too affected Jornet.

'I had also been on Everest in 2016,' he said. 'That year I took more risks, I did things I wouldn't do now. When you assess risk on the mountain, it depends on different things, on how you feel in yourself, in your capabilities, but also in the point you are at in your life. At this point, after Ueli's death, I am more cautious.'

But all this won't stop Jornet continuing to seek to push himself and break barriers. 'This is a risky thing,' he said. 'But life is risky. Life is not sitting on a sofa being safe. If you tell someone: "I love you", that is a risk. On the mountain, I try to find the small space between being safe – because it is good to stay alive – and risk, the place where you can find your limits and challenge yourself.'

For now, Jornet's challenge was a return to racing, and a face-off against Jim Walmsley and the rest of the world's best mountain runners. He hadn't run the UTMB for five years, but he said that when he saw how competitive the field was, how many great runners had signed up, he just had to be there.

And so, while I was shivering and feeling sorry for myself in a village hall in Anglesey, one of the greatest trail races in history played out in the Alps. In the early stages, Jornet, Walmsley and 6ft 4in Frenchman François D'Haene ran together at the front. They were flying along, way under the course record, when Walmsley was heard saying: 'It's too slow.' Jornet, the three-time winner, replied, according to the people watching: 'No, it is too fast.'

But it was D'Haene who made the first big move, forging ahead shortly after halfway. Walmsley, again struggling over the longer distance, started to drop back and in the end it was left to Jornet to chase the big Frenchman hard. But it was to no avail. D'Haene kept the pressure on to the end, finishing back in Chamonix in just over 19 hours for his third UTMB victory, putting his name up there with Jornet's as a legend of the race.

Jornet came in 15 minutes later in second, while Walmsley, after struggling badly at around 80 miles, managed to pull himself together to finish in fifth place – his best 100-mile race so far. Zach Miller was never a factor at the front after his injury-hit year, but he still ran well to finish ninth. Sage Canaday didn't fall or get stitches, like in his previous UTMB, but he had a bad run and finished back in fiftieth position, which he said was probably his worst ultra result ever.

In the end, it was a race that lived up to the hype and cemented the UTMB's status as the biggest mountain trail race of them all. Next year, it will be my turn to toe the line with the greats. First I just have to bag six more points in a little race in the Pyrenees called the 100 Miles Sud de France.

This race, of all the races I've signed up to, scares me the most. It will be my first mountain race. My first time running in the dark. My first 100-mile race. And it's my third big ultra in five weeks.

Tom Payn and his now-wife, Rachel, are running it too, both hoping to bag their final six points so they also can be at the UTMB next year. They've been a lot more thorough than me, though. A few months before the race they ran the entire route in preparation, to get to know the course. Tom tells me, as we sit in a café in Font Romeu the night before the start, that it was a lot harder than he was expecting. 'It's harder than the UTMB,' he says, which is not what I need to hear right now. He tells me I should expect it to take me around 35 hours. 'You may be quicker,' he says. 'But best to prepare to be out there that long. As a worst-case scenario.'

The race finishes on the beach in Argelès on the Mediterranean coast. It starts at 10 a.m., so I calculate that 34 hours would bring me in at sunset on the second day. That would be a nice time to finish. I could drop my bag and run straight into the sea.

I conjure up that image many times during the race. I keep reminding myself to make sure I take my phone out of my pocket before I crash and tumble into the waves. But I'm thinking too far ahead. One step at a time.

We line up on a bright morning by a sports hall outside Font Romeu with about three hundred other runners, nearly all local French men and women used to these mountains. As we mill around, even Tom looks apprehensive, a cloud casting a shadow over his usually sunny disposition.

The race is started by a local dignitary with a shotgun,

and we're off, bouncing through some woods, down easy trails, out of the village and into the mountains. My legs, as I feared after my recent exploits, soon feel tired. My ankles, my quads are creaking, already complaining. *Early days, boys*, I tell them. *Go back to sleep. I'll need you to be strong later.*

The early miles tick by easily, nonetheless. We go down a lot, through the walls of a castle, past aid stops manned by soldiers. After about seven miles we head up a steep path. Up a mountain. Here you can only walk. I pull on the rocks and grass with my hands, trying to help my legs. I seem to be the only person in the race without hiking poles, which already gives me something to be negative about. I'm working harder, I think. I'm not prepared; it shows how out of my depth I am. But I realise I'm holding my position, even passing a few people with their poles, people breathing way too hard this early in the race.

The views as we climb are stunning, and I allow myself to stop here and there to take pictures. These little rests, this reining back on the relentless urgency, will help me in the long run.

Over the top of the first mountain comes our first serious descent. I go cautiously, still a baby on these trails, wobbly and unsteady, as the other runners come streaming by. Let them go, I tell myself, fearful that trying to go too fast could lead to a fall and the end of it all. I just need to get around. The speed is not important.

I must cut a pathetic figure, however, taking tentative steps as everyone else crunches and leaps past me. At the bottom is an aid stop with picnic tables set up outside a long-abandoned farmhouse. I sit down for a moment, grabbing some bread and cheese. Just as I'm contemplating moving on, Rachel turns up. She looks surprised to see me.

'I expected you to be way ahead,' she says.

'I'm trying to hold myself back,' I half lie. I am, it is true, but also I don't think I can go any faster on these steep trails.

I get up and head back out, up another mountain. Rachel catches me near the top. She seems full of energy and we run together along the ridge before we hit another tumbling decent, crumbly earth, jagged rocks, loose stones. Again people stream by. They seem to have one of two techniques: either quick, nimble steps, light on their feet; or big crunching strides that seem to show disdain for the trail, crunching the stones and rocks that jut up to meet them.

Rachel is even worse at descending than I am, and by the time I'm leaving the next aid station, at the bottom of the hill, she still hasn't appeared.

Up we go again. This is the game. The climbs are a rest from the downs, at least. And fewer people pass me on the climbs. We're 20 miles in now and I'm doing OK. I feel calm, composed, though these are early days. The sunlight is slowly turning into evening yellow. The night is coming.

I arrive at the first of the three big aid stations, in the small town of Vernet-les-Bains, just before 7 p.m., running strongly through the streets, passing people already reduced to walking, even though it's a gentle downhill slope. This is my terrain. I'm still a road runner at heart. Passing people gives me strength and I turn into the town's main sports centre like a man on a mission. First base reached. Feeling strong.

I see Marietta, and our friend Charlotte, who has come along with us to help crew. Charlotte's a massage therapist, so she massages my legs as I load up on food: pasta, cake, peanuts. I shove it all down together. It all takes longer than planned, but as I leave the aid station I feel refreshed, as though I'm just starting out again. I have my jacket and head torch on, ready for the night. Ready to face my fears.

As I walk towards the exit I see Rachel. She is also preparing to leave. Her eyes look wild. Scared. 'I'm just going to fill my water,' she says.

'I'll start walking,' I say. 'This next climb is a big one, you'll soon catch me up.'

She just nods. But it's the last time I see her in the race. Tom, meanwhile, is up in fifth place, Marietta tells me, somewhere far, far ahead.

As soon as I get beyond the lights of the town, I realise something is wrong with my head torch. At first I think it's some clever lighting trick. This is a brand new torch. But I quickly realise that the batteries are flat. I feel like an idiot. Every race I've made some basic mistake. I can't believe I didn't test the batteries. I have some spares, but they only last six hours. Luckily the organisers also make you carry a spare torch, but the one I have is old and has a weak light, and worse, I haven't checked the batteries in that one either.

In the end they last the night between them, but I spend a lot of time and energy worrying about being stuck on the mountain, pleading with passing runners for their spare batteries.

Once I get my light on, I start up the climb out of Vernet-les-Bains. I have a vague recollection of being told that this is the biggest ascent of the race, so I hunker down and settle into a slow rhythm. Climbing in the dark is not too difficult – as I'm moving so slowly, there's no risk of losing my footing. But the darkness seems to darken my thoughts, and bring in a sense of foreboding. I occasionally pass people sitting by the side of the trail. They're just resting, but they appear suddenly from the darkness like the gaunt, frightened survivors of some terrible ordeal.

On it goes. The steepness is unrelenting. I stop every twenty minutes for a two-minute rest, and then haul myself on. One man, who is about sixty, is following a similar pattern and we keep stopping next to each other. We don't speak, but just sit there, staring into the darkness, and then we go on again. Hang in there, I tell myself. One step at a time.

As I climb, the wind begins to pick up. At first I take it as a sign I'm getting near the top, but I soon realise it just means we're getting higher. The top could still be a long way off.

It blows cold through my jacket and sweaty T-shirt. I remember reading a blog by the US runner Dylan Bowman, about his race at the UTMB, where he said his only mistake was not putting enough clothes on the moment he felt the cold. Once your body temperature drops on the mountain, it's hard to get it back up. So I stop and pull on an extra layer, and hike on.

It is almost two hours before the steepness abates. Lights, voices ahead. I climb out of my hole to find a great big fire with a group of teenagers sitting huddled around it. I go over and sit down. This isn't an aid station, just a brief respite. The kids speak Spanish. It's another five kilometres, they tell me, to the aid station.

'Going up?' I ask. 'Or down?'

'Up,' comes the reply. I stay calm. Up or down, it doesn't matter. I have to deal with whatever comes to get to the finish. Up is fine.

To my relief, however, it is a gentler slope from here. I'm too tired now to run, but I can walk quickly, and an hour later I arrive.

The wind is tearing at me now as I approach a stone building. There's a light in a window, I can see faces, runners, sitting around a long table. I go in and find a pew and sit down, smiling at the two men opposite. They ignore me and carry on eating. I'm not hungry, but I take some stuff here and there from the paper bowls on the table. Crisps. Cake. It is slim pickings. Most of the bowls need refilling, but I'm in no state to do anything about it. I drink some Coke and put my head in my hands. For a brief moment I'm hit by a rush of despair. I can't do this. I suddenly feel sick. I'm overcome with weakness. I hold myself, trying to stop myself caving in. I haul myself out of my seat and pull on my bag. It is dangerous to sit here any longer. The desire to stop, to stay in this warm refuge, is growing too strong. I grab some chocolate and step outside. Which way? I can't tell. I can't ask anyone. I stand there shivering madly, the wind slapping me like a wet sheet on a line. I have to move.

I see a reflective strip marking the way. I follow it. The path is flat here, traversing a ridge. The stars fill the sky, but I keep my eyes on the ground, following my light. I try eating the chocolate but it makes me gag. I almost get sick, so I spit it out, moving on.

The path is smooth for a while, but soon it begins to descend over piles of rocks. The steep slopes were bad enough in the day, but in the night they're perilous. I keep catching my feet on rocks and tree roots, almost toppling over. Almost every minute it happens and I have to catch myself. My god, I have to be careful. People catch me and pass me. They seem to be moving easily. I try to follow for a while, but everyone is too surefooted and so I stumble on alone.

After another hour it levels out, to my relief, the path winding its way around the edge of the mountain. Here on the flatter section I make better progress, except that I still keep stumbling. With a 500ft drop to one side, it's scary. At first I feel like a comedy drunk, but then I start to lose my sense of humour. Why can't I run longer than a minute without nearly killing myself?

At some point in the early morning, about 5 a.m. and still in the dark, I arrive at the second big aid station, 55 miles and 19 hours into the race. I'm making steady progress. Tom and Rachel told me the first 40 miles were the hardest. I've broken the back of this race. I still feel OK. By late afternoon I'll be on the beach. Everything is going to plan.

Charlotte massages my legs again, but my psoas muscle starts spasming. One of the officials sees me grimacing in pain and insists I go to see the medics. In the medical room a man with badly cut knees is being hooked up to a drip; another looks dazed, like he has just been punched. The doctor examines my hips and tells me the muscle is inflamed. He shakes his head and says I should stop. I want to tell him that my feet, my quads, my ankles, all hurt much worse, and that I'm struggling to eat, but I keep it to myself. I'm going on, I tell him, so he rubs some cream on the muscle and gives me a painkiller and sends me on my way.

Before I leave, however, another official warns me that there's a big climb coming up. Then a steep descent and then another climb. '*Muy duro*,' he says in Spanish. Very tough. Tom told me it was easier from here, but I suppose I have to expect a few climbs. They can't be like the ones before, though.

'And after the two climbs, it's easy?' I ask him. Yes, he says, but he doesn't sound very sure.

'I've got two more big climbs,' I tell Marietta. I can handle that. And so, an hour after arriving, fed and rejuvenated, I'm back out into the dark, back on the path to the sea.

Daylight seems to take forever to break. This next climb is tough and I'm glad I was warned. I have to climb over lots of jagged rocks. The sun finally emerges as I'm running down the other side. With the light it seems easier and I start skipping along, overtaking people. I imagine I'm Jim Walmsley on the charge. Rather than just trotting along, I start pushing the pace, bounding down the slopes. I'm crushing it. Almost 24 hours in and I'm rising. Bring it on.

I'm buzzing with energy at the next stop. Marietta is there again.

'You look great,' she says. I feel great. I don't linger, but pull my pack back on and I'm off. The last big climb.

The official was right, this one is *muy duro*. The higher we go, the steeper it gets. It's all smooth mud and grass, nothing to hold on to. One man asks me why I don't have poles. Up and up. The top never seems to arrive. I keep thinking I can see it, glimpses of sky between trees, but then the path twists and heads up again in another direction.

Eventually, of course, we get there. From the top, in the far distance, we see the sea. I stop along with everyone else to take it in. It looks a long way away.

After ten minutes scrambling along a rocky ridge we come to the tiniest aid station – just a table with water and Coke – and then it's a steep, concrete road down. People let themselves go, flying off into the distance. I try, but I can't. My quads are too shattered.

The road seems to go down for hours and I start long-ing for another climb. But when it comes, even though it's short, it's hard to manage. For the first time in the race I feel like I'm really struggling. Like I won't make it. The path is gentle here, mostly flat, but when I try running I quickly grind to a slow walk. I sit down and phone Marietta.

'I may need some new batteries for the head torch,' I say. It's now 5 p.m. and there is still no sign of the final big aid station in the town of Le Perthus, right on the Spanish bor-der. 'I may be going into a second night.' I sound panicky. On the verge of a breakdown. I'm doing well, she tells me. Just keep moving. I get up and soldier on. Fifteen minutes later, I arrive at the aid station.

Marietta grabs some chairs and we begin the now familiar

routine of massage and food. By my reckoning, and the sign outside the door, I have 15 miles to go. I'm within striking distance of the finish. If it really is all easy from here, I could be on the beach by 9.30 p.m. After dark, but only just. There might still be time for that dip in the sea. I ask Marietta to make sure she brings me a towel and some spare clothes.

They agree to next meet me at the penultimate checkpoint, with six miles to go. I should be there soon after 8 p.m. I wave goodbye as I walk off, chewing a banana. I have a spring in my step. Maybe 100 miles is not that far after all, even in the mountains.

The sun is still hot as the route ducks off the road and begins to climb a dry, dusty trail. I try drinking from the tube coming out of my bag, but it isn't working. I haul my bag off, re-attach the tube and try again, but it still doesn't work. I take it all apart and try again. I can't go on without water. Then I see the problem, there's an air pocket in the bottle. I open it, spilling half the energy drink all over myself, but I get the air pocket out. I put my bag back together and carry on. But two minutes later, it has stopped working again. Bloody hell. I look behind. A group of runners are coming up the hill behind me. I try to stay calm, but my mind is frazzled. How is it still so hot? I sit down on a clump of earth and look at the water bottle, turning it around in my hands. Then I realise, it's upside down. I turn it the right way, reattach it and this time it works. I stand up and carry on.

The hill goes on longer than I was expecting. I wonder why we aren't at the top yet, but still going up. I walk faster, hitting a little jog. 'Come on then,' I say, out loud. 'Is this all you've got? This little hill? I can take this.'

But the little hill goes on, and the bravado sounds hollow. I need to be sensible, 14 miles or so is still a fair distance. The group behind catch me. Five men, walking in silence, one behind the other. I stick on the back of their train and match their steps, one for one, until the next aid stop. It's manned by two immaculately dressed old ladies who fuss until I agree to take a cup of noodle soup. I stand eating it in the warm light of evening. This must be the last high point, surely. But as we head on from the aid stop, the path takes a violent twist and heads straight up a huge, steep climb through some trees. I look around in disbelief, but the other guys barely blink, setting off up the hill.

'Try to be strong,' one of them says to me. So I buckle down and join the climb.

It's sunset, about an hour later, when we reach the top. The sky is on fire in every direction, blazing over the jutting Pyrenees to one side, and glowing pink over the Mediterranean on the other. I stop to take it all in. It's a piece of luck to be up here at this exact moment, the air cold and fresh. It may just be the most magnificent sunset I've ever seen. But I have to go on.

I try to calculate how long it is until the next checkpoint with Marietta. Maybe another hour. For the next mile the path is incredibly steep going down and I'm thankful to be doing it before dark. Making a tricky descent like this with these battered legs, in the dark, is a scary thought.

After a while I hit a dirt road. It's dark enough now for the head torch, so I put it on. I try to run but it's too much effort. A quick walk is enough. I'm nearly there.

On I go, into blackness, trees, silence, a road winding

around the mountain, but never seeming to go down. Eight o'clock comes and goes. Then 9 p.m., and still no sign of the checkpoint. Occasionally I pass a lone figure, walking slowly, hands on hips. Or someone, running smoothly, comes by me. But mostly I'm alone. And then I begin to see things.

I'm hauling along the trail thinking I must be close when I spot the checkpoint ahead. I can see a building with a light on in the window, and people with head torches milling around outside. I check my watch: 9.15 p.m., about time. But when I get to the checkpoint, it's not there. The empty blackness is like a cold shiver. I imagined it completely. There's nothing there, not even a house-shaped rock. Some-how that would have felt better.

Shaken, I run on. Oh, there it is. Again I see lights, a building. Again, it isn't there. I stop dead. Now I'm scared.

The third time, I'm prepared. OK, I just have to accept this. Keep moving. I should be there soon. I keep expecting to see the lights of Argelès somewhere in the valley below. Why is it all so black? Nothing but the thick, swamping darkness. Am I losing my mind? Am I trapped in some kind of time warp?

To my relief, I start catching someone ahead. I watch as he, or she, runs under a huge wooden arch across the trail, with the words 'Welcome to . . .', while the name of the place is lost in the branches of a tree. The entrance to a town. This must be it.

But the arch isn't real.

I push on, trying to run. I have to get off this moun-tain quickly. A few minutes later I see a tent flapping in the wind. I approach it with caution. But it's real. I pull back the flap. Inside is a table with food. It's the checkpoint.

It feels dangerous to sit down. I have to keep moving. Marietta and Charlotte aren't here. I guess they went ahead to the finish. This spot must have been too remote for their small hire car. I try to remember: was it six miles, or six kilometres from here? I ask one of the volunteers manning the station.

'*Quinze*,' he says. I stand there unable to work out what he is saying. What was that? Kanze? Kilometres?

'Is that French?' I ask.

He nods. 'Fifteen kilometres.'

A cold wind blows through my skull.

'Fifteen?!' I stammer. I head for the exit.

'Are you leaving?' asks a man, appearing in the doorway with a smile.

'Er, yes,' I say, barely knowing what I'm doing.

'You follow to the right, then it's five kilometres down to the next checkpoint.'

'Is the hill gentle?' I ask.

He shakes his head. 'Not really,' he says. 'But you'll be fine.'

Minutes later I'm slipping and sliding, grabbing on to spiky bushes to stop myself falling. I realise I've lost the path. A couple of men go bounding past nearby and I follow after them for a while, until I see a light heading up a hill in front of me. I try calling the men over, but they go off the other way. I follow my light, until I realise there is no light. There is no hill. Just the sky.

I'm not going to make it out of this alive. Everywhere I

look I can see lights, people on verandas with trays handing around drinks, people chatting, sitting on rocking chairs. I can't move.

Suddenly a woman appears in front of me and cheers. A man comes from behind me and they kiss and embrace, chatting excitedly in French. They're real, I realise. I have to keep them close. It's my only hope. I charge through the undergrowth and tag on to them. I have to stay close, no matter what. So close I fill my field of vision with their backs. I'll ignore everything else.

They move quickly down the steep rocky slope. I follow behind the woman, my eyes fixed like beady devils on her feet. My feet follow, step for step. She is going fast and my quads throb, but I can't let her go, so I zoom in closer, my eyes stuck like glue.

Down we go, one after the other. Later, someone tells me that locally they call that hill *la descente de la mort*, the descent of death, because it's so difficult. And that's in the daylight. As we pass people, stopped, frightened, watching us fly by, a strange thing happens. The pain in my quads beings to ease, my feet become nimble, and I begin to feel a warmth, like a rush of wellbeing washing over me. I feel suddenly calm, completely and utterly in the moment.

The French couple chat together matter-of-factly like they are out for a Sunday afternoon stroll, while I track them in silent concentration. The hill is so steep there are ropes in places, but nothing fazes me, I am in flow, I am more focused than I have ever been. It feels amazing.

We emerge finally at a stream and a small village. It's 11.30 p.m. As I walk along the road, the doors of a car open and Marietta and Charlotte climb out. I can't believe I'm finally here.

Marietta and Charlotte have been here for hours, so the checkpoint volunteers have heard all about me. They're happy to see me arrive. I take a seat. Finally, six miles to go. I try to ask if it is just along the road now. Surely now it's that final easy bit. But I can't get a clear answer.

After some more noodle soup, I get up from my seat and say my goodbyes. 'See you at the finish,' I say.

For about half a mile we follow a gently sloping road down. After what I've just done, it's a big relief. But then I spot a route marker in the woods beside the road, high up among the trees. *You must be joking?* But no, a small path peels off the road and goes straight up. We have one more mountain to climb.

I take a deep breath and choose not to panic. Accept. One step at a time. I've been going now for over 37 hours. Time no longer has any meaning. My finishing position is irrelevant. I just know that if I keep going, through whatever is thrown at me, eventually I'll get there.

And so it is, at 1.45 a.m. on Sunday, that I clamber down some steps onto a marina next to the beach. I am so close, running along the seafront. There it is, the finishing arch. I run towards it, stumbling over the line. I stop. I've done it. Thirty-nine hours 53 minutes. I stand there and for a moment nothing happens. Nobody says anything. The place is deserted.

Two old men appear, smiling. One puts a medal over my head and shows me where my result has appeared on the computer screen. Ninety-third place out of three hundred starters. He offers me a drink, sliding open a small fridge. There is a choice of flavours. I don't care, any will do. He smiles and hands me one.

Marietta comes over and gives me a hug. We have done it. Oh my god, we have bloody well done it.

I expected to be in floods of tears at the finish, but it didn't happen. It all felt calm. I gathered my things and we walked back to the hotel, where I had a bath and went to bed. The next morning, however, I'm sitting on the hotel room balcony. It's 9.47 a.m. – almost at the final 48-hour cut-off – when I spot a man with a number pinned to him, a bag on his back, running through the car park and down some steps onto the marina. A couple out for a Sunday morning walk look at him, at his pained, anxious face, and walk on. He glances around, looking for something, and then, spotting it, he runs on. And sitting there, watching him go, I burst into tears.

To see that man and to know what he has just been through, to see it in his eyes, and to know he is going to make it, is too much. I sit there sobbing, letting it all out, all those moments when I thought I might die, when I realised we were going up again, over yet another mountain, when I hauled my bag back on and set off again, when Marietta told me how I looked strong, and Charlotte massaged my legs, when kind people at aid stations hustled around making sure I had what I needed, when that couple let me follow them like their shadow, it was all written on that man's face, so much strength, so much effort, so much kindness, that it brought me to tears.

And what of Tom and Rachel? They disappeared from my race early on. It turns out that they had an even tougher time of it than me.

We meet them on Sunday afternoon, in a café by the same marina, to share a beer and tell each other our war stories.

Tom raced off hard at the front, as he does, and says he was going really well for most of the race. 'Coming out of the last big aid station at Le Perthus I was still in about fourth or fifth and I could sense the finish. But on the next descent my knee started to get quite painful.' By the bottom of *la descente de la mort* he could hardly bend his knee. 'I had to walk. Every time I tried to run the pain was too much.'

For the rest of the race he was basically on one leg, using his poles as crutches. The pain got so bad that at one point he decided to lie down on the side of the road for a ten-minute sleep. 'I just needed a break from the pain,' he says. By the end it was so bad that the last kilometre along the seafront took him 35 minutes.

After the finish, he was taken to the medical tent where he spent the next eight hours on a camp bed, until Marietta turned up.

'It was like a scene out of the war,' she says. 'All these people, in a tent, lying on metal camp beds, under woollen blankets.' She found Tom under one of the blankets, gaunt, his lips blue, his eyes closed. 'He looked close to death.'

'I kept waking up,' says Tom, 'confused about where I was, but just happy to be off my feet. I'm not sure how long

I would have been there if it hadn't been for Marietta coming along and taking me back to the hotel.'

Rachel, meanwhile, is still shellshocked, a glazed look in her eyes as she tells her story. She had left the first big aid station at Vernet-les-Bains soon after me, heading up the long climb, into the wind. But she didn't stop to put on extra layers, instead forging on as she was. By the time she reached the top, she was suffering from hypothermia and the officials pulled her from the race. They took her number, and in the hut on the top of the mountain they made her a bed and she went to sleep. She woke up five hours later and demanded to be let back into the race.

'They told me it will be difficult to go on. But I told them, no, it will be more difficult to stop,' she says, laughing. But she sounds affronted. 'You know what I mean? I didn't come here not to finish. I wasn't going to quit.' Rachel has entered the UTMB race lottery twice before and both times failed to get a place. It means this year she is guaranteed her entry, as long as she gets the points. She wasn't going to let it go.

After a five-hour rest, she was running close to the cut-off times, but she raced on, moving strongly through the field the rest of the way, to finish in 44 hours. So in the end, all three of us have the points and a place in the UTMB – Tom qualifying as an elite runner, while I was promised a media place if I got the points.

'Onwards to Chamonix,' says Tom, as we all give a luke-warm cheer and toast our drinks to the fact that we can now do something just as insane all over again.

13

Watching the top runners line up side by side at the start of the Ultra-Trail du Mont-Blanc in Chamonix is stirring stuff. These men and women are incredible athletes, their bodies seemingly chiselled from the mountain rock.

But listening to the pre-race hype and all the talk of how impressive these superstars are, hearing people refer to them as the greatest endurance runners in the world, something seems not quite right. As the camera swoops over the crowded square at the start of the UTMB, and pans along the front row of the top athletes preparing to take off, I can't help thinking: if these are some of the greatest endurance runners in the world, why are they all white? Where are the Kenyans?

Watch any conventional long-distance race – a major road marathon, an international cross-country, or the Olympic 10,000m on the track, for example – and, with the odd exception, all the runners at the front will be from East Africa. In the marathon, Kenyans and Ethiopians dominate to an extent almost unparalleled in any sport – in 2017, for example, ninety-two of the top hundred men's marathon runners were from East Africa, while for the women seventy-six of the top hundred marathoners were from the region. Yet in ultra running, there are virtually no top East African runners.

The one exception is the Comrades Marathon, where occasionally a Kenyan or Ethiopian will venture along, but they don't tend to do very well. Comrades, and South Africa's other road races, are the only big ultra marathons in the world where the front of the field is not all-white, with the top black South African athletes fully embracing the country's ultra running culture. But in ultra trail running there is a complete disconnect.

Thinking about this, I begin hatching a plan. It's potentially disastrous, but it might have a big impact for both the Kenyans and ultra running. I decide that if no one else is going to introduce them to each other, then it will have to be me.

My idea is to convince a few Kenyans to try running further. More and more of the top ultra runners are moving into the sport from track and road running, particularly in the US. So it's certainly possible. I've also noticed an odd trend that a lot of the top ultra runners were previously steeplechase specialists in their youth: Zach Miller was, for example, as was Jim Walmsley. This is the track event where you have to jump over barriers, including a water jump. I guess it makes sense, as it shows from a young age that part of their strength is in dealing with obstacles, rather than simply just running.

And if there is one event the Kenyans dominate more than any other, it is the steeplechase. Kenyan men have won every Olympic steeplechase gold medal – except at the Games the country boycotted – since 1968. I think we can safely say that they can deal with obstacles when running. As for the uneven terrain, both in Kenya and Ethiopia the athletes train almost exclusively on hilly, dirt trails. It's a perfect match.

When I start asking the athletes in Iten, the town at the epicentre of Kenyan running, if they would be interested in taking part in an ultra marathon, however, they seem confused by the whole concept. Running for 50 miles? They look at me like I might be trying to trick them. Is that possible? One runner, Duncan Kibet, who has a best marathon time of 2hrs 4mins, initially shows some interest. I'm looking for someone to run a 50-mile race, to start with. 'How many days does it take?' he asks. A marathon is 26 miles. This is less than twice that distance. 'It won't take you days,' I tell him. But it illustrates how far out of their normal sphere of operation it is.

But the big sticking point is money. Pretty quickly the question is: 'What is the prize money?' And the answer, in the case of most ultra races, is: 'None.' Even the UTMB offers no prize money to the winners.[2]

In Kenya, promising marathon runners are signed up by agents, usually Europeans, who send them to races abroad and take a cut of their winnings. But with the lack of prize money, there are no agents looking for ultra runners. Part of the reason there are so many good Kenyan runners is because it is a way to change their lives, to escape poverty, and to help their families and communities. Even a relatively small cash

---

[2] In 2018, for the first time, the UTMB gave out prize money to the first ten finishers. The prize for first place was €2,000.

prize at a second-tier city marathon in Europe goes a long way in Kenya and can change an athlete's life. So money is a key motivator. They don't have the luxury of running just for the love of it.

Yet, as the sport of ultra running grows, the opportunities to earn money are also growing. A handful of elite ultra runners now have agents securing them big sponsorship deals, and more races are putting up cash prizes in the hope of luring the top runners. For those thousands of Kenyans who live like professional athletes, completely dedicated to their training, but who are not able to secure an invitation to a road race, ultra running could offer another outlet for their talents.

Not everyone in ultra running is enamoured with this idea of mine. One senior person in a leading trail running apparel company, who I approach about possible sponsorship for some Kenyan runners, is particularly blunt. He sends me an email saying he hopes Kenyans never discover ultra trail running.

'Trail running is attractive because there is excitement, and each athlete has a real story, human, emotions, values. They are not "machines" made for running fast.'

I'm shocked by his response, and I shoot off a quick reply: 'Kenyans have incredible stories to tell. They are people, not machines. Incredible people. Every single one has "a real story, human, emotions, values".'

Backtracking, he says he knows they are human, but the problem is that the brands are not creating interesting content around them, telling their story. This is exactly what I'm offering him the chance to do, as the head of a well-known brand. But clearly, he isn't interested.

To have top Kenyans competing can only elevate the sport. Imagine two Kenyan athletes standing at the front of that UTMB start line next to Jornet, Walmsley, Zach Miller and the rest. It would bring added excitement, added competition. And if these ultra guys really want to be considered the world's greatest endurance athletes, then surely they have to take on the best. That is what elite sport is about, seeing the very best, the titans, going head to head. If ultra running wants to become a truly global sport, it needs to embrace and welcome competitors from the greatest long-distance running nations on Earth.

Luckily, others in the ultra running community are responding more positively to my plan. I decide to set up a crowdfunding page to pay for a Kenyan athlete to travel to an ultra race, and two of the first people to pledge money are Gary Gellin and Sage Canaday. When I speak to Zach Miller about it he is excited, saying he would relish the opportunity to race some top Kenyans, and even invites them to train with him up at Barr Camp. I contact Jim Walmsley about it, and he too is excited by the challenge. But, as a man who knows about the time it takes to adapt to ultra running, especially 100-mile races, he sounds a note of caution. 'The Kenyans are talented runners,' he says. 'And there's nothing to say they can't crush it, depending on who you pick. But you can't just take a 2:08 guy and plug him in and expect him to win. He needs to be willing to take the time to adapt.'

In the end, it is indeed a 2:08 guy, Francis Bowen, who decides to take me up on my offer. He may just be the fastest marathon runner ever to tackle a trail ultra, which is an exciting prospect in itself. The race I line up is called the Wendover Woods 50 in Buckinghamshire, England. It's five laps of a 10-mile loop, which will reduce the risk of him getting lost on his first ultra. He only has about four weeks to prepare, but he says he will do some longer training runs and that he will be ready.

And so, on a chilly morning in November, I meet Francis at Heathrow Airport and we make our way to the house of a couple of runners in London who have agreed to host him. On the train there, he is clearly still unsure what is in store for him, asking me again about the distance. I leave him at the house with some new trail shoes and kit such as a backpack, which I suggest he tries out over the next day or two before the race.

It's still cold, the sun just coming up, as we pull the car into the field where the race starts. Tom Payn, who knows Francis from Kenya, is driving. Tom has agreed to come along to help me crew. The frost in the field is so thick it looks like snow, and the ground crunches under our feet as we get out of the car. Francis is amused and asks me to take a photograph of him standing in the white field. He has never seen anything like it.

As we wander over to register him, you can see people doing a double take. It's not often an elite Kenyan runner turns up at a race like this. Despite being forty-three, Francis still has the powerful look of a serious athlete, and combined with his dark black skin, it's clear who he is. He seems calm as we help him with his number and get him to the start. This is not a big race and I feel like we're over-egging it a little as we both stand around in the woods holding his kit. It's like Chris Froome has turned up at the start of a village cycle race wearing battery-powered heat pants, while his two assistants hold up his bike.

Francis is not enjoying the cold. He keeps telling me he can't feel his feet. But the sun is out, it looks like it will be a nice day. I've told him just to follow the leaders for the first lap, not to rush off. This will help him get a feel for the race and stop him going off too fast. He looks at me like he's not taking in a word I'm saying, but nods anyway. 'Yes,' he says.

And so they race off, in a blur of about four hundred runners. As they go by me, about 100 metres down the course, Francis is right in the middle somewhere. I almost miss him. I hope he hasn't taken my instructions the wrong way.

We get a coffee and wait in the car. Tom is excited to see what will happen. The plan is that if Francis wins, he'll have the qualifying time for a big race in California next year called the North Face 50. It's another 50-mile race but this time with a $10,000 first prize. First, though, Francis has to post a result here that gets him entry into the elite field in California.

'If he runs fast here,' says Tom, 'it will cause a stir. People will notice.' A few journalists have already contacted me about Francis, and interest on social media is buzzing despite my efforts to keep it as low profile as possible. As I had hoped, the ultra running world seems intrigued by this new Kenyan runner.

After about an hour we make our way over to the tent that acts as the checkpoint and refreshment area at the end of each lap. The sun is out now, and soon we hear people clapping and look over to see the first runner approaching. It isn't Francis. But he's not far behind. He has done exactly as I said, followed the leaders. He's in third, just behind the first two runners. He comes into the tent and sits down smiling. He looks like he's been out for a morning jog. We give him a banana and some cake. Tom refills his bottle.

'Ay, it's cold,' he says.

'Otherwise, you OK?' I ask.

'Yes, good, good.' He spots the other two runners heading out on lap two already, so he jumps up and follows after them. After he's gone we look at each other. He looked easy. It's all going to plan.

Lap two ends exactly the same, with the same three runners in the same order and Francis looking easy and relaxed.

At the end of lap three, Francis is the first runner to appear. He has made his move. As he runs towards us he looks strong, easy, powerful. Thirty miles in and he's barely breaking sweat. But he's waving his hands like he's trying to tell us something is wrong. He comes into the tent and sits down.

'What's happened?' I ask.

'I stop,' he says. 'My toe hurts.'

Wait. What? Your toe? 'It's OK,' I tell him. 'You're doing great. Only two laps to go.' He looks at me like I'm mad. Like I didn't hear him. He shakes his head. 'My toe hurts,' he repeats. He looks straight at me this time, to make sure it's registering.

'Francis, this is ultra running. Things hurt in ultra running, that's normal. But you push on.' The other two runners are in now, and soon heading back out on their way. Tom realises he has the same shoes as Francis but half a size bigger. He runs to get them from the car.

I try telling him about the $10,000 race in California. He needs to get a good time, then he can run that. And win some money.

'No,' he says. 'My toe hurts.' He takes his shoe off to show me. I can't see anything wrong.

Tom is back, but Francis is refusing to try the new shoes. 'I need to look after my body,' he says. 'If I carry on, I might get injured.'

Tom, too, tries telling him about the race in California. Francis looks at him patiently. 'My toe,' he says, spelling it out. 'It hurts.'

And so we sit there, while he eats his banana. He explains that the cold at the beginning meant he couldn't feel his toes. Then on the downhills they pressed against the shoes. But after all I've been through to finish ultra races, after all I've done to get him here, I don't want to hear it. I look around the tent, which is full of mid-pack runners now, some just finishing their second lap. They pull off their shoes and look at their blisters. They hobble around the room. Yet they all cheerily lace back up and head back out. After another ten minutes or so, we head over to the car and back to London.

For a while, after Francis has flown home to Kenya, I keep thinking about the way he stopped. In some ways it illustrated a lot about the difference between a marathon and an ultra. In a marathon, you will have to fight fatigue, your muscles will get tired and rebel, and your mind will battle with you, but usually that's it. But in an ultra marathon, all manner of problems can strike, and usually do. Running through pain at some point is almost inevitable. Not only tiredness, but actual pain.

But is this a good thing? I was annoyed with Francis at the time for flaking out, as I saw it, at the first sign of trouble. But actually, was he simply listening to his body and responding in a rational, sensible way? He knew his body was his livelihood. As a professional runner, he couldn't risk any damage. So he stopped.

It also makes me think about the way a top Kenyan experiences running. I remember seeing an interview with the former marathon world record holder Wilson Kipsang in which they asked him at which point in a marathon it starts to hurt. He smiled and said: 'The last kilometre.' He may have been joking, or making light of the question, but it made me wonder if the Kenyans are used to operating in a relative comfort zone. Of course, they get tired, they fatigue, but they run so smoothly, in that way people always describe as 'effortless', that perhaps it isn't the same struggle as it is for the rest of us.

Joe Kelly once said he didn't think 'endurance running' was a good label. He said it implied suffering, and then coping with it, *enduring* it. A better term would be 'efficiency running', he said. Because to run long distances well, you needed to be efficient with your energy, your body, not fight and struggle with it. That's what the Kenyans do so well. But in an ultra, with the increased distance, the uneven terrain, the greater number of variables, it's harder to achieve.

And perhaps many of us want to suffer, and that's what attracts us to ultra marathons in the first place. People talk about enjoying the difficult parts, looking forward to them. The US runner Timothy Olson, in an interview after finishing fourth one year in the UTMB, said with relish: 'I like going to those dark spots and overcoming it. In ultras, you think you've hit your lowest low in the last race, but ultras just keep surprising me how dark it can really get.'

In an essay in *The Philosophers' Magazine* in the US, Professor Pam R. Sailors quotes a paper by the celebrated psychologist Dr Arnold Cooper, entitled 'The Psychology of Running', in which he says one of the reasons people are motivated to take up long-distance running is that they have 'narcissistic and masochistic needs', which are 'beautifully gratified by running distances which are clearly beyond the intended uses of the human body'.

Leaving aside the narcissism for now, ultra running and the pleasure ultra runners derive from the pain of their efforts certainly fits some definitions of masochism. In her essay, Prof Sailors recalls going to watch a friend running the Chicago Marathon and being struck by a Nike card handed out after the race that said: 'Bloody nipples are a trophy.' And in ultra running, bloody nipples are just the beginning.

Paul Rozin, a Professor of Psychology at the University of Pennsylvania, calls the enjoyment derived from the pain of falsely threatening experiences 'benign masochism'. In a paper titled 'Glad to be Sad', he says overcoming the pain 'leads to pleasure derived from "mind over body".' Although his examples are eating hot chilli peppers and watching sad movies, he tells me the term can equally be applied to the enjoyment of long-distance running. One man's self-transcendence, it seems, is another man's benign masochism. He also uses the term 'hedonic reversals', which I rather like.

Many ultra runners have also told me that by suffering in a race they are breaking out of the comfort and mundanity of their normal, everyday lives, that they are being challenged. It makes them feel alive, they say. There is a moment in the documentary about the gruelling Barkley Marathons in which one of the runners says bluntly: 'Most people would be better off with more pain in their lives.'

But to Francis, coming from an already hard life in rural Kenya, perhaps the need to find pain and suffering in running was less enticing. He didn't even get within a mile of the pain cave before he was calling time, packing his bags and heading for home.

Not long after the race, I go to see Gary Ward again, to check on my movements. When I tell him about Francis pulling out, he says it is amazing to hear of a professional athlete with so much respect for his body. Just listening to the story gives him goosebumps, he says.

It all brings me face to face with a question I've been asked many times since I started ultra running, almost always by non-runners: 'Surely,' they'll say, looking a little horrified when I tell them my last race was 100 miles, 'that can't be good for you?'

After my race in the Pyrenees, I could barely walk. That night, despite having been awake for two days, and despite necking a dose of Ibuprofen, my legs ached so much I couldn't sleep. Months after the race my nerve-damaged toes still tingle like I have permanent pins and needles. When the medics examined my psoas muscle 55 miles into the race and told me it was inflamed and I should stop, I paid no attention, pushing on instead for another 45 miles. And in the medical centre, there were a lot of people much worse off than me, still wanting to go on.

Many runners get through ultra runs by popping pain-killers along the way. I saw it at the 24-hour track race, crew members handing out pills as a matter of course to their runners as they went by.

Robbie Britton tells me this is a big problem in the sport: 'In my first 100-mile race I remember someone saying that normal painkillers no longer worked for him and he had to get prescription ones. Ibuprofen is such a danger during ultras and I can't believe anyone would willingly take NSAIDs [nonsteroidal anti-inflammatory drugs]. It's just dangerous.'

Indeed, studies have shown they can cause kidney prob-lems, damage your intestines and increase the risk of heart attacks. Pain is our body's way of telling us to slow down, but as ultra runners, we ignore it. That may help us find our limits, achieve our goals, or win the race, but it isn't good for our health.

And even those who survive relatively unscathed – who don't fall, pull muscles or push themselves until they need to take painkillers – don't necessarily escape unharmed. In 2012, cardiologist/runners Carl Lavie and James O'Keefe caused a stir when they released a research paper that found that while moderate running was clearly healthy, those health benefits began to tail off and possibly reverse if you ran 'excessively'. Initially they defined that as more than two and a half hours a week – though Lavie later revised it after further research to more than five hours a week. Ultra runners, of course, undertake much more than that, often in a single day.

Lavie and O'Keefe's main concern was heart damage and a hardening of the tissue around the heart brought on by extreme exercise. In a TED Talk on the subject, O'Keefe says that while exercise is one of the best medicines for good all-round health, 'like any drug, there's an ideal dose range. If you don't take enough, you don't get the benefits. If you take too much, it could be harmful. Maybe even fatal.'

To illustrate his point, he brings up the story of Pheidippides, the man who inspired the marathon by running from Marathon to Athens in 490 BC to proclaim victory in a battle against the Persians, only to then drop dead. O'Keefe also recounts the story of Micah True, the hero of the book *Born to Run* and an American ultra runner who lived and ran with the Tarahumara people in Mexico. The locals named him Caballo Blanco, the White Horse, for his famed running ability. But he too dropped dead, age fifty-eight, while out on a run in 2012.

'When they did the autopsy, they found an enlarged, thickened heart with scar tissue,' says O'Keefe. 'I'm a cardiologist, I'm in the business of finding out the ideal diet and lifestyle, and I'm coming to the conclusion that running marathons, and extreme endurance athletics, don't fit into that recipe.'

It's scary stuff. The only issue, however, in relating O'Keefe's study to ultra running is that he combines intensity and duration to define 'extreme running'. Ultra running may be extreme in duration, but it is usually undertaken at a very low intensity – with walking forming a large chunk of most ultra races.

O'Keefe says 'moderate' exercise is good, and goes on to make the comment: 'You can exercise all day, it seems, without getting yourself in trouble, if you keep it down.' His definition of 'keeping it down'? Ten minutes per mile pace, which is actually a pretty fast pace for an ultra marathon.

The problem with drawing firm conclusions is that there are not many studies looking specifically at ultra running, with most instead focused on marathon running, where a lot of people run and train at a pace faster than 10 minutes per mile.

One 2009 study by Liverpool John Moores University examined athletes taking part in the Lakeland 50 (mile) and 100 ultra marathons. Its findings would chime with O'Keefe.

All the selected runners had been running marathons and ultra marathons for over two years and had no known heart problems. In the end, 25 of the 45 runners completed the course. Ranging in age from twenty-four to sixty-two, they had blood tests taken for cardiac Troponin I, and electrocardiograms (ECGs) were performed before and after the race.

After the race, the cardiac Troponin I levels rose significantly in twenty-one of the twenty-five runners, and in three it was high enough to suggest significant cardiac damage.

O'Keefe says when Troponin I levels go up, it means heart muscle has died. 'Normally we jump into action because that generally means there's a heart attack going on. In this case they're little micro tears. Not a big deal if you do it once, they heal, and a few days later it's gone. But if you do it over and over again, heart chambers get scarred.'

The ECGs at the start of the Lakeland ultra races displayed the typical features of a healthy heart commonly seen in athletes. At the finish, however, there were significant electrical changes in over 50 per cent of the ECGs, and in some there were bizarre changes not commonly seen in ECGs, either at rest or during exercise.

Professor John Somauroo, one of the study's authors, said the results suggest that 'running continuously over 50 or 100 miles may not be good for the heart'.

Before you bin your running shoes, however, plenty of other studies have come up with contrary results. A 2013 study from the University of Ballarat in Australia found that ultra runners have a life expectancy of up to sixteen years longer than the average person. The research, led by Dr Fadi Charchar, was based on the impact of distance running on telomeres in the human body.

'Within our cells, telomeres are structures that work similar to the plastic parts or aglets of our shoelaces – that is, they protect our genes from fraying,' Dr Charchar explains. Telomeres get shorter with age, and the shorter they are the more prone we are to disease. 'The trick,' he says, 'is that we can actually do things to make our telomeres last longer. And we found that doing running – and lots of running – can do wonders for telomeres.'

The researchers found that ultra runners covering 40km to 100km a week had 11 per cent longer telomeres, which they said equates to sixteen more years' life expectancy.

'The ultra-marathoners from our study had an average age of 43,' says Charchar. 'According to our results, their biological age would be 27.'

In 2014, Dr Martin Hoffman, professor of physical medicine and rehabilitation at the University of California, ran a study on a range of self-reported health issues in over 1,200 ultra runners. He concluded that they were healthier than the non-ultra running population, with a low prevalence of virtually all serious medical issues, and that they missed fewer days off work each year due to illness. I asked him about those studies that had linked ultra running to heart attacks, but he said he wasn't convinced.

'At present,' he said, 'there is no good evidence to prove there are negative long-term health consequences from ultra running.'

The thing is, we know, just as Francis knew, that when something starts to hurt, it's our body's way of telling us to stop, that we may be causing some damage. But few ultra runners are doing it primarily to be healthy. Most of us know that, even taking out the risk of injuries, of falling off a mountain and losing a leg, of getting blisters the size of tennis balls, ultra running is putting our bodies through the wringer in a way that may not be completely healthy. The question is, do we care?

Hoffman recently followed up his 2014 study with a fascinating question posed to another 1,394 ultra runners. He asked them: 'If you were to learn, with absolute certainty, that ultra marathon running is bad for your health, would you stop your ultra marathon training and participation?'

Seventy-four per cent of the runners responded: 'No.'

Despite Francis dropping out of the Wendover Woods race, I'm not giving up so easily on my idea to introduce ultra running to the great endurance athletes of East Africa. Hearing about the project, Conyers Davis, an American reader of my first book, *Running with the Kenyans*, reaches out to say he'd like to help organise for a few Kenyans to run a trail ultra in the US.

Conyers lives in California and is keen to set something up quickly, so we target the Lake Sonoma 50, a 50-mile race in Sonoma County, California. It was last won by Sage Canaday a few weeks before I was in the US to run the Miwok 100K. It would be a good, tough challenge for a rookie Kenyan ultra runner.

This time we decide to line up two athletes to increase our chances of success. Francis says he is keen to try again, as is a female runner called Risper Kimaiyo. I first met Risper after she won the Edinburgh Marathon in 2013 and we have kept in touch ever since. She has a best marathon time of 2hrs 29mins but, more intriguingly, in 2016 she ran the 50km World Championships in Doha and won. She is an ultra running world champion.

That this has gone completely under the radar illustrates

how little attention 50km road races get in the ultra world. A victory on the trails at Lake Sonoma would have a much bigger impact.

One problem we have is dealing with the fact that the race has no prize money. Unable to convince our two runners to see the bigger picture – the potential sponsorship opportunities, the fact that they will be breaking new ground, and who knows where that might lead – we strike a deal to pay them a small allowance towards their training costs, and we promise them a small bonus if they win or do well in the race.

But, alas, it never happens. Francis gets injured, and despite getting him some intensive physio treatment, a few weeks before the race he is still hurt and unable to run. Then, just a week before the race, after we have crowdfunded for financial support among the ultra running community, after I've done interviews on podcasts and done everything to convince the ultra running world that this is an exciting development, Risper sends me a message to say she is pulling out as her agent has got her an invite to run the Rome Marathon.

A win in Rome is worth €10,000. It's a road marathon. This is the Kenyans' stomping ground. They gobble up these big city marathons for breakfast. It doesn't require any explaining to their friends and family. It makes sense. Unlike this strange ultra marathon malarkey, where you have to run twice as far for nothing.

But if I've learned anything from ultra running, it's that when things seem hopeless, you can always get back up and carry on. After a quick chat with Conyers, we realise that our mistake was not getting the athletes' agents on board.

So we talk to Risper's agent. The next suitable ultra race is the North Face 50 we tried dangling in front of Francis when he dropped out in Wendover. It has a $10,000 first prize. Now we're talking.

The good thing about dealing with Kenyan runners is that they generally assume they can win virtually any race. They seem to possess a wonderful confidence, completely free of arrogance. Of course it's often unrealistic, but they don't beat themselves up if they fall short. They just get up and try again. It's why a race in Kenya is an insane stampede right from the start, because everyone is racing to win and so is trying to run at the front.

In any case, Risper is keen to race, and her agent gives it the green light. She says she used to train in South Africa, where ultra running is normal, and so she understands it in a way many other Kenyans don't. It doesn't feel weird to her, which is why she put herself forward for the 50km World Championships in the first place. 'I went to Qatar and I came up liking it [ultra running],' she says.

Francis, it turns out, no longer has an agent, but his interest in ultra running is waning rapidly each time I speak to him. Eventually he tells me to find someone else. He wants to go back to road marathons, he says, while he still has a few years of running left in him.

Hearing about this, Risper's agent, Antonio, suggests another of his athletes, an Ethiopian called Mohammed Teman. With a marathon best of 2hrs 12mins he's a strong runner, and like Risper he already has some impressive ultra running credentials: in 2015 he finished second in the Comrades Marathon.

While the ultra success for both these runners has come on the roads, I'm not worried about them coping with a trail ultra. Having run in both Kenya and Ethiopia, I know the athletes there train almost exclusively off road, so I don't envisage the smooth, runnable trails of the North Face 50 presenting any problems. They have six months to prepare. We're on.

But again, alas, the gods of ultra running are not kind. After we asked all the people who had pledged money for Lake Sonoma to transfer it to this new race, and worked hard to secure visas and flights and race entries, Mohammed arrives in California a week before the race to find the worst wildfires in the state's history raging 150 miles away. Risper, meanwhile, is camped out in Nairobi waiting for her US visa, ready to jump on a flight if it comes through.

It never does. And in the end it doesn't matter, because the race is eventually cancelled. The smoke from the fires has been blown down the coast and the air in the San Francisco Bay area and the Marin headlands where the race was due to take place – the same headlands where I ran the Miwok 100K – is barely breathable. Residents are being told to stay indoors. Running any distance is strongly discouraged, let alone running 50 miles.

Like a boxer who refuses to go down, we stagger on, still swinging. As Mohammed is in the US already, we try to find an alternative race for him. Conyers is from Philadelphia and realises the city's marathon is on the same day as the cancelled North Face 50. The prize money for a win is also $10,000. He calls the race up and they say they're happy to invite Mohammed to run.

However, people online start pointing out that the JFK 50 – the oldest ultra marathon in the US – is on in Maryland the same weekend. Mohammed could run that instead. Zach Miller, who was down to run the North Face 50, is shifting his plans to run the JFK 50. We could do the same. Again we contact the race and again they say they'd be happy to invite Mohammed to run.

Mohammed, however, now has his heart set on the Philadelphia marathon. The prize money calls, but so does the fact that he knows where he is with a marathon.

Antonio is a little confused by the prize money, questioning how it is only $1,000 at the JFK 50. The maths don't seem to add up. 'One thousand dollars to run 50 miles!?' he asks, a little incredulous.

It's funny, this idea – which I came up against repeatedly when looking for potential ultra runners in Kenya – that the prize money should increase with the distance. They must think 100-metre sprinters get paid very little.

Antonio points out, however, that regardless of the prize, the online funders have pledged money to see Mohammed run an ultra marathon, and so he should do that. But Mohammed is the one who actually has to do the running, and I know from experience that you can't run an ultra marathon unless you are fully committed to it in your mind. We can't force him to run and expect him to do well, especially against a fighter like Zach Miller.

In the end our chin has to take one more sucker punch. Conyers decides to look into the cost of flights to the east coast, where both races are taking place, and realises that we're now entering the weekend before Thanksgiving – the biggest travel week of the year in the US. Flights are going to cost thousands of dollars to get to either race. The project's funds have long since run dry and Conyers has already been digging into his own pocket to cover the costs.

So in the end Mohammed runs a local marathon in a wildfire-free part of California. After all the chaos and disruption, we shouldn't be surprised when he gets sent the wrong way while leading, and ends up finishing a few seconds behind the winner. His consolation is a $500 prize to bring home to Ethiopia, a confusing whirlwind of a trip to California, and a few new friendships, not least with Arnold Schwarzenegger, with whom he somehow ends up sharing a stage the day after the race and together handing out hundreds of free Thanksgiving turkeys. That's not quite how I envisaged this whole thing ending up. But then again, maybe it's not over yet. Conyers is already talking about trying again for a race next year . . .

14

One runner who has gone quiet recently is Elisabet Barnes. I contact her and ask if she is still going to run the Ultra-Trail du Mont-Blanc. She has entered and is on the official start list. But I haven't seen her competing in any races since she went back to the Marathon des Sables nine months ago and won it again.

'No, I'm not running,' she says. 'I'm taking a break from the sport. To recover.'

To find out more I arrange to meet up with her. Sitting outside on a chilly morning in London, she brings me up to date with her story. A lot has happened since our run along the Thames path.

'I still don't know what's wrong,' she says. 'After the MdS I got really tired. A week after, I could still hardly walk, I was lying in bed all day. Mentally and spiritually I felt connected to something out there [in the desert]. So after I felt very deflated.'

Since I last saw her she has separated from her husband, had another relationship that didn't work out, taken over the business she shared with her ex-husband, started training to be a coach, hosted a number of altitude training camps, run a six-day race in the Rockies, run 360km across Sweden, and travelled to the Himalayas to run the Everest Trail race for the second time. Is it any surprise she's tired?

'Yes, it was a lot of things at the same time,' she admits. After the Everest race she got a cold, which she says she couldn't shake for weeks. She was losing a lot of training to illness and was struggling to get ready for the next year's MdS. So she got a blood test, read up a lot about nutrition, and became vegan.

It's amazing how many ultra runners I meet that are vegan. Tom and Rachel are vegan. The most famous vegan ultra runner is Scott Jurek, a seven-time winner of the Western States 100. There are many others. If you start typing 'why are ultra runners . . .' into Google, it autofills the next word as 'vegan'.

Elisabet says she used to eat a lot of meat. 'I loved a good steak, a lot of fish, I had eggs every morning,' she says, laughing at the memory, as though it seems funny now, even though it was only a few months ago. 'I can't see me going back,' she says. 'I can't imagine eating meat now.'

Elisabet's new boyfriend, the Norwegian ultra runner Sondre Amdahl, is also vegan. 'He was an influence,' she says. 'He opened my eyes a bit.' Although she won't be running the UTMB, she will be there crewing for Sondre, who is one of the elite runners.

'I read a lot of research linking animal protein to cancer, heart disease, etc,' she says. 'My dad had heart disease, my mum had Alzheimer's, so I used to think: life is short, I'll probably get some disease when I'm in my sixties, so I'm not going to sit in an office wasting my time.'

But she says she realises now she was victimising herself,

thinking she had no control over whether she got these diseases. 'But we can have some control,' she says. 'That's a difficult thing for people to accept. We don't like giving up things we enjoy. For some people giving up bacon is unthinkable.'

I ask her why she thinks so many ultra runners are vegan.

'It's the mindset of someone who runs ultras, that they're comfortable with change. Actually for me giving up meat was a small matter in the grand scheme of things.'

The big rival diet to veganism in the ultra running world is the LCHF (low carbohydrate, high fat) diet. To follow it usually involves eating a lot of meat. The basic theory is that your body's fat reserves are an almost infinite source of energy, but they are hard to tap into. So you have to train yourself to burn fat by restricting your carbohydrate intake and eating a lot of fat. I've always been intrigued by the diet, which is often known as the Paleo diet, because, according to its proponents, it is how early humans ate, and fits with how our bodies are designed to function. As with barefoot running, I like the idea of following the most natural approach. But I've always had two issues with this diet. One, it involves eating a lot of meat. As a lifelong vegetarian, someone who has never even tasted meat, this is a problem. People say you can be vegetarian and LCHF, but in truth that is very difficult. And my second issue is that eating a lot of fat never feels good in my body. When I eat something fatty, I usually want to go and lie down, not run.

I once asked Scott Jurek about it and he was pretty unequivocal: 'It's not a diet for long-term health. People can get results initially, because they're cutting out sugar and processed foods, but studies have shown that eating meat in those quantities is not good in the long term.

'People are always looking for a quick fix, but veganism has stood the test of time. Carbs are not the enemy. Even people who follow the Paleo diet will use carbs on race day, because that's what we need. The brain needs glucose to survive.'

Top US ultra running coach Jason Koop is more scathing: 'The whole LCHF thing is a load of garbage. As a professional coach, I've seen it come and go three times in my career. It's nothing new and the reason it goes away is because there are better approaches.'

Yet for every Scott Jurek proving you can win big ultra races on a vegan diet, there's an athlete out there showing you can win races eating mostly fat. Jeff Browning, for example, started eating an LCHF diet in 2015 at the age of forty-four and within a few months won the tough Hurt 100 ultra in Hawaii.

And he's just as convinced of the benefits of his diet, saying in a recent interview: 'I'm lighter and faster than I've been in years. I feel ten years younger. I'm winning races and setting records as an elite ultra marathoner – at age forty-four.'

Elisabet says she tried LCHF a few times. 'I even tried it again in January when I first started getting tired,' she says. 'I did the two-week Maffatone diet. But I felt terrible. People say you need to give it time, but I think my body is really bad at metabolising fat. I just get fat.'

She says most LCHF ultra runners are men, and that women struggle with it. When she became vegan, she started eating more carbohydrates. 'I felt I had more energy. I can now run sooner after eating. Before I couldn't train in the evening as I was too tired. Now I can train anytime.'

I ask her about dealing with pain in a race. Is the pain

cave something she looks forward to? 'I hate pain, like I hate bad weather,' she says, laughing. 'When I'm struggling in a race, I always think, at least I'm not stuck behind a desk in London.' I'm nodding, but I'm not sure it's a thought that would get me very far. In those darkest moments, when I'm halfway up a mountain and my legs have gone, I think I would give anything to be whisked away to a desk in London. I wonder again if I'm really an ultra runner at heart.

'I've also learned that pain will come and go,' she adds. 'I know it will pass. Don't fight it, let it live its life, don't give it attention – it seeks attention. Pain is really needy, like a dog. Ignore it and it will behave.'

Now I have my UTMB points, I start to knuckle down to some serious training. One thing I now find, to my delight, is that ever since *la descente de la mort* I've become much faster at running down steep trails. Whenever I run on Dartmoor or the coast path, my days of tentative steps, almost slipping and cursing at the stupidity of it all, are gone, and I now delight in the joy of a quick-step descent. It's actually the best part of each run, a quick thrill ride. One day on the moor, in thick snow, I find myself laughing deliriously after a long downhill in which I flew down as though I was on skis.

Now that I can descend, I decide to take myself up to the Lake District for a weekend of fell running. This is England's original trail running scene, renowned across the world for its down-to-earth, good-natured community and its long history.

Of course, I never do things the easy way, so after working in London until late on Friday, I go home and grab a few hours' kip before setting off at 3 a.m. to drive up to Cumbria. I arrive at 8 a.m., an hour before the start of the Duddon Valley fell race. It's a fell running classic, I'm told. There's a long race of 18 miles and a short one of about nine. As I step out of my car in the bumpy field, surrounded by an old stone wall, the man directing me where to park comes over in his fluorescent jacket.

'Plenty of time,' he says. 'Registration is in the village hall up the lane.' He can spot that I'm fresh blood. 'First time doing this one?' he asks. I tell him it's my first ever fell race.

'Well, I hope you're doing the short one, then?' I want to tell him I've just run 100 miles through the Pyrenees, but I keep it to myself. In any case, as a fell running newbie, and because I want to do another race tomorrow, I am indeed running the short race.

An hour or so later, I find myself standing in a rough line across the field with about eighty other runners. All around, the mountains we'll be heading up are shrouded in a heavy mist. The starter warns us to keep to the right on the final descent, otherwise the way we go is up to us. 'And there's no water on the course as the farmer who usually puts it up there has gone to a wedding,' he says through his megaphone. It screeches and he puts it down, realising he doesn't need it as he's standing next to us.

'Right, ready?' And with that, he blows his whistle and we race off.

I've always known that fell running involved racing up and down crazy steep mountains, but I didn't realise how key it was to know how to navigate the route and terrain. Particularly on a day like this when the mist sets in.

As the race starts to spread out and I realise there are no course markings, I decide my best hope is to follow someone who looks like he knows where he's going. I overhear one man talking about the first time he did this race in 2007. Right, I'm sticking with him.

As we run, he is constantly checking his map, holding it out in front of him as we trot and stumble through the mist, making our way gradually up and along the sides of the mountains. After a while I begin to wonder if he minds me following him. Occasionally I run ahead for a short while and then stop and pretend to look at my map – on which I have no clue where I am – to let him pass me again. But in the end I decide to come clean.

I tell him it's my first fell race and that I'm following him as I don't know the way. He looks at me and says rather gruffly: 'As long as you're not in the over-fifties?'

I'm not, luckily, being a relatively young forty-four. I blame the mist for the confusion. He seems happier when I promise that if it comes to it, I won't out-sprint him at the end.

It turns out that part of the skill and challenge of fell running is picking your 'line', your path through the rocks, ditches and steep hillsides. Simply following someone else is not really in the spirit of things.

It can be a particularly sore point if you're competing to win the race. 'It does happen,' the man tells me. 'We all know people who do it.' I get the feeling those who do are not the most popular fell runners on the circuit.

In the event, I lose him in the mist soon after, and bumble along the rest of the way following the hazy figures of runners, doing my best to keep an unobtrusive distance, until eventually we drop down the final descent, out of the clouds and back to the field where it all started over two hours earlier. I'm still in one piece.

Sitting in a lakeside pub later that evening, local runner Ben Abdelnoor tells me that the gamesmanship involved when one person decides to follow another is all part of the sport. He says some people will stop to tie their shoelaces so the person following is forced to pass, then they'll shoot off in another direction.

Fell runner Ricky Lightfoot says he won a race recently by out-sprinting a local runner he had been following.

'It's not the best way to win,' he admits. 'But is it better to get my map out and stand around while he disappears, or follow him?'

Lightfoot says the great Joss Naylor – a fell running legend who I hear people talking about in every race, café or pub I visit during my weekend in the Lakes – would sometimes purposely run over the roughest terrain, as he knew no one could keep up with him on it, or he would hide behind a rock to lose his trackers.

Another local runner, Colin Dulson, used to be married to Joss Naylor's daughter and has some great stories of running with him when he was younger and trying to woo his daughter.

'I'd go around on Sunday morning for lunch and he'd say: "Fancy a run first?" Then he'd take me for 30 miles over the fells. And he'd kill me. I guess he was testing me. One time after we finished, this guy was passing and he saw Joss, this scrawny old man, helping me, a big strapping lad, into his car. He didn't know what was going on.'

Part of fell running is knowing the mountains well, and as such it favours locals. 'Part of the fun,' says Abdelnoor, who lives in Ambleside in the heart of the Lake District, 'is going out to recce the route beforehand, and finding some good lines. Not just turning up on the day with a GPX file and following your watch.'

A controversy is bubbling in the fell running world after a number of races recently banned the use of GPS devices to help with navigation. Abdelnoor says the ban is needed to protect the uniqueness of fell running.

Over the weekend, I don't meet anyone who disagrees, though Lightfoot says he can see both sides of the argument, in that GPS devices make races more accessible to non-locals. 'There are races in Scotland I simply don't have the chance to recce,' he says. 'It would be much easier if I could download the route on my watch.'

But that's just not cricket. Fell running is proud of its grassroots, no-frills style – where the farmer going to a wedding means no water on the course. Fancy gadgets like GPS watches were never likely to be a welcome addition.

'It's three pounds to enter, and you get some orange squash or a piece of cake at the finish,' says Lightfoot. 'That's it.'

'You don't turn up in fancy kit,' adds Abdelnoor. 'If I lined up with a race pack, trekking poles and compression socks, I'd get lynched,' he jokes.

No, this is a land of club vests, short shorts and bumbags

for the required waterproof jacket and gloves. Everyone seems to know everyone and it's a friendly, community atmosphere, full of hale and hearty people with big smiles and tree trunk legs. When I tell one fell runner that I'm doing another fell race the next day, he nods and says: 'Classic fell running weekend.'

Indeed, the next day I see many of the same faces at the Coniston Gullies race. This one requires no navigating and is more like I had imagined fell running. You go up the mountain, climbing over 900ft, turn around, and charge straight back down again. The whole race is just over a mile long and is going to test my new-found descending skills.

On the way up, my head is down and it's so steep that my hands, like those of everyone around me, are getting involved. I feel like I'm crushing it – my heart and legs do, at any rate – but when I get to the top, I turn around to find I'm nearly in last place.

As we look down over the edge from the top of the descent, I'm momentarily dizzy. 'Oh boy,' I think as I begin my quick-step skipping technique. I'm expecting to go past a few of the older runners at least – many of them are in their fifties and sixties – but everyone ahead of me disappears in a blur of leaps and skids through the scree. I end up finishing about three places from the back, and almost ten minutes behind the winner, in a race of a single mile. The whole thing is wonderfully chaotic.

I told Abdelnoor, in the pub the night before, about my experience in France, where I learned to descend – although clearly I still have room for improvement. He said it reminded him of a coach in the Lakes who used to take his athletes up the mountain one at a time and then tie them to him with a bungee. Then he would charge down the hill and they had to stay on their feet. He was laughing as he told me about it, but I can imagine it was similar to my experience. The risk of breaking their necks probably focused their minds to the point that something in their brain realigned. Although I'm still not fell runner standard, it certainly helped me.

One runner who lives near to me and who knows a lot about the Mont Blanc race is Damian Hall. When I started out on this journey, he was a bit of an inspiration to me. This is because he first started ultra running as a journalist in his late thirties looking for something to write about, and then discovered he was quite good at it. When I compared our times at shorter distances, they were very similar, and so part of me wondered if I may end up being as good as him. So far that hasn't happened.

In his first run in the UTMB, which is comparable in length and difficulty to the 100 Miles Sud de France, he finished in 26 hours (compared to my 39 hours). He returned in 2016, when he improved to 25 hours and finished in nineteenth position. That was pretty impressive going for a journalist.

Then in 2017, in one of the greatest trail ultra fields ever assembled, Damian finished twelfth, in 22 hours. I saw he was planning to run the UTMB again in 2018 and this time he was stepping up his training and shooting for a spot in the top ten. It was a lofty goal, as he was only ranked fiftieth out of the elite runners on the start list, but he knew the race as well as anyone. To get some inside tips, I arrange to join him for one of his Friday morning bimbles, as he likes to call his six-hour runs in the Brecon Beacons.

So that I'm ready to roll at 4 a.m., the time he sets off from his home just outside Bath, he invites me to sleep on his sofa the night before. As he makes it up with a sheet and duvet, we talk quietly so as not to wake his wife and children, who were already asleep when I arrived. I tell him I'm nervous about keeping up with him, but he tells me not to worry. 'You'll be fine,' he says, like it's a silly concern. Like he's not really an elite ultra runner. I get the feeling that he still doesn't consider himself in that bracket, but more as a plucky amateur who just keeps getting lucky breaks on the big days. But twelfth in the UTMB, that's serious. I'd better get some sleep.

I hear his alarm go upstairs and then something dropping on the floor. I'm straight up, sitting on the edge of the sofa, shaking my head awake. Damian comes down the stairs. 'Morning,' he says, unnervingly chirpy. He makes some tea, finds me a spare base layer – 'It looks a bit chilly out there' – and we're off.

It's a two-hour drive to a desolate car park beside a big

hulking hill buried in cloud. We get out and munch down a few biscuits and nuts. And then we shuffle off, nice and easy.

We spend the next six hours running and chatting through the cloud-sodden hills. At the end we've covered 23 miles and over 8,000ft of ascent. It's a decent run.

Damian ran his first ultra marathon for a magazine article, and says he instantly loved it. He's surprised when I say that part of me is looking forward to doing a road race again when this is all over. 'I'm sad about that,' he says, only half joking. 'I've never met anyone who started ultras and then went back.'

Well, I like both, I tell him. But sometimes I crave the feeling of just running, with no bag, no food, no bumps, no walking. As we stand on the top of one of the peaks in the driving rain, completely drenched, four hours into our run, I ask him if he enjoys the experience of running miles and miles out here for its own sake, or is he doing it so he can succeed at the UTMB?

He looks at me like it's a trick question. Like I'm being underhand. 'I think I love it,' he says. 'But do I? Or do I just tell myself that?' We run on.

I decide to try him again. We have plenty of time. 'What keeps you coming back for more?' I ask him. 'What is it about ultras that you like?'

Again he's not sure. He says his wife tells him he sounds like an addict when he talks about it. He's not the first ultra runner to have been told that. We clack up Jacob's Ladder to the top of Pen-y-Fan and more mist-filled views of the emptiness.

'I guess I'm attracted to the idea you can be like a hero,'

he says after a while. 'The stories that stuck with me from childhood were Robin Hood and King Arthur. Then, as an adult, I liked the stories of Scott and Shackleton.

'It may sound silly, but my favourite scene in *Star Wars* was always when Luke had to survive out in the blizzard overnight and he crawled into the belly of some beast for warmth.'

I tell Damian about my hallucinations in France and we compare stories of losing our minds. Damian has heard a few hallucination tales in his time, but his favourite is one he heard from the Irish runner Gary Dalton. It took place in the Tor des Géants, a race of over 200 miles across the Alps. During the race, Gary became convinced that he was responsible for setting up the course and that the flags marking the way were in the wrong place, so he started collecting them up. He ended up with an armful of flags, which he then started placing back in the ground, satisfied that he was doing a great job.

With all the chatting the time flies and we're soon back at the car. It's the longest training run I've ever done and, although my legs are tired, I've managed to keep up with one of the world's best ultra runners – even if he won't admit that's what he is. I'm beginning to feel like I might finally be getting somewhere. I have two more races before the UTMB, starting with a 45-mile run along the coast path in Dorset. It's the first time since I started all this that I've come back down in distance. Forty-five miles should now be a breeze.

The race starts at the Portland Bill lighthouse, on the Isle of Portland, jutting out into the English Channel near Weymouth. The sun is out and right from the gun I'm off ahead at the front, feeling good. I'm Zach Miller, letting loose. Maybe I'm over-confident, but in the back of my mind I can't help hoping I might sneak a top five position or even a place on the podium. I don't say it out loud, but sometimes you just get that feeling, that this is your day.

I get to the first checkpoint in good spirits. Just before I arrive, I pass a young guy who had shot past me a few miles into the race, up some steep steps cut into the cliffs. I notice he has a regular rucksack on, not a running one, which swings from side to side so much he has to hold the straps as he runs. He looks hot and is running quite slowly as I pass. 'You OK?' I ask.

He looks at me. 'It's a bit hilly, isn't it!' he says, sounding shocked. I don't know what to say. Apart from one big hill at the beginning, it has been mostly flat so far. The hills are all ahead, and they're huge.

I'm pretty sure, right there and then, that this guy won't finish the race. In almost every ultra I've done I've seen a few people who have no business being there. By that I don't mean they're too slow, but people who are clearly unprepared for such a long race. They have the wrong equipment, they shoot off like it's a 10K, they don't know you have to eat, they don't know the course, they don't know there are hills along the way. Many ultra runners probably go through this when they first start – as I did in Oman when I was completely unprepared to run on sand. Even though the race was in the desert.

But there have been worse cases than mine. Like the runner who turned up at the Marathon des Sables, and instead of food for six days, all she had was Werther's Originals sweets. The race stipulates how many calories you need each day and the sweets matched the requirement. But you can't run for six days in the desert just eating sweets, and in the end she didn't even make it through the first day.

Another runner tells me about the time he entered the seven-day Amazon Jungle Marathon. He says he had never heard of an ultra marathon, and had never run further than 13 miles. 'I took all the wrong kit, my rucksack broke 20 metres into the first stage, I brought the wrong food and my running gear was shocking. I got to stage four somehow and dropped out. I felt so out of place on the start line, I still cringe about it now.'

When I ask him what possessed him to even enter in the first place, he laughs and says: 'It looked like a great idea when I saw it in a magazine.'

Back in Dorset, as soon as I pass the young man struggling with his rucksack, the hills start. My new descending powers help me make good ground, although the ascents still burn. However, I'm making solid progress by the time I come to the second aid station in Lulworth Cove, 20 miles into the race. I come hurtling down the chalk path into the checkpoint. A quick water refill and I'm off. Marietta tells me I look strong. See you at the next one, I say. One aid station at a time. Let's go.

The route then traverses a stony beach, which isn't quite what I was expecting. At the end of the beach we head up some steps to the cliff top, and about halfway up my leg starts cramping. I stretch it out and it seems to go, but that's a bit of a shock with 25 miles still remaining.

I start worrying, and slow down a little. Maybe I'm getting carried away, going too fast. Something unexpected always comes up, and I find a way to tell myself it's fatal. This time it's the cramping. But I can't run with cramp. I could get stuck on my own on the side of a cliff. It would be irresponsible to carry on. I decide I'm going to pull out at the next aid station. There are no UTMB points on the line here; this is just a training run. I'm getting towards 30 miles now. That's a decent training run along these trails.

As I climb the last few steps up to the car park where the next checkpoint is, my body decides to seal the deal and my legs cramp up worse than ever. Oh god, it's agony and I have to sit down on the grass.

A couple come over to see if I'm OK.

'You need some salt,' the man says, offering me some Hula Hoops. I munch them down. 'Thanks.'

'Do you have salt tablets?' the woman asks. There's always something I haven't got. No, I don't, I tell her. She goes to her car and comes back with a tub of pills. 'Here, take one of these.'

I take it without question and it's only after that she starts showing me the label. 'I got them from the ultra running shop,' she says. 'I take them all the time.'

Right now I don't care. The cramp lifts, and I feel better, so I decide to carry on.

With about 10 miles to go, I come through a gate to find the coast path sign pointing inland, away from the coast. I look around but can't see any other runners. The organisers had told us to follow the coast path signs unless another sign pointed a different way. There's no other sign, but it seems a bit odd. Just then another runner comes through the gate and starts heading down the path towards the coast.

'The sign says this way,' I say, pointing inland, up a big hill. He stops and comes back. We stand there looking at it.

'You're right,' he says. 'Must be that way then.'

We walk together and start chatting and before we know it we've come to a road, with no signs anywhere. We decide to turn right, back towards the sea. But something's not right. We're lost. We look at our phones, but it's impossible to work it out. A one point we enter a field and run around until we realise the only way out is the way we came in. We're getting a bit flustered now.

Eventually we find a town and run along a busy promenade. It's a hot day and we have to weave our way in and out of happy weekenders eating ice cream. We've missed an aid station somewhere and I ran out of water about thirty minutes ago, so we stop at a shop and buy a drink. We look at the map and try to work out where we are.

Just then another runner comes by and sees us sitting by the path. 'The finish is up on that hill,' he says, pointing at the cliff right in front of us. It is? Let's go. It's only about another mile, but I still have time to unleash my trademark fast finish up the last hill, passing a couple of people on the way. I cross the line to see Marietta taking my picture.

I look at my watch. It says we ran 45 miles. Despite our

detour it looks like we still ran the right distance. The man I got lost with finishes a few minutes later and I cheer him in, but he looks annoyed. He starts talking to the officials, arguing with them. He thinks we cut a corner, that we should be disqualified. Bizarrely the officials are having none of it. They ask to see our watches, and when they see we've run the correct distance, they tell us not to worry. But my friend won't leave it. 'It's not right,' he keeps saying.

I don't say too much. If we cut a corner then I don't mind being disqualified. But I don't really want to be. We didn't cheat. We just got lost. It turns out I've finished fifth, which I'm quite pleased with. It's not a big race, and I did it as a training run, so it's not that important either way, but I'd rather the result stood, if that's what the officials think.

Later, I wonder, did my relaxed attitude reveal a crack in my moral fortitude? Did my friend have a stronger sense of fairness, of right and wrong? Or was he being too inflexible? The organisers may have just not wanted the hassle, or to acknowledge the fact that the course was badly marked and people went the wrong way. And it's possible that by taking an inland route we missed out a few steep climbs. Should I have stood in solidarity with my friend and demanded to be disqualified?

It's an interesting question when I think back to the stories of people cheating and doping in ultra running, and the idea that if you can justify it to yourself, and can get away with it, most people will cheat. Here the justification was easy: we still ran the full distance, give or take a few hundred metres. And I could get away with it because the organisers were insisting we forget it. But where was my line? My friend's was in a different place, closer to the letter of the law, whereas I was in a greyer area. I also think back to the salt tablet and how I accepted a pill without question from a complete stranger. But I was cramping. I needed help. Was it that simple?

15

In my continual quest for good running form, one thing that I keep hearing about is an exercise therapy called Feldenkrais. Even though my Achilles are now better, my form is still, I assume, not perfect. Interested to see what Feldenkrais can offer, I book myself a session with practitioner Jae Gruenke, who specialises in applying the therapy to running.

I meet her on a sunny day in Covent Garden in London, where she starts by getting me to run up and down the street outside her clinic. After a few easy sprints, I feel the need to point out that I've been working a lot on my form and that's why it's pretty good, just in case she's struggling to spot any obvious issues. But she gives me a withering look that suggests she can see a bucketload of them.

After the running, we go into the clinic and she gives me what she calls a 'rolling lesson' in which I mostly lie on my back on the treatment table with my knees bent, and she pulls and rolls my legs very gently from side to side in slightly different ways. After she's done we head back out to the street and she gets me to run up and down again. I have to admit, I feel great. Before, she had asked me to listen to the sound of my feet, as a point of reference. I had thought they were extremely quiet, but now they positively purr, and I seem to skim silently along the ground. How is this possible after such a gentle session of rolling around on a table?

Gruenke says that in Feldenkrais you don't fix form simply by telling people to change how they move, because movement happens at a subconscious level. Over our lifetime, she says, we've all developed habits to achieve the movements we need in the best way we can, and – most importantly – without getting hurt. If we suddenly try to change these, even if the changes would be more efficient, our nervous system, which is always trying to protect us, will set off warning lights, causing us to tense up and reject the changes. For example, if she had just told me to run lighter on my feet, this could have caused all sorts of issues, because I wouldn't really know what to change to make it happen, or whether these changes were going to cause me any pain or discomfort. What the Feldenkrais lesson did was allow my body to explore the new, more efficient movements in a way that felt safe and comfortable, so my nervous system knew they were not dangerous and could be adopted.

Gruenke tells me that in the lesson she had been working on the movement of my pelvis, which she noticed wasn't moving optimally, and that the quieter foot strike was just a by-product of better rotation of the pelvis. 'You weren't necessarily landing lighter on the ground either,' she says. 'You were just making a better contact.'

The reason I had restricted movement around the pelvis, she says, could be from an injury, but is most likely simply the consequence of the many, many hours I spend sitting at a computer or slumped on a seat somewhere.

Another thing she tells me as I run up and down after the session, is to hold my arms in a slightly different position, with my hands higher up. I try it and it feels great. I feel like Eliud Kipchoge. And in the weeks and months after the lesson, I hold my arms in this way on every single run and it continues to feel easy and natural.

'I wouldn't have told you to do that before the lesson,' she says. 'Without the lesson, you would have tried it, but it would have felt weird, and you would forget and probably give up after a while. But after the lesson your whole body was moving differently, and the higher hands fitted in perfectly. So when I suggested it, you could do it immediately. It made sense and felt good.'

With all my new tricks, my functioning Achilles and new, powerful Kipchoge arms, a few weeks later I meet up with a form coach to get myself assessed. I first met Shane Benzie at the British 24-hour running camp at the youth hostel in Berkshire, where he was giving a talk and had the runners excited about all the ways he could help them improve their form. He has worked with many of the top British ultra runners and comes heavily recommended.

We meet in a park in London and he sticks sensory pads on my legs and sets up his iPad camera and gets me to run around while he films me and records all sorts of data. Then we sit down and look at it. It's a lot of numbers and angled lines drawn on the iPad, but the upshot is that I have pretty great form. He films me on the downhills and I'm great there too.

'You have balance to die for,' he says, pointing out the identical impacts of my left and right strides, while my rotation and cadence are spot on. My arms, too, are moving just as he would want them to. I'm certain that a few years ago this would have been a crushing disaster movie of bad form. But things, it seems, really are working.

Of course, I'm not perfect, and digging around Benzie finds some room for improvement. Even though my foot strike is excellent, it happens a split second too late, he says, which means I'm losing a bit of momentum with each step. He tells me to bring my legs down quicker when I run. I try it and he records me again, and it's better. But it feels like an effort, both mentally and physically.

I go away thinking I will try this, and I do, but the fact that I'm making this change so consciously concerns me. I like the way Feldenkrais and Anatomy in Motion encourage adjustments to my form through movements that work on a more instinctive level, in my nervous system or my fascia. Trying to change things consciously feels like a less precise tool. No doubt the key is to take it away and play with it on my easy runs, and not to force it. That way it will hopefully become a natural and subconscious movement. As Gruenke says, my body needs to experience changes in a way that feels safe. My central governor system, it seems, is not only over-protective and forgetful, but sensitive too.

So far in my journey I've yet to experience the razzmatazz of the Ultra Trail World Tour, the series of trail races that culminate each year at the UTMB. Until now I've being learning my trade quietly in mostly smaller races, where you sleep in sports centre halls and finish in a field under an inflatable arch. But now I'm ready to unleash myself on the grand stage, starting with the Lavaredo Ultra Trail in the heart of the Italian Dolomites.

In the week before the race, the town of Cortina is over-run with lean men and women in trucker caps and tattoos, tiny backpacks and running tights. I see one couple walking around with matching tattoos on the backs of their arms that read 'test' on one arm, and 'life' on the other.

Marietta, feeling a little out of place, finds a café to do some work, while I wander around soaking it all up. I spot Paddy O'Leary, whom I met on the top of Cardiac Hill 30 miles into the Miwok 100K. He tells me he's going to the main square where the elite athletes – himself included – are being introduced to the crowd. He has to bustle through the packed square to get to the stage, where the runners leap up, one at a time, waving to the crowd, all grins and cool handshakes. I find myself somewhere to stand to one side, when I hear a voice I recognise, and turn around to see Zach Miller behind me. He's rummaging through a plastic bag, before pulling out a carrot and handing it to the woman next to him, who starts eating it whole. It's Hillary Allen, his former girlfriend. Or perhaps not former. 'We're seeing how it goes,' he says when I venture to ask him about it later.

Zach and Hillary are both doing the 'short' race here in Cortina. The main race, which I'm doing, is 78 miles, or 120km, while their race is a mere sprint at 50km. Zach recently ran the Trail World Championships and, true to his style, was leading until near the end when he crashed badly. So he's not ready for another big race so soon. Hillary is just happy to be able to run at all.

About three months after I spoke to her in Boulder, she went to run the Tromsø Sky Race in Norway. She was leading the Sky Race World Series, and a decent result in Tromsø would see her claim the overall world title. The course there is considered extremely technical, and as she neared the summit on an exposed ridge she stepped on a rock and the ground fell away beneath her.

'I felt my bones breaking and then I felt like someone was kicking me in the chest,' she says. She broke both wrists, three ribs, bones in her back and in her foot, badly twisted both ankles, and needed a lot of stitches including some in her head. It was months before she could even walk again unaided, yet ten months after her accident she was lining up at a big 53km Sky Race in California. That was a week ago. Now she's here in Italy for another 50km race.

I ask her how it felt to stand on the start line less than a year after doctors told her she might never run again?

'I was so nervous,' she says. 'But excited, and extremely scared. I told myself I just needed to try, and the result didn't matter.' In the end she finished sixth.

For months she had felt depressed; without running it felt like part of her was missing. 'Like I was a shell of myself. But I got the chance to re-discover how much I love running and what it brings out of me.'

While she was injured and couldn't run, Hillary wrote a blog titled 'Who Am I Without Running?' which was shared widely on social media and stopped a lot of ultra runners in their tracks.

'Since I'm not running, I feel as though I have lost my identity,' she wrote. 'I'm . . . trying desperately to prove that this emptiness I feel would be fixed if I could just run again.

'The biggest impact of this rebuilding process has been that I no longer look at myself through the lens of singularity. I can see a more complete and complex person beneath the brightly coloured running shorts and shoes.'

For many people in this sport, running around in the mountains has become so central to who they are that they can't imagine life without it. Dave Mackay, the injured runner I met in Colorado, was so determined to get back out there that he asked doctors to amputate his leg.[3] The call of the wild is strong, but Hillary sounded a note of caution: that life is bigger than this one activity.

The story of her journey to get back running has been followed closely by many people in the ultra world, so it's wonderful to see her fit and well. In the end, both Hillary and Zach win their 50km races here in Italy, despite strong competition. Hillary is a bona fide star of the sport, and her face is plastered over posters and shop fronts across Cortina.

As the elite athletes in the main races come down off the stage, many of them come over to see Hillary and Zach. I feel a little out of place – and a little overweight – standing in the middle of them all. Clare Gallagher is there, who I

---

[3] In August 2018 Dave Mackay achieved his ambitious goal of completing the Leadville Race Series in the US, including running the Leadville 100-mile race in just over 24 hours.

missed when I was in Boulder. I say hello, mentioning that we spoke over email, that I'm the one writing a book.

'Oh yeah,' she says. 'Make sure you mention the environmental problems. That's the number one issue for this sport.' Clare is a strong campaigner who believes that trail runners who spend all their time out in nature should be at the forefront of the campaign to protect it. 'We tend to think these trails are just here for us and they'll always be preserved and never sold off to private extraction companies,' she says. 'But these threats are real, and it's occurring in America right now. We can't just blindly keep running and not address this issue.'

With all the stars milling around, it's not a surprise when a woman comes over with a T-shirt and a pen looking for an autograph. 'Excuse me,' she says. Everyone stops talking and turns around. 'Er, which one of you is Zach Miller?' she asks. When he's pointed out, she smiles, and says: 'Will you sign my T-shirt?'

Despite all the stars in town, there is one person I want to speak to more than anyone else. I've been hoping to meet her at some point, so I can't let this opportunity slip. I manage to get hold of her representatives through her sponsor, and they arrange an interview at her hotel. So an hour later, I'm sitting in the lobby waiting. I can see her at the far end of the empty dining room, being interviewed by another journalist. I'm next in the queue. But she is so chatty, she won't let the journalist go. She wants a selfie with him. In the end her minder has to go over and explain that I'm waiting. I feel bad, as they seem to be getting on so well.

I sit down and she smiles at me like I'm her long-lost best friend. 'Hi,' she says, beaming at me.

Mira Rai is a former child soldier from Nepal who ran away from home to fight for Maoist rebels in an uprising against the government.

'I wanted to do something to support my family,' she tells me, her face as concerned and genuine as though it is something she has just done. She may have told this story a thousand times, but she still feels its pain. 'In the village it was very hard to manage – not enough to eat, no money to go to school.'

She had to quit school when she was twelve to help her family and would carry heavy bags of rice across miles of rugged trails to the local market. At fourteen she ran away.

'Mum was very sad when I left,' she says. 'She sent my dad to find me. But he didn't find me.'

In 2006 the war ended. Mira wanted to stay in the army, but under the UN-brokered peace agreement she was too young, so she returned to her village. Unable to settle back into village life, however, she went to live in Kathmandu with her former karate instructor from the Maoist rebel camp. While living there she used to go out running. One day she met a group of runners and ran with them. Afterwards, they invited her to a 50km race that was taking place that weekend.

'I didn't know it was a race,' she says. 'They said it was just training. Everyone was running with rucksacks and water and everything. I was just . . . simple, nothing.' She was just wearing shorts and a T-shirt and a cheap pair of shoes that were full of holes. 'But I started, and I won.'

She won 7,000 rupees, which is about £45, and a pair of Salomon shoes. 'I was happy with these new shoes,' she says. 'They were too big, but I didn't care.'

Richard Bull was the race director that day. He says she was so smiley and happy that he decided to help her get to another race in Nepal a month later, the 112-mile Mustang Trail Race. She won again. After that, she told him: 'Europe, can I go, sir?'

Bull says he had no thought she would be a particularly special runner, but he helped fund her to get to two races in Italy and France. 'I was worried about her going with limited English,' he says. He linked her up with an Italian woman who got kit for her and taught her about refuelling and aid stations. Mira won both races.

'It was incredibly exciting and amazing,' says Bull. 'It brought tears to my eyes, I tell you.'

The ultra world was captivated by Mira's story and Salomon signed her up as a sponsored athlete. A year later, she became the subject of an award-winning documentary simply titled *Mira*, and in 2017 she was named National Geographic's Adventurer of the Year.

'I'm so lucky,' she says. She says this about twenty times in our short interview, every time she recalls the kindness of those who have helped her along the way, funding her first races and helping organise things for her.

Now she is a star in her home country. 'Yeah, everybody recognises me,' she says, wide-eyed like she still can't believe it. 'In Nepal no family ever told their children to do sport. "In sport there is no life," they said. But now they say: "Do like Mira." But it is difficult. Trail running still has no support.'

Mira says she is living and working with young runners, mostly girls, in Kathmandu, working to get them races abroad. She also organises a couple of trail races in Nepal. 'I have a programme supporting girls to do training and learn English to give them an opportunity,' she says. 'Many runners are very strong but they don't have a chance.'

With the race here in Italy looming, I wonder if she can offer me any advice. I tell her that when I'm running, at some point my mind always tells me to stop, that I should quit. I ask if the same happens to her.

'No!' she says, laughing at the whole notion. 'I really like to keep going, keep moving. I am enjoying myself.'

I tell her that sometimes, if I look at my watch and there's still a long way to go, it makes me want to give up.

'Oh no!' she says, feeling my pain. 'Don't look at the watch. Just run. Don't think about why you are running. You just have to think, go, I am enjoying it, or wow, I'm so lucky to be running.'

It's an amazing perspective that I may find hard to replicate, but I love the spirit of it. I leave her to prepare for the race and I head back to my hotel, carrying her advice with me in my back pocket. Out there in the mountains, once the race starts, it may come in useful.

A week or so before flying out to Italy, I met up in London with a journalist colleague and ultra runner, Kieran Alger, who had run the Lavaredo race twice and dropped out both times. Perhaps he could help me avoid a few pitfalls particular to this race.

'Don't shoot off up the first hill,' he said, smiling. 'I thought that was a big hill. It's not a big hill.'

He said the big hill came at around 90km, and in his two attempts he hadn't got beyond it. 'I remember being sat on a rock halfway up, my head in my hands, in a dark place. I was smiling at people when they went by, but I was in total misery.' Yet, despite all this, he said he was desperate to go back and try for a third time.

'I think I enjoy the pain,' he said. 'I'm actually really jealous of you going out to do it. There's such a reward from knowing you've been to that place.'

He promised to buy me a pint if I finished the race in under 24 hours. I do love an arbitrary target time, so that would do. My goal was to finish in 24 hours.

It's 10 p.m. and I'm standing in the main square in Cortina an hour before the race is due to start. It may be late, but the place is heaving. As well as the 1,600 runners, the whole town has come out. There is music pumping, people dancing on balconies. At the start of a road race I usually feel like one of the few serious runners as I push my way to the front.

But here everyone looks fit, mean, with that I've-seen-things look in their eye. Rather than try to push myself into the crowd huddling around the start, with plenty of time still to go I find a bench in the shadows off to the side and sit down. It will be good for me to start near the back, to stop me shooting off with the elite runners like one of those riderless horses at the Grand National who think they're in the race, but actually have no idea what they're doing.

Everywhere people are filming, livestreaming, tweeting. Yes, at this point, social media matters. They want to show off. But later, much later, there will be less filming, less tweeting. It's funny that the rise in this sport is at least partly driven by ego, by a desire to impress, because so few sports can destroy the ego so ruthlessly.

Later, about 90km in to the race, halfway up that hill Kieran warned me about, I pass a young guy in his late twenties. He looks every inch the ultra runner, with the dark beard, the long hair, tattoos down his legs, his powerful yet lean frame bristling with muscle. But the light has gone out. He's walking slowly, a picture of hopeless self-pity. The sun is baking and he has thirty brutal kilometres to run. Maybe I pass him a little too quickly, maybe I'm too old, a pasty English writer with floppy hair. Whatever it is, as I go by he chucks his poles on the floor in disgust and sits down, his ego shattered. No promise of Strava kudos or thumbs up on social media will motivate him now. If he is going to make it – and I don't know if he ever did – he is going to have to dig deep. Once you descend into that dark place out on the trail, where everything is crashing down around you, you need to find something real to keep you moving. It could be love or pain, but it has to be real. It certainly won't be Facebook likes.

But back at the start a thousand glowing phones are held aloft under the night sky, as the race's anthem, 'The Ecstasy of Gold', soars through the streets of this small mountain town. And with that, to cheers and the sound of whistles and cowbells, a hooter goes and we trundle off up the road out of the town and into the darkness.

With so many runners, the narrow trails are congested to the point where I'm often forced to stop and walk. Uphill and down we traipse in silent single file, a march of the condemned. It's surprising how quiet it is, even in a country where people love to talk so much. But each person is on a personal journey, the descent into the well, to find that connection with the buried self. It needs quiet.

Dawn breaks among giant boulder fields of mountains, and the runners begin to spread out. The mood lightens. I bask in the majesty of the world, exhilarated. I take Mira Rai's advice and think about how lucky I am.

I fall into a general pattern of holding my position on the climbs, hiking anything even vaguely steep, just like everyone else this far back in the field – and then, on the descents, moving past people. The hills are similar to those in the Pyrenees, but here I'm the one flying past everybody. People hear me coming, a galloping mountain ox, and they step aside. One of those crazy local guys, is what I would have thought. But this time it is me. It feels so easy. Quick, nimble footsteps, I'm back on *la descente de la mort*.

In an effort to stay in the moment, I haven't started my watch, and most of the time it works. One step at a time, the next aid station, don't think ahead. Of course, I'm no Zen master, and there are moments of doubt, when I teeter on the edge of a crisis. On the very first descent I feel a sharp, stabbing pain in my knee. Surely not. It feels so real and for a moment I think I'm done. Then it moves to my heel, and I know it is my mind playing tricks. It will have to try harder than that.

But generally, this time there are no moments of despair. This is it, finally, an ultra that doesn't drag me to the edge of the cliff and kick me over. Instead, the time melts away and I exist in the perpetual motion.

At some point I realise I might finish before dark, before the dreaded second night. The thought gives me a lift and I press on harder, faster. I keep expecting my legs to suffer from the descents, for my quads to start buckling. But they never do. Looking back afterwards, at my position at each checkpoint, I gain about 100 places on each big downhill, moving from 900th at the first checkpoint to finish in 366th position. As I pass runners slumped on the ground with their heads in their hands, I know their pain too well. But this time I'm holding it together, on the right side of the line. I know one false step, one moment of weakness, and it can all come caving in. I need to stay focused, to stop myself falling. And for once I do. I hold my line. Even after 110km, with the final 10km all downhill, I'm still moving well. I can see people almost annoyed with me as I rush by, as though I'm showing off. How can he still be so fresh, they ask, shaking their heads. I'm as confused as they are.

After 21 hours, I arrive back in Cortina, still in daylight, racing through the crowds, high-fiving children, leaping over the line, hugging a smiling Marietta, my whole body buzzing to have done it. To have set off and come back standing, this time not broken, not whimpering, but in one piece. Finally, I'm beginning to get this thing. I'm beginning to feel at ease running for hours and hours in the mountains. Slowly I'm turning, it seems, into an ultra runner.

I shouldn't pat myself too firmly on the back, however. Hayden Hawks, the winner, still finished over nine hours ahead of me. How is that possible?

In an emotional interview straight after the race, in the main square in Cortina, Hawks said that for the first 30 miles of the race he felt horrible. 'I thought, argh, this is not a good day,' he said. 'But it was a lesson, don't ever give up. If you're feeling down, and you're feeling like you're not going to be able to make it, don't give up, because it can change.'

It seems that no matter how good you are, these races are never going to be easy. But it is the epic, challenging nature of them, the way they force you to dig so deep, that makes them special.

16

In the world of ultra running, sitting alongside the races is the separate realm of Fastest Known Times, or FKTs. Without the rules and restrictions of races, without needing to turn up and register, or win points, or pay to compete on a set day along with hundreds or thousands of other people, in an FKT you have the world – or the trail – to yourself. You can start when you want; you are alone, free in nature. It is the original Into the Wild spirit of ultra running, just you testing yourself against the mountains or the deserts or whatever it is. At least, for a while it was like that.

'The do-it-yourself and vaguely subversive, underground nature of FKTs is the primary attraction for me,' US ultra runner Anton Krupicka wrote on his blog back in 2011. 'It's a very primal and largely unfettered way of being in the mountains and testing oneself.'

In 2005, ultra runners Peter Bakwin and Buzz Burrell started the Fastest Known Time website, bringing the term into wider use. In the US, a scene grew up around it, with people tackling and setting records each year on some of the most iconic trails in America, such as the 223-mile John Muir Trail through California's Sierra Nevada, and the epic 2,175-mile Appalachian Trail.

Runners taking on an FKT are expected to document their trips to prove they've broken the record, or have set a new one if there is no existing record on their route, but the unofficial, relaxed nature of the exercise is implicit in the name: Fastest Known Time. Someone may have done it faster, who knows?

On the FKT website, however, it gives some key guidelines for anyone wanting to establish a new record and have it generally accepted. It says: 'For the renowned routes that receive publicity, please announce your intention in advance, and provide the link to *real-time tracking* . . . photos and a trip report immediately following the effort are the standard procedure.'

Bakwin says: 'These rules do not "prove" you have done anything. They just make it easier for a good person to believe you.'

Setting records on long trails, of course, has a history going way back before 2005. The Bob Graham Round in England's Lake District, for example, was one of the most famous FKTs long before the term FKT was ever coined. In 1932, hotelier Bob Graham ran up and down forty-two peaks, covering a distance of 66 miles, in under 24 hours, setting a challenge now considered the Holy Grail of British fell running. In 1982, the legendary Billy Bland ran the same route, setting an almost impossible FKT of 13hrs 53mins.

When I was in the Lake District, I asked fell runners Ben Abdelnoor and Colin Dulson if they thought anyone could break Billy Bland's record, which had stood for over thirty-five years despite thousands of people attempting it. Kilian Jornet had been saying he might give it a go. In the past many of the great ultra runners, such as Scott Jurek, had tried and not come even remotely close.

'It annoys me when people just rock up and say I'm going for the Bob Graham record,' says Abdelnoor. 'It shows a lack of respect.' Like almost every fell runner, Abdelnoor has had a go, finishing the round in 18 hours. One man who has been touted as a possible contender to beat Bland's time is local hero Ricky Lightfoot. So far he has only tried once, in the middle of winter, which meant not only terrible weather but doing most of it in the dark.

'I thought if I did a winter one first,' he tells me, 'then a summer one would be easier. It's a funny way of thinking, but that's how my mind works.' He completed his round in 21 hours.

'Until recently people thought breaking Billy's record was impossible,' says Dulson. 'But then last year Rob Jebb did it in 14 hours. And Jasmin Paris shattered the women's record, running around in 15 hours.'

'Yeah, people have started to think that maybe it is possible,' says Abdelnoor.

And indeed, that proves to be the case. Just a month before the 2018 UTMB, Kilian Jornet does indeed rock up in the Lake District for a surprise attempt at the record. Although it has been kept a secret from the media, to avoid too many people turning up and getting in the way, Jornet has a group of local pacers to tag-team sections of the route with him – which is how these rounds are usually done. All he has to do is keep up.

In a piece of running history, on his first attempt the Catalan superstar smashes the old record by over an hour, arriving at the finish at Moot Hall in Keswick in 12hrs 52mins to be greeted by a huge crowd and Billy Bland himself. After touching the door to mark the finish, Jornet sits chatting with Bland on the steps of the hall, and together they open a bottle of champagne and share a celebratory swig or two. And, just like that, another chapter in the incredible story of Kilian Jornet has been written. It seems the normal rules of what is possible don't apply to him.

In an effort to grab myself some sort of FKT glory, I manage to join an attempt organised by *Runner's World* magazine to set a record for scaling the highest peak in every borough of London. It's more for fun than a serious athletic endeavour, especially as we're doing it in a relay between about twenty runners. The joke is, of course, that the highest points in some boroughs stretch the definition of a 'peak' so far that the only response is to take a picture of yourself looking exhausted and oxygen-deprived while planting an imaginary flag in the middle of a speed bump. The lowest peak of all is just sixteen metres above sea level, in Tower Hamlets. FKTs are becoming so mainstream, it seems, that they're now inspiring parodies.

Despite the 'fun' nature of the attempt, the logistics of getting everyone to their hand-over points smoothly and on time means it still needs to be undertaken with a degree of professionalism. There are also lots of serious runners getting involved, including Damian Hall, who recently set an FKT on England's South West Coast Path, running the entire 630 miles, with climbs totalling more than three times the elevation of Mount Everest, in just ten days.

In total the London round covers 150 miles, and like the Bob Graham Round the primary goal is to finish it in under 24 hours. As such, I find myself with another early start, getting up at 3 a.m. to meet my running partner, my work colleague Kate Carter, in the middle of Wimbledon Common, where we stand around waiting like two lost running goons for the baton to arrive. Are we in the right place? It's hard to tell. We're still trying to align our Google Maps when we hear a shout in the darkness: 'Hello? Anyone there?'

The overall schedule is not too arduous, but once we get the bag with the tracker in it, we're off, out of the park and through the quiet London streets, crossing empty dual carriageways, feeling suddenly like this is something real and serious after all. Being part of a team brings its own pressure and we do our best not to get lost as we race to the top of Richmond Park. Kate knows this area better than me, so I'm really just following on. We run for about an hour before handing the tracker on in a flurry of crazy, wacky poses for the photographer, who appears suddenly from nowhere.

OK, it's not as impressive as some FKTs, but it's a new route that people may take on in the future and try to set their own record. We meet up in the pub later that evening, pioneers in FKT land, having turned something that started as a way to get out into the wilds, to test yourself against nature, into an urban, team-bonding session/jolly good laugh followed by drinks and food down the pub. I wonder what Anton Krupicka would make of it all.

The next record attempt I find myself involved in is more in keeping with the original FKT spirit. It takes place in Scotland a few days after my six-hour training run with Damian Hall in the Brecon Beacons. My mountain running brother, Govinda, has his eyes on what he perceives to be a weak FKT in the Galloway Hills. It's a 45-mile route called the Ring of Fire[4] and he wants some help with it.

As yet Govinda has never run further than marathon distance, so this is a big undertaking. But he has been running sections of the route, which goes over difficult terrain – lots of marshy hills with no trails, where the ground can give way unpredictably, and where everything looks the same, making navigation an issue. The plan is for me to run the first few miles with him, and then to meet him later so we can do the last and the trickiest 10-mile section together. The only problem is that my quads are still trashed from my run with Damian. I can barely get up and down the stairs in the house the day before, but I keep this to myself, not wanting to cause him any unnecessary anxiety.

So I set him off on his way as planned at dawn, taking a photograph at the start and making a note of the exact time. Then, later that afternoon, I go to wait near a loch with both our wives and children. It's a scorcher of a day, the sky pounding blue, reflecting on the water, where the children are swimming and playing happily. It's such a

---

[4] This has nothing to do with the similarly named race in Anglesey, which was named after organiser Quentin's favourite song.

relaxing, idyllic scene, while my legs still feel like two concrete blocks, that I'm secretly hoping he'll get to this point and decide to call it a day.

As the clock ticks past the time he planned to meet us, my hopes grow. Half an hour goes by, then an hour. Then two hours. We try calling him but either his phone has died or he has no reception. He had wanted to finish the whole thing in daylight, but that's now looking less and less possible.

Finally he appears, lumbering towards us, still smiling. We have food and water for him. He stands there looking as happy as anything, but not saying what he plans to do next. I should be getting my bag on, not giving him the option to stop, not even allowing him to think about it. I feel terrible about it afterwards, but instead, I ask him: 'Are you going to continue?'

It's the kiss of death. Of course he has been thinking about stopping. He has been planning it for hours. My job, as his crew, is to push him on. But my legs. I'm not sure I can even run 10 miles. I might be a liability.

He looks at the scene. The children splashing in the water, the mountains standing around, bathing the world in their calm serenity. There's not a sound. How could anyone continue?

'I've done enough,' he says. 'That was awesome. I loved it. But I'm done.'

'Are you sure?' It's the best I can do. 'If you want to carry on, I'm ready to go.' I may as well be taking his shoes off for him and passing him his towel.

'No,' he says. 'I know who I am.' And with that, he stops.

It's an interesting statement. *I know who I am.* He enjoyed pushing himself, taking on the challenge, but he didn't feel the need to prove anything to himself or anyone else.

Long before he turned up to smash the record on the Bob Graham Round, Kilian Jornet was the man most responsible for bringing FKTs to a wider audience. His Summits of My Life project, to scale seven of the world's most iconic mountains, has been gold dust to magazine editors and TV producers since he began it in 2010, with the whole project being meticulously recorded and photographed, including in a series of documentaries and books.

Once he started things off, others followed, with a host of films appearing with titles such as *Made to be Broken* about incredible, inspirational FKT attempts. But nobody does it quite like Jornet. The footage of his FKT up and down the Matterhorn in 2013 looks like something out of a James Bond movie. There he is, running down snow slopes, across the top of a death-defying ridge – not slowly, but leaping from rock to rock, his arms pumping as though he has seconds in which to save the world.

One of those magazine editors, hearing about Jornet's exploits, calls me and says he wants an article on this new phenomenon of FKTs. 'Just make sure you interview Kilian Jornet,' he says.

I run into a problem when I contact Jornet's press people only to find that he is on a trip to Everest to practise for an eventual FKT attempt on the world's highest mountain. He's halfway up Everest, they tell me. Out of contact. I dig around some more, and I'm surprised to discover that, good as he is, someone has been following Jornet around breaking his records. That man's name is Karl Egloff.

A mountain guide from Quito in Ecuador, with Swiss parents, Egloff was sent to accompany groups of hikers who wanted to ascend Kilimanjaro. In the afternoons when his guests were sleeping, however, he would head out for a run, up to the summit. 'Word got out about what I was doing and so I got a call from my boss,' he says. 'I thought I was going to get fired, but he said he wanted to sponsor me.'

Although he was a former international mountain biker, and not a runner, he decided to give the record a go and started training. After two practice runs he made his attempt. 'I made a lot of mistakes,' he says. 'I didn't even have running clothes, I was wearing my cycling clothes. My socks were too thick.' But despite this he ran up and down Kilimanjaro, a route people usually take seven days to hike, in six hours and 42 minutes, beating Jornet's record by over 30 minutes.

'I'd never even heard of Kilian,' he says. 'Afterwards, everyone was telling me I'd broken Kilian's record. So I Googled him and I was like, wow.' We're sitting in the same restaurant in London I took Jornet to almost a year earlier. Egloff is no more comfortable in the city, with a big rucksack on the seat next to him. But he likes talking and has just returned from filming his first ever TV chat show interview, in Switzerland. People there have heard of him at least.

His boss, cashing in on the publicity being generated by the Kilimanjaro record, suggested Egloff try Aconcagua next, the highest mountain in the Andes, and another one of the peaks in Jornet's Summits of My Life project. The Spaniard had set an FKT there just two months before, but this was a mountain Egloff knew well from many guiding trips, and he broke the record again, this time by a full hour.

Capturing the sense of astonishment in the mountain running community, *Outside* magazine in the US published an article headlined 'Where in the World Did Karl Egloff Come From?'

'Kilian was the first to tweet my record,' Egloff says. 'That set my social media going crazy. The TV people were knocking at my door. I was scared. Everyone wanted me to race Kilian, but he's a runner and I'm a mountain racer.'

After his two records, Egloff got a kit sponsor and went on to claim the FKT on another of Jornet's summits, Mount Elbrus in Russia. In total, Egloff has taken the record on three of Kilian's seven summits.

But rather than wrecking Kilian's project, the two are friends and they once even attempted to break the Mont Blanc record together, but were stopped by bad weather. I ask Egloff why, if he has more records, he is known only to the keenest observers of the sport, while Jornet is a huge star all over the world. He looks at me as though he has thought about this a lot.

'He is a shy guy, but he started very young; at fourteen he was already racing. And he has a huge marketing team. His sponsor, Salomon, are like his family.'

In an effort to grab some of the limelight, Egloff has now hired a marketing manager. Next year he is going for Jornet's ascent record on Denali, and eventually he wants to go for the ultimate record: Mount Everest.

By racing up these huge mountains, Egloff and Jornet are crossing into the world of mountaineering, where FKTs are nothing new, but where they are simply called speed records. By repackaging it, however, Jornet and his team have grabbed the media's attention the world over. Our drink in London was arranged for a *Financial Times* interview about his record attempt on Everest. They wanted a full-page feature on him.

Despite the media furore, however, I remember it was surprisingly unclear whether Jornet had actually broken any existing record on Everest. It seemed there were ascent-only records, and then round-trip ascent and descent records, and different records from different starting points. But as far as I could tell, he hadn't broken any of them. The big thing the news outlets and his sponsors were all going with was the fact that he ended up summiting Everest twice in six days. Was that a record? I couldn't tell, but the headlines everywhere ran with it.

But not everyone was happy. An American climber called Dan Howitt started questioning online whether Jornet had even got to the summit at all.

I was initially surprised that someone had the audacity to question Jornet. If anyone was capable of superhuman feats, it was him. He had proven his powers again and again. It hadn't even crossed my mind when we met to ask him for evidence of his Everest exploits. Like everyone else, I was sure he had done it. He was a man of integrity, a living legend. When we met he was generous, charming and self-effacing, exactly as I had been told to expect. It was hard to fault him. So when I first heard about the doubts, I assumed he had been targeted by one of the many overzealous online sleuths who seem to have emerged as these FKTs become more and more popular and incredible.

Nevertheless, when Howitt contacted me directly, after reading my article in the *Financial Times*, with his charge sheet against Jornet, I felt I had to at least look at it. And I have to admit, it was a pretty compelling read.

In a detailed 22-page report, Howitt said it was odd that such a voracious documenter of every training run, race and previous record in his Summits of My Life project, had no photographs or video footage at or even near the summit of Mount Everest. Even in 1953, when Tenzing Norgay and Edmund Hillary were the first people to scale the world's highest mountain, a photograph at the summit was a priority. 'Camera and video technology have improved dramatically since 1953,' Howitt pointed out.

On top of this, Jornet's own GPS files were incomplete and suggest he didn't reach the summit. The files were automatically uploaded to the Movescount website, just as with all Jornet's other GPS-tracked activities.

Jornet responded to Howitt's claims in a public statement, taking the issues one at a time. He said the GPS files were incomplete because the batteries in his watch died due to the cold and the length of time he was alone on the mountain.

Howitt also questioned why Jornet chose not to bring a satellite phone with him, which he could have used to make a call from the summit to prove he had arrived on the top of the world.

Jornet responded by saying that his priority was to be alone on the mountain, to cut off contact with the rest of the world, and to rely on himself to make decisions. 'It was a matter of style,' he said in his response. 'I could [have] organized a big expedition, with sherpas on the route . . . and some cameras . . . [on the] summit to have nice images. I could [have] had a satellite phone call from the summit to "announce". But the major goal of the expedition was far from that. It was for me to see if I was able to climb Everest with no external support . . . and by myself.'

That was an admirable intention, and in many ways true to the original spirit of FKTs, to leave the paraphernalia of races and crowds behind and to go it alone. But still, to have nothing, not even GoPro footage or a camera phone image from the top, did seem a little strange. As Robbie Britton said to me: 'If I was going to spend all that time and effort on one big project, when it came to the crunch, I'd be sure to have a lot more evidence.'

Questions were also raised about the time of day Jornet opted to summit Everest, not just by Howitt but by another experienced mountaineer with numerous speed records on high mountains, who told me he didn't want to be named for fear of being seen as critical of Jornet. On his first ascent Jornet said he arrived at the summit at midnight and on his second ascent at 9.30 p.m., but both Howitt and the mountaineer I spoke to point out that no one ever climbs through the afternoon and into the night to arrive at the summit so late in the day, because it is so cold and dangerous. But then again, Jornet is no normal athlete, and in his defence, he said he had planned to reach the top earlier but got stomach issues along the way that slowed him down.

A few months later, an independent investigator called Andy Tavin asked for and was given access to the original pictures and videos from Jornet's GoPro camera – it turned out there were some after all. Tavin produced a forensic 56-page report which concluded that Jornet did summit Everest on the first attempt, but at 12.32 a.m. and not midnight as claimed. He then concluded that there remained little evidence to support the second ascent to the summit, and that if it did happen it most likely took two hours longer than Jornet claimed. The Spaniard again responded and his case was again that he was doing it for himself, and that he wasn't thinking about the timings or taking pictures because he was in an extreme situation and had other priorities.

It's not up to me to judge whether Jornet did or didn't summit Mount Everest twice in a week, or to begin to speculate why, if he didn't, he would claim that he did. This is a man with enough verified success to his name to be able to ride out a failed summit attempt, a man who is always happy to cheer on rivals who beat him or break his records. The ultra running community has certainly rallied around him and the doubts have done little to dent his reputation. When I asked Buzz Burrell, co-founder of the FKT website, what they thought about it all, he said: 'His [Jornet's] style and ethics I believe match his ability and training – he is the best mountain runner of his generation, and is highly respectable in every sense.'

All Jornet's case proves beyond doubt, is that as the stakes continue to get higher in this game, anyone planning to do something remarkable should plan on gathering some solid evidence. In the realm of FKTs, it seems the old-fashioned reliance on trust and goodwill alone is no longer enough.

17

And so on to Chamonix where, for a week in late August, the ultra running world comes together for its annual celebration at the foot of Mont Blanc. People bustle around stalls selling ultra-light backpacks, compression wear, the latest graphene-soled shoes. Runners are collecting race numbers, bumping into friends, eating pizza. Everyone looks lean, prepped, ready to take to the mountains. I try not to look too out of place.

I've come to France with Marietta and the children, my super crew. After setting up our tents in a campsite just outside Chamonix, we head in to town to meet Tom and Rachel at a café straight out of Byron Bay, with falafel and tofu burgers, and sweet potato wedges with everything. Tom and Rachel have spent the last few months in Australia, after Rachel's dad was diagnosed with cancer. They almost didn't come back for the race, but her dad insisted, knowing how much it meant to her after waiting three years to get a place.

'He keeps saying the cancer is his UTMB,' she says. 'He says things like: "This must be what it's like running at night when you can't see what's around you."'

Rachel tried to tell him that she didn't need to race, that she would stay with him in Australia. 'But he wouldn't let me finish the sentence,' she says.

Rachel's parents live on a tiny island off the coast of Brisbane with no shops or roads. Everything is run by solar energy and they grow their own vegetables. 'There are lots of kangaroos,' says Tom. 'But no mountains.' So for the three months leading up to the race, they've done all their training on a flat stretch of beach. As a result Tom has ditched any hope of being competitive at the front of the race and has decided to run it together with Rachel.

Moments after they arrived in Chamonix they got a phone call from Rachel's mum, saying she wanted them to come back as her dad had been rushed in to hospital for a second operation. 'But I felt if I went back,' Rachel says, 'he would be so upset that I hadn't run, so I said no, I'm staying. I'm going to run it for him.'

After lunch, as we walk through the town, every now and then I catch sight of one of the elite runners milling around. They seem to stand two foot taller than everyone else, decked head to toe in the latest gear from their sponsors. There's Hayden Hawks, the winner of the Lavaredo ultra in Italy, slapping big handshakes with people stopping him for selfies. For a few weeks, in this one town in France, the top ultra runners are like rock stars. All the talk among the fans is of another showdown between Kilian Jornet and Jim Walmsley. François D'Haene, who beat them both to win the race last year (when Jornet was second and Walmsley fifth), is not running, but these two have been winning everything again this year and both seem to be in the form of their lives. Everybody wants a piece of them – a photograph, an autograph, a handshake.

'If I want to get anywhere,' Walmsley tells me when I track him down at the elite athletes press conference, 'the trick is to not go out wearing my Hoka gear. Then people look at me, but they're like, not sure.' He says he takes the back streets or the long route to avoid Chamonix town centre. 'If it's raining,' he says, 'the hood definitely goes up.'

When I ask him about his fitness heading into the race, he tells me he is coming fresh from one of the best training blocks he has ever had. He says he has just spent six weeks living in a tent in the mountains outside Silverton in Colorado.

'Very few of my training blocks have been perfect,' he says. 'But this one has been.' During his six weeks in the mountains he was running an average of 140 miles (225km) a week, with 15,000m (50,000ft) of climbing. Those are huge numbers.

'I feel good about doing my best performance. And on my best day, I can beat anyone.'

Walmsley is known for his fighting talk, which hasn't always gone down well, but he now has the records to back it up.

'When I first started out,' he says, 'people were like, "Man, you're full of it." But now that people know me, it doesn't seem so crazy. But I was never trying to stir things up, I was just trying to be honest and candid, not give BS answers.'

Only a few months before the UTMB, he finally did what he had been threatening to do for two years, break the course record at the Western States 100 – and he did it on one of the hottest days in the race's history. All that despite coming across a bear on the trail late in the race. It was at exactly the same point where he missed the turning in 2016. In 2017, he didn't make it that far due to stomach issues, so when he turned the corner the right way in 2018 and saw the bear, he says his immediate response was: 'You have got to be kidding me!'

'I had waited two years to get back there,' he says. 'If it was a training run, I would have turned around and gone another way. But it wasn't.' The bear's two cubs had climbed a tree over the trail, so she wasn't about to walk off. He tried shouting and throwing rocks, but to no avail.

'Then I just thought, "What the hell." The bear's body position seemed a little less aggressive, and after 13 hours' running I didn't want to throw it all away.' So he just ran straight past it as fast as he could.

'I remember thinking, in the worst case scenario at least it will make a good story: it finally took a bear to stop him.'

While Walmsley was living in his tent in the Rocky Mountains, Jornet, despite breaking his leg in a skiing accident less than six months earlier, was winning races all over the place. He had recently set the incredible Bob Graham Round record, and just five days before the UTMB, while everyone else was dialling back their training to give their legs a rest before the big day, Jornet was racing the Trofeo Kima, a 32-mile, extremely technical and demanding sky race in Italy. He won, again in a course record.

His powers of recovery seem extraordinary. A week after finishing second in the UTMB the previous year, when almost every other runner would still have had their feet up eating ice cream, he went and won the competitive Glen Coe Skyline race in Scotland. And the day before the Glen Coe race, just for a little warm-up jaunt, he ran to the top of Ben Nevis.

Another of the bona fide A-listers here in Chamonix, just behind the Jornet versus Walmsley title fight, is Zach Miller. I arrange to meet him one evening a few days before the race at the house of one of his sponsors, Buff. I'm let in to the luxury chalet just outside the town centre by Buff's marketing director, and find Zach sitting on a leather sofa going through his nutrition plan with a representative of another of his sponsors, like a schoolboy getting extra tuition after class.

'I'm terrible at planning, so I'm doing my homework,' he tells me. 'Trying to learn my nutrition plan.' What everybody loves about Zach is that he just runs. He has no strategy, he just puts his foot down and relies on his heart and his will to get him through. But in his effort to become the first American man ever to win the UTMB, he's working on the details.

'I really like races like the North Face 50 [the 50-mile race in California, which he has won twice],' he says, 'where you can just turn up with a few gels and run. But here at the UTMB it takes a bit more planning.'

The Buff team is mostly Spanish men and women from the company's head office in Barcelona. They've laid out a buffet supper and barbecue and I'm invited to stay. Also here is the filmmaker Billy Yang, who is making a documentary about Zach's attempt to win the UTMB. While all the focus may be on Zach, he doesn't exactly embrace it, preferring when he can to sit to one side and talk quietly, letting the general jokes and banter of the rest of the house pass him by.

As we stand around waiting for our turn to get some food, I ask him if he ever gets moments of doubt in a race, moments when his mind tells him he can't go on, or that he needs to slow down. I rarely hear elite runners talk about this, and I wonder if they're just focused on practicalities the whole time, or if they spend time out there fighting off the demons like the rest of us?

'Sure,' he says, piling his plate high with meat and salads, and taking a seat at the end of the table. I grab some food and sit down next to him. 'But I'm very hard on myself when I run,' he says. 'At the North Face 50 last year, I was running at the front with Hayden Hawks and Tim Freriks, and they both started pulling away from me. It was the place where in previous years I'd made my move. So I was like shouting at myself: "No! This isn't happening. Catch those guys." Sure, part of me was hurting and wanted to just let them go, to give it up, but a bigger part of me wanted to be at the front. It's just stubbornness, I guess.' He ended up catching Hawks, but not Freriks, and he finished second.

Why did he want to win so badly, I ask him, a little mischievously. What, deep down, was driving him?

Further down the table the beer is flowing among the non-runners, and the conversation is getting louder, with lots of laughing.

'Ego plays a big role, I guess,' he says. 'That feeling of winning, the adulation, the attention, it's addictive. And you want more, because it doesn't last.'

It's an answer as honest as his running. In Billy Yang's film, a more considered Zach says he is driven by a desire to do his best, in everything he does. He says that this is just his nature, that he has been that way since he was a child. Of course, both answers can be true at once. One thing I've learned in this journey through ultra running is that putting our finger on why we do this seemingly mad sport is almost impossible. The real reasons seem to lie just beyond the reasons we give. Sure, we want to win, we want to finish, we want to do our best, we want to find our limit, we want to make people proud. All of that. But none of it quite explains it. It's an unfathomable urge, a deep, primal call, to be out there, to stand facing oblivion, and to come through to the other side. And the feeling that we get when we do it can be addictive.

The time flies chatting about these things and I realise it's almost 11 p.m. I say my goodbyes and leave the comfort and warmth of the Buff house for our chilly campsite in the mountains, where Marietta and the children are already asleep, still unsure what their role in all this is.

The day before the race, after getting my kit checked and collecting my number, I work my way around the town, meeting as many people as I can while I have everyone in one place. My first stop is a coffee with a real rising star in the sport, the British runner Tom Evans. A soldier in the British army, a few years ago he was sitting in a pub in London listening to two friends regale him with their stories of the Marathon des Sables and how well they had done. A little naively perhaps, he said: 'Yes, it's not bad, but there were still 290 people in front of you.' Affronted, they told him that if he thought he could do better, he should run it the next year. So he did.

Not considering himself in any way a serious runner, he just ran when he could. 'If I had an hour, I ran for an hour,' he says. 'I didn't have a coach or follow a schedule or anything.' Without any specific ultra or desert training, he turned up in the desert and finished third – the first time a non-North African man had finished on the podium in four years. He then went on to finish third in the 2018 World Trail Championships, beating some of the biggest names in the sport. His burgeoning reputation is at odds with the tiny sponsorship deal he has with Hoka, but he has recently signed up with a top sports agent – the former agent of David Beckham – and is still being supported by the army to train for races, so he's fairly relaxed about it all.

His agent later tells me that what attracted him to Tom, apart from his huge talent, was his age – he's 26. 'Tom is ridiculously young [for an ultra runner], and he has digital appeal,' he says. He tells me he wants to work with Tom in the way he worked with Beckham, building a brand over many years. 'We're already planning 2020, 2021,' he says. It's heady talk for the sport of ultra running, but the agent says he sees it continuing to grow. 'There are a lot of big brands in this sport,' he says.

Indeed, on the day I meet Tom in Chamonix, Red Bull announce that they have signed him up to their roster of sponsored ultra runners. If he does well in his event here at the UTMB festival – he's running the 63-mile Courmayeur Champex Chamonix (CCC) race – I'm sure his agent will see that Hoka look again at the amount they're paying him.

As I sit talking with Tom in the café, another elite runner, Tim Freriks – the guy who beat Zach in the North Face 50 – walks in and sits down with us and orders the same huge slice of vegan pie and salad. He's a team-mate of Evans and after they've eaten they have to do a signing with the rest of Hoka's roster. We take a slow walk together through the crowds towards the towering Hoka stand in the outdoor expo area, where a long queue has formed for the signing. I lose Evans and Freriks as they join the rest of Hoka's mostly American stars, including Jim Walmsley, Hayden Hawks and Magda Boulet, who gave me a lift home from the Miwok 100K. The crowd swarms in, jostling to get close enough for signed photographs, or for a word and a joke with their idols.

I leave them to it and head over to a smaller, altogether more British gathering at the Inov-8 stand. Inov-8 is a firm based in the Lake District, firmly embedded in fell running and the all-weather, no-frills British approach to trail running. Fittingly, by the time I get to their stand, the brilliant sunshine has been replaced by a faint, British drizzle. As people mill around preparing to head out for a short group run, it's hard to pick out the stars. Unlike Hoka's line-up, here they're a little more understated. One is fell running legend Nicky Spinks, who holds the overall record (male or female) for running the Bob Graham Round twice in one go. She is not racing the UTMB, but is here crewing for the brand's big star, who is none other than my friend Damian Hall.

'Alright?' he says when he sees me, grinning happily. Damian has a film crew following him around this year as he attempts to fulfil his dream of finishing in the UTMB top ten. Looking at the elite field, it's a lot to ask. He's ranked fiftieth in the official ITRA ranking system, but that's a lot higher than when he ran it last year – and ended up finishing twelfth. The film they're making about him is called *Underdog*.

With a smile, Damian tells me he has no chance against the 'fast guys', as he calls the favourites for the race. 'Unless they mess up, which I hope they will, of course,' he says. He points out to anyone who will listen that he is not a full-time athlete, that he is in his forties, he has children, and he doesn't live in the mountains. 'That's the mindset I like to get into,' he jokes when it's suggested he's playing himself down a little. 'It takes the pressure off.'

Damian is introduced to the gathering of about thirty people who have turned up for the chance to run with him and Nicky, and to try out some new Inov-8 shoes. Tom Payn is also here. Tom is also an Inov-8 athlete, and in some ways he is a faster, more accomplished runner than Damian. But despite living in these mountains he has never got it quite right here in the way Damian did last year. In the Orsières Champex Chamonix (OCC) race in 2016 – one of the shorter races during UTMB week – he finished twenty-fourth, after running the first half pushing the pace alongside the eventual winner, Xavier Thévenard. This has been Tom's story in all his big races, pushing hard from the front early on and then falling away near the end. I'm sure it comes from his belief that he's as fast over a marathon as any of these guys, but the mountains are a different beast.

This year, with his lack of training, Tom isn't going to improve his status in the ultra running world, so he stands in the background with the rest of us mortals and seems a little crestfallen. He is only in his late thirties, though. His time is not up. After the UTMB he plans to shoot for some fast times on the road – aiming to break the British over-forties marathon and 50km records. These are worthy goals and would earn him plaudits, but I can't help hoping he will get it right here in Chamonix one day and find his rightful place among the stars of trail running.

After the introductions, Damian takes us all off for a short run in the rain. As we hike up a steep climb, which Tom skips up like a goat, Damian tells me about his UTMB playlist, which he likes to put on his headphones when the race gets tough. 'What is on it?' I ask. 'Mostly Phil Collins, and Kate Bush, of course,' he says, with that wry, disarming smile.

Before we all disappear to our quiet corners to gather ourselves for the race, I have time to catch up with one more person in the mêlée of pre-race Chamonix. It's late in the day and the café where I met Evans is closed, so I find Elisabet Barnes and her boyfriend, Sondre Amdahl, standing outside like two giants. Next door is another café, and we go in and sit down. Elisabet orders tea and raspberries. It's a delicate combination.

She tells me she met Sondre at a number of races –

including in Oman when she returned the year after we met there – and then together they ran across Sweden. 'As friends,' she says. Sondre can't help smiling, at this. 'Well, maybe Sondre had other ideas,' she says. 'But something clicked between us.'

So as she continues to recover and take a break from running, she is here in Chamonix to crew for Sondre, who says his goal is to run the race in under 24 hours, which he hopes will be good enough for the top twenty.

I wish him luck, and then, with all my meetings and interviews done, I head back to our campsite, where it's pizza night. We sit in the cool evening on a bench with our pizzas, the mountains like huge backdrops hung all around us, the children excited at the thought of going horse riding in the morning. My race is still an abstract concept to them.

I need to get to sleep. Luckily once darkness descends there isn't much else to do on the campsite, so I settle down on my roll mat one last time and somehow manage to get a solid eight hours of deep sleep. I wake up on Friday morning, the day of the race, with my legs feeling fresher than they have in a long time. I'm ready. I've got this.

And then my phone beeps.

18

Ping. I reach for my phone and look at the message that has popped up: 'UTMB Weather deterioration: bad weather until Saturday afternoon, very cold, windy, feels like -10C (14F). Cold weather kit essential.'

All across the valley, runners give a collective shiver as they read the message. The challenge of the race was already looming as big and foreboding as the mountains buried under the black clouds, which have been gathering for the last few days. But now it is worse. Much worse. Rain means muddy, slippery descents, wet clothes, in -10°C, at night.

'I am the storm,' I whisper to myself, trying to believe it.

'Did you get the text?' Rachel says as I step into her and Tom's tiny studio flat in central Chamonix later on Friday afternoon. They have invited me around before the race – which starts at 6 p.m. – and suggested we all set off together. It's a nice idea. We can start together, sure, it will stop me from shooting off too fast. But I'm a lot stronger now than when we all ran the 100 Miles Sud de France. I'm planning to go a lot faster this time. I was still raw then. Now I'm an ultra runner. A hundred miles is not so far if I can stay in the moment, keep a cool head. I've learned my lessons. It's just a matter of cruising the descents, staying steady on the ups, and moving quickly through the aid stations.

'Sub 30,' Damian Hall suggested when I told him I wasn't sure about my goal time. 'You should do that,' he says, as though it's easy. The number becomes fixed in my head, and I begin to think of it as the UTMB equivalent of the sub three-hour marathon. Tough, fairly impressive, but within my reach. I have the experience of Lavaredo in my legs, where I stayed strong for 21 hours and 78 miles in the mountains. This is only another 27 miles, a little over a marathon. I can run that in nine hours.

Rachel is a bag of nerves, hopping around on her bed re-checking the weather forecast on her laptop. After what happened in the Pyrenees, where she got hypothermia, and after two months on a baking Australian island, her fears about the weather are understandable. This cold and wet isn't ideal. Tom laughs jovially, saying the forecast for later on Saturday is better, but he too seems a little flustered. He keeps trying to decide how many layers to wear at the start. He keeps changing his mind.

Outside the rain is already coming down, so we zip up our rain jackets and, after one more loo stop, we make our way out into the corridor, three rustling explorers heading into the unknown. We take the lift down and walk out into the street to make our way to the start.

A heaving mass of runners is already there, shunting and shuffling to find a position behind the starting arch. Tom pushes right into the middle. He's used to being an elite runner making his way to the front. We both follow. Once we have our space, it's just a matter of waiting.

Overlooking the square is the town hall, with a balcony at every window and people standing on each one watching.

'That's where we got married,' says Tom, pointing at it. Chamonix and running are ingrained in their story. Rachel recalls the time she met Tom in London. 'We were allocated into teams and I was gutted because I wasn't with any of my friends,' she says, smiling at him. 'But there was this randomer there who seemed very excited.' Tom just laughs at the memory. 'After, I didn't remember who he was. I kept asking my friend, "Who is this Tom Payn? He keeps messaging me on Facebook."' For both of them, this moment, standing together at the start of the UTMB, has been a long time coming, and I try not to feel like a gatecrasher as they hold on tightly to each other. But I, too, have been part of their story and Tom pulls me over and we all take a picture together. I'm getting emotional already.

Big screens around the square show the elite runners turning up at the front. They stand like gods among us. There's Jim Walmsley looking serene, already holding his hiking poles like two spears. The camera stops on Kilian Jornet, smiling, relaxed. There's the American Tim Tollefson, joking with Xavier Thévenard. There's Zach, his moustache trimmed, wearing only shorts and a T-shirt despite the rain. He looks edgy, pumped. I spy Sondre standing behind him, towering above everyone. The Nordic king. Each one is like the leader of a planet at an intergalactic summit of super beings. Tom should be there too. He has an elite place, but he is back here with the rest of us, the cannon fodder about to be fed to the mountain. Yet we all have our own stories to write. For Tom, this one is for Rachel. Her dad, back in hospital, will be following her every step online.

As I stand among the crowd, deep down I feel a rising confidence in my body. It all seems so simple. I just have to stay focused on the present moment, be like a monk. The knowledge that this can work, as it did in Italy, feels like a secret weapon. Only my mind can defeat me, and I have learned to control it. It is time to do this.

Right on cue, a man steps onto a large platform above the start with an electric guitar and starts the first screeching, soaring notes of Vangelis's 'Conquest of Paradise', the race anthem. The black clouds swirl about the mountains, as the song builds and guitar riffs meld with thumping classical strains. I feel the stirring, the adrenaline rushing through me, as I stand, alone, among the crowd, facing the mountains, the rain. I am the storm.

Pap. It's a rather muted sound amid everything else, but the starting gun has gone. We're off. At the front, caught a little by surprise, they stutter for a moment on the big screens, before racing off.

We don't go anywhere. It takes time for the movement to filter through. Tom laughs. He has never started this far back in a race before. We fist bump, pat each other on the back, and then slowly, at first at a walk and then a slow jog, we start to move off through the streets of Chamonix, and out into the mountains.

It doesn't take me long to lose Tom and Rachel. I'm letting myself go on the small descents along the relatively flat first eight kilometres, as the race follows the river through the Chamonix valley. I skip past people when I can, but often it's too crowded and I have to slam on the brakes. This feels like it's working my quads, as I stutter and catch my momentum, and is frustrating, as I'm ready to go faster. But it's still early, I tell myself, just roll with it.

The towns and villages are raucous with cowbells and people tipsy on wine cheering us on in a stream of languages. *Allez, allez! . . . Vamos! . . . Gambate! . . . Go on, Finn!* I have my name on my number. It's nice when people pick me out to cheer. I smile back, relaxed. 'Thanks,' I say. I'm not tired, I'm enjoying myself.

The first climb looked small on the map before the race, but it's a long trudge to the top. I pull out my poles and join the steady train of people, single file, just keeping my place in the line. I've finally practised using poles and I can see why most runners in these races carry them. It's like having something to pull on up the steepest climbs, though I fold them away on the descents, where I feel they only get in the way. I'm like a fell runner on the descents, free falling, skipping, loose. I don't need poles.

Every now and then, as we go up, the path winds through some trees or over a false summit, and then rises up more, surprisingly so, steeper and higher and more endlessly than I was anticipating. Each time it's like a weight added to my pack, causing a weakening of my stride.

'Find your strength,' I say to myself, as if some inner Obi Wan Kenobi is speaking to me. It seems to help. I hike on.

Over the top, finally, and then it's four kilometres down to the next checkpoint. It's now getting dark, but I've been waiting for the first big descent to unleash my downhill skills. This is steeper than I was expecting, though – perilously so, especially with the rain. It's all mud and wet grass, tipped up at a dizzying angle. I try to skip and waltz down but I have to keep stopping myself. In the end, I'm no faster than anyone else and it's a relief on my braking quads to get to the bottom.

The hours tick by, short chunks of time that come and go, marked in these early stages by snacks, aid stations, toilet stops. I'm having stomach trouble, which is a little concerning, and I need to keep stopping at every portaloo I can find. I keep wondering whether Tom and Rachel have passed me during one of these stops, or whether they're still behind me. But my dedication to the moment, to staying present, means I'm not tracking anyone on my phone, not myself and not Tom and Rachel. It's just me and the gnarly, rocky path that climbs now into the night.

This second climb is the longest of the race and so for two and a half hours we wind our way in the rain and the dark, up through different landscapes. Each time I think we must be nearing the top, it goes on, up more. At one point I stop to look behind and see a string of lights hung out for miles along the zig-zagging trail, an army of foot soldiers marching to our destruction. Aware of the coming oblivion, we walk in an eerie silence, nobody talking, just the crunching of shoes and the click-clicking of poles in the blackness.

I start to long for the morning, to be able to see again. Then I'll unleash my descending powers. For now I just

don't want to fall, so I continue to brake and swerve on the
next downhill, trashing my legs to hold myself back. The
path is too crowded to let myself go. Stick, don't twist, bide
my time. Patience. Find your strength.

Meanwhile, up at the front, the men's race has started at a
blistering pace. On those first, flattish eight kilometres, it is
Jim Walmsley who takes a commanding lead, running like
a 5K runner, as the rest of the group follows a minute or so
back. Up the first big hill, however, Walmsley is caught by
Kilian Jornet and Zach Miller, the three of them gapping the
rest of the runners behind them. Footage of the race shows
Kilian joking with people along the trail, relaxed, while his
two US rivals stay focused, both pushing hard.

It was interesting before the race to ask these two Americans about their great rival and nemesis Kilian Jornet. In
contrast to Walmsley, who is known for his competitive-
ness, always focused on winning and winning big, Jornet is
famously laid back. If he doesn't win – like the year before
when he was second – he never seems to mind, and is apparently just as happy celebrating his rival's victory. In the press
conference before this year's race, he played down the fact
that he was going for a record fourth win at the UTMB,
saying he just liked to run different types of races. This was
just another day out in the mountains for him.

Walmsley doesn't completely buy it. 'I think he's more

layered than he gives off,' he told me. 'It takes a super-competitive guy to want to keep coming back to do these races, to keep winning them.'

Zach has even developed a theory to explain Jornet's prowess.

'Fitness and strength is like climbing a ladder,' he says. 'The more you do, the more your body can handle, the quicker you can recover, the more you can do . . . and it goes on. But the ladder has rules. You can't miss a rung. Well, only by doping, but we're not doing that. So as I run more in the mountains, I'm getting stronger, and I'm recovering quicker. But Kilian has been on the ladder for years, since he was sixteen.'

Whatever it is, Jornet seems to be cruising in the early stages. As they head down into the town of Courmayeur in Italy before dawn breaks, far, far ahead of me, it's Jim Walmsley who seems to be hurting the most, and who starts dropping back.

Zach later tells me that heading up Col de la Seigne to the pass into Italy, he suddenly noticed that Walmsley had dropped away. 'I said to Kilian, "Where's Jim?" He looked around. "I don't know," he said.'

Getting slower and slower and being passed by others on the way down into Courmayeur, Walmsley spends a full twenty minutes in the aid station there trying to revive. 'I hoped that getting some caffeine in would help, but the race just wasn't coming back,' he later tells *Runner's World* magazine. He ends up heading back out onto the course in about twentieth position and hiking for a few more hours before dropping out.

Meanwhile, another American favourite, Tim Tollefson, who finished third in this race the two previous years, is also hurting after falling and gashing his knee, but he is still pushing on behind the front two, a permanent grimace on his face.

Looking relaxed and gaining ground on the leaders is the Frenchman Xavier Thévenard, who has won the UTMB twice before. He was recently leading the Hardrock 100 in the US, when he was disqualified after 91 miles when someone on the course handed him some water. It seemed a harsh penalty and there was talk of Thévenard being even more determined to do well here as a result. Pumped up to beat the Americans, perhaps. In interviews before the race, he didn't want to say too much, but it was clear he was still upset to have been disqualified.

Dawn breaks, for me, on the descent to Lac Combal, 13km before Courmayeur. By now it has stopped raining and the trail seems drier, so I finally start making some ground on the way down, relaxing and skipping past people. Overtaking people gives me energy, and by the time I reach the aid station I feel like I've moved into another part of the race. Rather than being stuck in a long procession, here there are fewer runners and they seem somehow faster. Nobody lingers at the aid station, we just grab at the food, stuffing it into our mouths like hungry gerbils. I don't realise it at the time, but I've moved into the top 1,000, of the 2,500 starters, and I'm gaining places rapidly as people ahead of me drop out of the race.

From here it's a relatively short hike up, before a long, steep descent down to Courmayeur and the halfway point. Tom and Rachel, aiming to run the whole thing in around 34 hours, said they planned to reach Courmayeur by midday. It's still not yet 7 a.m. I start doing the maths. Bloody hell, I'm well ahead of schedule. I whip out my poles. That sub-30-hour time is on. I quicken my step up the slope, Mont Blanc emerging into the cold morning light behind me, its huge glaciers suspended, half falling, its rocky outcrops like the turrets of a huge castle. But I'm eating up the ground. I take your mountains, I chew them up and I spit them out.

One of my poles won't open, however. They're collapsible, and need to be opened with a firm yank, but one of them just won't work. I pull at it again and again to no avail. But I'm in full action hero mode. It doesn't matter, I'll just use one. I shove the broken one back in my bag and march on. Nothing can stop me.

It's actually OK with one pole. It still helps. In fact, I quite like it. I feel like a shepherd, striding across the mountains. This is just what I do. I look at these ultra runners, with their two poles, struggling up the hills, desperately racing on towards some arbitrary goal. I pity them and their strange behaviour.

It's a daydream that keeps me moving, but it makes me realise that I'm still not completely comfortable with this whole world of ultra racing, with all its paraphernalia. I still have the lingering sense that it's all too complicated, too removed from the pure simplicity of just running, from the freedom of not caring about anything but the movement, racing from point A to point B as fast as my legs will carry me.

I live out my shepherd fantasy all the way to the top. Then, with the sun fully out and the trail dry, the warmth on my back and the wind in my sails, I fly down to Courmayeur.

Shortly before the bottom, before the last, steepest section, is an aid station, where a rock band are in full flow, at 8 o'clock in the morning. I have a plan to meet Marietta and the children at a place called Champex Lac at 5 p.m. It's only 35km away. I call her up.

'Hey, I'm flying around,' I say when she answers. I can hear the excitement, the energy in my voice. 'I'm three hours ahead of schedule. You'd better get to Champex Lac a bit earlier or you'll miss me.'

'You sound great,' she says. 'I hope you're not pushing too hard.'

'No, I'm fine. Another downhill coming up, so I better go. This is my speciality. See you soon!' And with that, I race on.

The final section into Courmayeur is one of the steepest, most technical on the course, twisting through trees with roots spiralling all over the trail, creating big steps. It's dry and dusty but I'm like the Dukes of Hazzard now, leaping and hooting along. I can't help thinking that perhaps I'm overdoing it, but when I try to control my pace a little and put the brakes on, it feels much harder on my legs. Those braking muscles are tired from the early part of the race, so I find it better to let go and move more quickly. People talk of trashing your quads in a race like this. 'If you do it right,' Joe Kelly tells me, 'your quads shouldn't come in to it. They only get trashed if you're braking.'

So I roll, skip and run the descents, rather than brake. As the fell runners in the Lake District say, 'Brakes off, brain off.' They're right, it's faster and easier.

And so I breeze into halfway at Courmayeur in 15 hours. I have a drop bag here waiting for me. A fresh T-shirt, socks and shoes. I plan to be quick. One more loo stop. My stomach seems to be feeling a little better. I'm smiling and high-fiving people. So far, I think, so bloody good.

Drama is unfolding at the front of the men's race, meanwhile. Kilian Jornet has dropped out. The story that comes out is that he got stung by a bee a few hours before the race and had an allergic reaction. Wary of using anything that may include a banned substance, his team doctor uses a medicine he has never taken before. After the race he says he felt fine until after Courmayeur, but when he was heading up the hill after the aid station he began to get a heavy allergic reaction, saying it was difficult to breathe, and that he felt chest pains and nausea. In the end he said he felt it was dangerous to carry on and he decided to pull out.

With the two titans gone, Zach is left out in front and pushing hard in his inimitable style, grunting and breathing hard the whole way. After crossing over the highest point of the course, however, he is caught by Thévenard, and then from the aid station in La Fouly until Champex Lac the two of them run side by side, one pushing and then the other.

'In hindsight, I got excited and pushed too hard,' Zach tells me later, sitting outside a bar in Chamonix late on Sunday night. It was his third attempt at the UTMB, and despite everything he says he felt better this time than in his previous attempts. But in dramatic footage of the two of them racing up to Champex Lac, the contrast is stark – Zach is running hard while Thévenard seems to glide along easily, biding his time, letting Zach lead if he wants.

Sitting in the aid station at Champex Lac, Zach looks destroyed while Thévenard, standing at the next table, is a picture of calm efficiency, drinking, changing his top. Zach keeps glancing over at him with a bemused look on his face. He comes out of the aid station stumbling and lopsided, as Thévenard races away in the lead. Over the next few hours an injury in Zach's lower leg, which he says had been manageable up until then, starts to hurt more and more until eventually he has to stop. He ends up being helicoptered off the mountain.

'I didn't want to be taken down by helicopter,' he says ruefully. 'It felt unnecessary. I mean, I could still walk. Tim didn't want that either.' Tim Tollefson is also evacuated, after falling again. It's carnage up at the front, with Thévenard the only one of the main contenders left running.

Hillary Allen, who was crewing for Zach, tells me later: 'He really believed he was going to win. And I believed he was going to win, especially how the first half played out. He runs with so much heart and passion, but I think his passion got the better of him and he pushed too early.'

She says he was confused when he came into the aid station at Champex Lac. He was cramping, couldn't eat and could hardly run. 'I think he knew then that his race was over.'

All this carnage is playing into the hands of Damian Hall, who is playing his usual game of moving steadily but surely through the field. By 9 a.m. he's up to seventh place and still moving well, joking with everyone who tries to film him, offering them chips, drinking cups of tea, saying how much he loves this 'British' weather, Phil Collins and Kate Bush going around and around in his headphones.

I feel tired and stiff coming out of Courmayeur. I sat down for too long. It was hard to find a place on the long benches and I ended up opposite an English guy called Martin who recognised me. He had once been to a talk I'd given about ekiden running at the Japanese Society in London. He tells me that the year before he pulled out of the race at Champex Lac after he cut his ankle and it became infected. So he is back to finish what he started. It is a common story, people who don't finish and feel compelled to return, who refuse to be defeated by the race. After the dust has settled, the regrets begin to bubble to the surface. *I should have started slower, I should have eaten more.* The reasons for not finishing are rationalised, and in the cold light of day it begins to look simple to fix. The memories of the pain and struggle, the torment of the mind, the doubts, the despair, are all forgotten. *Next time I'll drink more, I'll pace myself better.* For Martin it was his head torch. Last year his torch had been too dim and he had fallen. In any case, he seems within himself this time. When I arrive he tells me he has already been sitting in the aid station for an hour.

'I should go,' he says. 'I don't know why I'm still here.'

'Well, you're making good time,' I say. 'Halfway already.'

He looks at me.

'But it's not really halfway,' he says. 'I mean, they call it halfway, but it's only 80km.'

It's like a punch in the gut. I try to stay calm, but I'm suddenly fretting. The minutes are ticking by as I sit here in this sports hall. I've got a cup of soup, but it's too hot to drink. People sit around me on all sides, changing socks, rummaging through bags. I need to move. So the halfway point is another 5km away. And it's all uphill. It may be close to midday – Tom and Rachel's halfway target – by the time I get there after all.

The hill out of Courmayeur is steep, and for the first time in the race I'm feeling a real, sinking tiredness. I keep getting flashbacks to the races in Lavaredo and the south of France, but always the worst bits, the stretches that seemed to go on for ever. My mind is scattered; my monk-like focus gone. I remember Sondre saying his big problem is that he always thinks about the finish too soon. At the time, sitting in the café in Chamonix, I asked him why that was a problem. Didn't thoughts of the finish spur him on? He couldn't quite explain why it was an issue. But now I can see why. I keep thinking of the finish, but it's not a good thought, because it is still so far away, and the distance remaining looms up, rising like an insurmountable storm, its spiky winds pushing you back, making you want to pull your coat tighter and sit down.

In essence it is the same old problem: it takes you out of the moment. I need to re-focus. I try plugging myself in to some music, but it's just another thing to deal with, so I put my headphones away and walk on.

A few tough hours later I arrive at the aid station in Arnouvaz, 95km in to the race and the beginning of the steep climb up to the highest point on the course, the fabled Grand Col Ferret. As I make my way into the large white tent for my periodic food grab, one of the marshals holds his hand up.

'Finn, long leggings are mandatory from here. It is very cold at the top. Minus 10.'

Coming down into Arnouvaz I kept glancing up at the towering mountains ahead, disappearing into black clouds that seethed angrily, rushing over the rocky outcrops. The thought of heading up there, in -10°C, is daunting. But I have to accept it and keep moving.

The tent is a hive of people pulling on leggings, water-proof jackets, hats. I put on everything I have and head back out, following the line of tiny humans making their way up, up until they're just dots of colour disappearing into the clouds. It's hard to believe my legs can carry me all that way up, but I start slowly, steadily, one trudge at a time. It takes forever.

Occasionally I get a burst of energy, my steps quicken and I pass people by taking the steeper, less trodden part of the trail. But it doesn't last.

At the top we enter the clouds, which bluster and fret around us. The wind seems intent on pushing me over the sheer drop in front of me. I'm glad I'm not up here at night, where the edge to certain death would be less visible. I push back against the wind and cross over the ridge to the summit, where a man inexplicably sits in a glass box. I'm thirsty, so I mime drinking to him and he steps out with a bottle of water. I thank him before starting on my way back down the other side.

My descending legs are weary now, whether I let myself roll or not, though I still make some progress. But it is another hour before I arrive at the village of La Fouly down in the valley. It's 6 p.m. I've now been moving for 24 hours. I try running the last flat section of road into the aid station, but nothing happens. A fuse has blown, my legs have shattered. I can barely walk.

The aid station is a small, crowded barn with a few benches and tables. I struggle in and find a seat.

'Hello.'

I look up. I'm sitting next to Martin again.

'I can't seem to leave these places,' he says. He seems a little spaced out. I sink into my seat. The urgency I had at the other aid stations has gone. I just want to stop. To lie down.

'The good thing,' says Martin, 'is that we're well ahead of the cut-off.'

I look at the sign on the wall. In five hours, the course here will be closed and anyone not already through will be disqualified. Until now cut-offs have not entered my thoughts. The final cut-off, at the finish, is 46.5 hours. I plan to have eaten, slept, recovered, played chess with my son, Ossian, and bought a dozen ice creams by then. Why is he talking about cut-offs? But the more I think about it, the more I realise how far I'm slipping from my 30-hour goal.

'Oh, it's raining again,' says Martin, staring out of the barn door. I look outside to see grey sheets across the sky. I give a little shudder. I still have over 70km to go. On the map it's three big climbs. I ask Martin what they're like.

'Yeah, not good. Pretty tough,' he says. 'Some of the worst of the race. I better go.' And with that he stands up.

'Go,' I say, trying to muster some enthusiasm. 'Go get it!'

As he leaves, I feel broken. A big screen has been erected in the barn and is playing recorded goodwill messages at high volume. Mothers and small children on white sofas, whooping and giggling in French or Italian. I need to sleep. I remember Gary Gellin saying that it's the lack of sleep that kills you. Even a two-minute power nap can help. A few Japanese runners are asleep sitting at the tables, their heads on their bags. I hoist mine onto the table and lay my head on it.

The barn jumps and crackles with noise. I open my eyes. I can't sleep. But I can't move either. A runner is standing nearby, talking loudly in Russian to his wife. She seems annoyed. An official comes over, a boy of about sixteen, and tries to tell her she can't be in here.

'I'm finished. I stop,' says the Russian man. His wife scowls.

'You want to abandon?' The boy asks, a little confused.

I stare at it all like a child, too tired to look away. But the idea lodges like a rock in my head. I'm going to pull out. The thought is delicious. I can end this now, pull the escape cord. It's so easy.

The Russian man has unpinned his number and handed it to the boy. His wife looks disgusted, but he just shrugs. I know how he feels. Who cares? You get to a point where only you can decide. I think of something Lazarus Lake says in the film about the Barkley Marathons, after most of the runners have dropped out. 'Everyone,' he says, 'after a certain point, has his own definition of success or failure.'

I have run eight ultras in eighteen months. I finished every one. I can DNF – not finish – one. That's OK. I realise I haven't moved in nearly an hour. I pull out my phone to call Marietta. She must have been waiting with the children at Champex Lac for hours. I wonder if they are still there. I imagine the children got bored, fractious, and she had to take them back to Chamonix. To think that I called her this morning to tell her to get there early. I might be there by 1 p.m., I said. It's now almost 7 p.m. and I'm still 14km away. But the phone won't call. I'm in Switzerland. It isn't part of the EU so doesn't take part in the free roaming system for making calls. My phone tells me I need to download an app and then alter my settings. I put it back in my pocket. I try to think. It's 14km, but mostly a gentle downhill, to Champex Lac. I can do that walking in three hours. And then I can stop. It can end there, this adventure in ultra running, at dusk, by the shores of the lake with my beautiful family. It will be a more fitting ending than this. If I can make it to 120km, that's a good effort. I can't always be the hero. That's just not me. I don't need to prove anything to anyone. I remember when Govinda stopped his Ring of Fire FKT attempt. 'I know who I am,' he said. Yes, I won't be defined by this. It's just a race. I'm still the same person whether I finish or not.

So I haul myself up off the bench and pull my bag back on. It's just 14km. Let's go.

I feel a surge of heroism as I walk back out into the race. A few people give me a clap. 'Bravo!' they say. They don't know I'm only doing 14km more.

Two minutes along the road I nearly turn back. Suddenly even walking – and the thought of walking that far – is too much. They'll drive me to Champex Lac, I think. Someone will.

But the rain has stopped. A few more people clap. Somehow I turn myself back to face the right way and carry on.

I know Marietta will try to get me to keep going. She will remind me of the time I revived in Tooting when I felt this bad. By the end of that I was sprinting. I said that day that I would never again accept that I was finished, that I couldn't revive. *But*, I say, to her, to myself, but, but, but . . . it's a big difference reviving on a track in London, or on the coast path in Anglesey, where it also happened, or in the last 10 miles in the coastal hills of California. Here I still have 70km to go, in huge mountains, heading into a second night without sleep, in freezing temperatures. I remember hallucinating in the south of France on a second night. I've been there before. I don't need to go there again. The thought of it frightens me. What if I walk off the side of the mountain?

I try not to think about it, but I once read a book about a man training to run a big ultra marathon. At the end of the book, he does the race, but he drops out. He's not injured, or dead, his mind just can't go on. I read that and I thought it was such a let-down. How can you write a book about this, and take me on this journey, and then just stop? It made me mad. I always knew my book wouldn't end like that. But, readers, I'm sorry. I'm so tired. My legs are broken. You understand, I hope. Over 40 miles at night in these mountains, it's just not safe. As I walk, I'm sorry to say, but my only thought is, who cares? It's just a damn book. My safety is too important. I'm sorry.

As I continue along the beautiful Ferret valley, I stumble on a tree root and my legs almost buckle under me. It confirms everything. Every step down is now killing my shattered quads. And this is a gentle slope. I think about stumbling on a steep descent, at night. It's irresponsible. I have no choice but to quit.

For a moment I wonder if I'm just being negative, letting my mind control me, letting my doubts weaken me. 'Find your strength,' I tell myself, and I begin to run. Forget the 70km ahead, forget the night, just be here, now. For a few moments the legs ease. I'm running. Oh, maybe. Just maybe.

I run on. But no, the tiredness is too overwhelming. This is not an invented pain. I truly am exhausted. The mind may impose limits, but at some point you must hit an actual limit. I'm standing right at the edge of endurance. I've come to the cliff, to the end of the road. It has been an amazing ride, but this is where it ends.

And so it is decided. I'm 100 per cent certain. I'm stopping at Champex Lac. I can't see how Marietta can argue. She doesn't want me to kill myself. It's just not worth it.

The people moving around me seem just as tired and I get in a little group to hike the last few miles up to the aid station, which is perched on a shelf a little way up the next mountain. Knowing it is the end of my race, I find some strength to push on, but I begin to feel sorry for the people around me. Surely they'll all be dropping out here too. They won't finish until late tomorrow morning if they carry on. Surely they can't face that? I'm convinced they will all stop. To go on is madness. I stumble again on another root. See, I say to myself.

Like every climb in this god-forsaken race, this one goes on further than I'm expecting. I keep seeing buildings emerging out of the trees in the fading light. But they're not buildings at all. Just more trees and rocks.

Eventually we emerge onto a tarmac road. There they are: Marietta, my daughter Uma, and Ossian, standing by the roadside. I raise my arms in the air. This is my finish. 'Yeah!' I yell. 'At last!'

They stare back at me in silence. What's wrong?

It's not them. It's three women, wondering what I'm doing.

'Sorry, I thought you were someone else,' I say, trying not to break down.

'Adharanand!' comes a shout. Is it real? Yes, it's Marietta with Ossian. I struggle over. They take me by the arm, one on each side.

'I'm stopping here,' I say, choking up. 'I can't go on.'

'You're doing brilliant, Daddy,' says Ossian. I look down at him. That's a kind thing to say.

'I'm not,' I say. 'I'm too tired. My legs have gone.'

'Let's just get to the aid station,' says Marietta, cajoling me. 'Get something to eat.'

'No, you don't understand. This is not like before.' I tell

her this is not like the track in London. This is dangerous. But she leads me into the aid station and sits me down and goes off to find the girls.

I look at the guy sitting beside me. It's Martin.

'Hello!'

'Hey, how are you doing?'

'I'm going to stop,' I tell him. 'I can barely walk.'

'Are you injured?'

'No. But my quads are blown. Completely blown. I can barely take a single step down.' This isn't quite true, I know. But almost. He looks more spaced out than ever, just staring at me.

'Yes, it's hard,' he says. 'But . . .' he hesitates, looking at me. 'It's just, you don't want to wake up tomorrow and think: "I could have continued."'

'No, honestly, I won't.' I don't think I'll ever forget this pain. 'I'm completely done.'

He nods, sympathetic. 'Yes, well, if that's the case.'

Marietta appears. 'Come and see the children,' she says, and leads me off.

Champex Lac aid station is a huge marquee with rows and rows of benches. It's a bustling, tense, post-apocalyptic dining hall, and there in the middle of it all, in the family section, are the three lights of my life.

I hobble over to them and they all hug me tightly. They keep telling me how well I'm doing, as we find a space to sit down. Uma strokes my arm, not letting it go. Ossian hugs me again.

'You can do it, Daddy,' Uma says.

'I can't,' I say, shaking my head, trying not to cry.

'You can,' says Ossian. 'We know you can.'

And I can't stop it, the tears. I'm sobbing.

'It's OK to stop sometimes,' I say. 'Sometimes you can't do things, and that's OK.'

I see the people opposite, watching us, touched by Uma and Ossian's affection. Uma hugs me tighter.

'It's OK,' she says, comforting me. 'You're doing amazing.'

Marietta is suggesting coffee, soup, anything. But it's over. Nothing can help.

'You could have a sleep and see how you feel after. They have beds here.'

It's already so late. 'I'll just get even more stiff if I sleep,' I say. 'The only thing that could possibly help is a massage.'

Even as I say it, I realise I've given them a chink of false hope. Marietta is off looking to see if there is a massage tent. But there are still 40 miles left of this crazy race, in the freezing night, hallucinating, alone on the mountain. It scares me, and a massage won't fix that. It's no good, it's over.

Lila, my eldest, who is fourteen, has been sitting quietly not saying anything since I first arrived. I imagine she is on my side, that she finds the whole thing ridiculous and just wants to get out of here and back to Chamonix.

'What do you think, Lila?'

She looks at me, measuring her words.

'What about Tom and Rachel?' she says. 'They should be here soon. You could run with them.'

Tom and Rachel. I've forgotten all about them. Are they still going? Something deep down flickers. I take a breath. It's an option I hadn't considered. Trust Lila, always thinking differently. With Tom and Rachel it would be safer. But are they still going? Marietta is back. She has found a massage tent. She says Tom and Rachel were about 30 minutes behind me the last time she checked. They should be arriving at any moment. She pulls me up and leads me to the massage tent. Inside, I lie back gingerly on a stretcher as the physio presses and rubs my dead quads, calling another physio over to help, one on each leg, the white lights of the medical tent spinning even when I close my eyes.

I open them to see Tom Payn standing over me. He looks wild, like a lion. He grabs my hand, holding it.

'We're going to do this,' he says. I can feel such power, such a surge of energy rushing into me as he continues to hold my hand.

'You can run with us. We'll do it together.'

Tom has run this route before. He knows what he's doing. I'll be safe with him. Oh god, what am I thinking? Am I really going to head back out, over the edge?

Tom has gone. Marietta is back, looking at me kindly, waiting to hear me say it. The massage is done. I stand up. My legs definitely feel better.

'OK,' I say. 'I'll carry on.'

Long before I even reach Champex Lac, the race leaders are home and dry, washed, showered and enjoying dinner in Chamonix. After Zach drops out, Xavier Thévenard has a clear run to the finish, taking his third UTMB title. Just before the finish line he turns and pours a little water on his head in reference to his disqualification at Hardrock. He's a quietly spoken man who looks about fourteen, but he's a fierce competitor who has made a point with this victory.

'As if a little water can affect the result of a 100-mile race,' he says afterwards. But it is all forgotten now as he basks in being the toast of Chamonix.

A few hours back, the irrepressible Damian Hall keeps his brisk shuffle going, moving through the field to finish fifth in 22 hours. The underdog has fulfilled his dream. The former journalist, who only started ultra running in his late thirties to write about it, is suddenly swanning around in the upper stratosphere of the sport. I may imagine it, but the next day as he does the interview rounds, he seems to have replaced a little of his self-effacing Englishness with some ultra star swagger. His trucker cap seems to fit him better than ever.

Meanwhile, our little three-person expedition is heading back out into the second night, joking and laughing, forgetting the task ahead of us, finding strength in each other.

Together we head up into the dark mountains. We ebb and flow, all waiting when one of us needs to stop, Rachel even sleeping for five minutes on the trail at one point, her head resting on a flat rock. Tom sets his alarm and we both sit and wait.

The path is longer and steeper even than I had feared and my legs whimper with every step, but Tom cajoles and encourages us, even though the lack of sleep is taking its toll on him too.

We both keep having the same hallucinations. We keep seeing buildings everywhere; small huts, chalets, tents, even telephone boxes. Each time one appears, I think: 'What's that doing there?' It seems unlikely, up here on the mountain. But it looks so real.

Every time, a few steps from being able to touch it, I get the same dawning realisation that it's not actually there. The odd thing is that after I realise it's a hallucination, and it's not a building, I can't work out what it actually is. Each time, it seems to warp first into the gnarled, mangled shell of a building. As I go by I reach out and touch it and only then realise that it's a rock or a tree. But it still looks strange.

A few hours later, on the descent to the next big aid station, I find myself dropping back more and more, going slower and slower. I feel like I'm holding Tom and Rachel up, so I tell them to go on. They've saved me, I can make it now. The crisis has passed. All my thoughts of stopping have gone. I'm resigned to a slow, weary plod that I'm sure will get me there eventually. I know Rachel's dad is following online in Australia, that she wants to make him proud.

My own parents, it turns out, are at a party in Brighton back in England and have everyone there logging on to their phones to follow my progress. People who have never heard of the UTMB or ultra running are suddenly obsessing about a dot on a screen. I hear that they all cheer and yell out each time I make it to the next checkpoint, toasting my progress with beer and wine.

Tom and Rachel agree to forge on ahead. I watch them disappear, and I'm alone again, climbing in the dark. It's crazily steep now. One of the hardest climbs of the race. But I'm past being defeated. My whole existence is focused on just moving. This is the pain cave, this is where ultra runners look to go, to dig, hoping to find out what they're made of. I'm made of a slow, grinding movement, weightless, thoughtless. Time has ceased to exist, to matter. I dig slowly, not looking for anything, just knowing that I must carry on. It's strangely peaceful.

Up, up I go, slow steps, stabbing the earth with my poles – the broken one started working again – like a tired, wounded beast close to death. But still I go on, something in me refusing to lie down and die.

Somewhere halfway up the mountain I decide to sit for a moment on a rock to get my breath back. I'm mindful not to delay too long. Tiredness, coldness, stiffness, I'm holding them all at bay through my movement.

In the silence, from deep in the blackness, comes a scratching sound. I see lights, legs, moving closer, switching slowly back and forth, one behind the other. They come by me like a train of ghouls, five men, hauling themselves up step by step. One of them beckons me to join them. It's a simple gesture, a quick wave of the hand. He has no energy to do more. *Join us*, it says. *Save yourself.*

And so I pull myself up and tag along, following their

rhythm. At the top we emerge out of the trees to the breaking dawn of the third day. The mountains reveal themselves tall and majestic, basking in blueness, mist snaking through the valleys below. The mountains seem gentler today, the clear sky calm. The storm, it seems, has passed.

On the path down I manage to move, not fast, but not broken either. Pained jumps, skips, trying to put weight into the poles, to save my legs. Down onto a stony road, into more forest. As I move gingerly through the trees, I come across a dejected figure sitting on a rock by the trail, leaning on his poles. It's Martin.

'Hey,' I say. He looks at me, confused.

'Oh, you're still going,' he says.

His shin is causing him a lot of pain and he says he's struggling to move. He must be if I'm catching him. I can't see how I can help. 'Go on,' he says. 'I'll make it.'

It gets warmer as we descend into the valley. The sound of cowbells and people cheering reaches us through the trees. The aid station is getting close. But never as close as you think. It's always further. Another climb down, another road to follow. Always more until you start to despair. Then more again. Until you give up hoping. And then you arrive.

Vallorcine is the last big aid station. It's 19km from here to the finish. I walk in, a zombie, looking around. It's now almost 8 a.m. and I've been in this race for almost 38 hours. And there, sitting on the floor, in front of an air heater, are Tom and Rachel. They look shaky and disoriented.

'Wasn't that last road the worst bit?' says Rachel. 'It was horrible.'

I don't know what bit she means. It has all been the same, up and down. But her legs have gone, blown. This is how I felt at La Fouly. But now we only have one more climb. She will make it. Her dad is watching. We regroup one last time and go again.

It's another five hours before we step onto the road back in Chamonix. Rachel is even more beat up than me now, but we've come too far, we're a team, we're going to make it together. We run three abreast through the town, actually running. I feel strangely easy. Not fast, but it's easy to run, to talk. It's like I'm just jogging along watching myself.

As we enter the final section, the streets are full of people cheering. I'm a little embarrassed to have taken so long, but the crowd are a joyous celebration. The closer we get to the finish, the louder it gets. We're grinning at each other. Over 22 hours since the winner arrived, the crowds are still cheering. It's overwhelming.

And then I spot them, Uma and Ossian, waiting for me.

'Come, come,' I call to them. My team. Ossian grabs my hand, and Uma runs at the other end, next to Tom. We all link hands, the five of us, and run through what is now a tunnel of noise. It's like we've won.

And then there it is, the finish. We lift our arms and cross the line. We've done it. From the depths of the abyss, we've made it out alive. Marietta is there. Lila. Friends of Tom and Rachel. We're dissolved into hugs, smiles, photographs. After all that, somehow, it's over. We don't have to run any more. There is nowhere left to go. We are there.

19

Later that afternoon, after sitting with Tom and Rachel and drinking a beer on the grass behind the finish, none of us saying much, but soaking up the afternoon, the people milling around, runners crossing the line still, each having his own moment with the crowd, we go back to the campsite. I'm walking around in a dream, still hallucinating, much to Ossian's amusement. I gently pull him away from a cow as we walk back from the bathroom block. 'What cow?' he says, shaking his head and looking to see if I'm serious. When he sees his sisters he shouts across the campsite: 'Hey! Daddy's still hallucinating.' Then he looks at me again. 'What can you see now?'

In the showers, I heard someone come in, enter one of the other cubicles and turn on a radio. I stood there listening, half shivering, the shower not nearly as warm and engulfing as I hoped it would be. It struck me as odd that someone would bring a radio into the shower on a campsite. It was playing the Bee Gees, but after a while I noticed it was the same song playing over and over. Not only the same song, but the same part of the song. I listened closer, trying to hear the words. Closer and closer, until I realised that it wasn't the Bee Gees at all, it was just the sound of the water in the shower.

I remember Kieran Alger telling me that after he had dropped out of the Lavaredo ultra in Italy, he stood in his hotel brushing his teeth and thought then that he could have done it. If only he had kept going. The memory of the pain dissolves so quickly.

Marietta had said as much to me at that last aid station at Champex Lac where I saw them all. You'll regret it if you drop out, she said.

I really won't, I thought. I'll know it was impossible. I'll remember how broken I was. It seemed so cut and dried in that moment.

But, yes, I would have regretted it almost instantly. Getting into bed that night I would have known deep down that I could have carried on. I wasn't injured. I wasn't sick. I would have felt terrible lying there knowing that people were still out on the mountain. Knowing that Tom and Rachel were still going. That Martin, dazed and confused, was still struggling along, getting stuck in the aid stations, but still in the race. He made it in the end, finishing in forty-five and a half hours.

Looking back, my demise came on suddenly. At La Fouly, where the Russian man dropped out and gave me the idea, I was actually still moving through the field and was in my highest position – around 800th – of the whole race. But everything somehow turned there. My mind, catching me with my guard down, moved in with a quick one-two. All the braking early on, because of the crowded trail, had killed my quads. In Lavaredo I could run freely, so that didn't happen. But here I had no chance. And I still had over 70km to go. It was too much on trashed legs.

The talk of the cut-offs knocked me further off balance. It was the clock again weakening me. Taking me away from the present moment. But the killer punch was the second night, the danger, the risk of death. It all seems so dramatic looking back now, but my mind knew I was too hardened to be floored by subtle, light jabs. It had to go straight for the knockout blow: death!

Weeks later, we joke about it. The children mock me about how I was wailing: 'I'm going to die!' But it's with kindness. They also know it was no easy thing to carry on. The 70 kilometres still remaining were an ocean.

It was only when Tom arrived, with his little rowing boat, that it seemed possible. I hadn't expected this whole experience to teach me so much about the power of friends, of people, of companionship.

From the depths of La Fouly, I sent a text to my family: 'Guys, I'm still three hours away at least, can barely move. Not sure what to do. I'm at an aid station called La Fouly. Think I might sleep for five minutes. Phone running out. Help!!'

The message was never delivered.

Reading it back, this is a man alone and struggling. In need of help. It came at the next stop, luckily, but it makes me think back to the Ring O' Fire when I struggled around on my own. If I had to pick a lowest point in my whole ultra running journey, it would be the end of that second day in Anglesey when I crawled fully clothed into my sleeping bag and spent the night shivering and aching under a pile of village hall tables. Not because that was my most difficult moment, or the point where I was most in pain, but because I had to face it alone.

Humans are social animals and it was something primal and fundamental to feel scared and weak on my own, but to draw strength from Tom and Rachel, and from the love and kindness of my family. 'You can run with us. We'll do it together,' Tom had said. That was the moment that dragged me back from the brink. It seemed to fill me with strength. Everything felt safe. The wolves wouldn't attack if we ran together in a pack.

A few weeks after the UTMB, I catch up with fifth-place finisher Damian Hall. I ask him if life has changed, now he's officially one of the world's best ultra runners. He laughs. 'Well, I did get interviewed by the *Wiltshire Gazette*,' he says.

He mentions the fact that a few sponsors have made quiet approaches, but he's not expecting a life-changing offer, and he's happy to continue as the plucky part-timer.

I ask him if he had any slumps or mental battles during the race. For some reason, I imagine him serenely running through the day and night, cruising along happily without incident. He was only running for 22 hours after all. But of course, a 100-mile race is never going to be without incident.

He says he started harder than in his previous three UTMB races, and thought he was doing well when someone in the crowd told him he was in about thirtieth position.

'My French isn't very good, so I may have heard it wrong,' he says. 'But I thought I was around fifteenth, so that knocked me for a bit. I was in a slump for about an hour after that.'

Later, revived, he passed a struggling Jim Walmsley coming down into Courmayeur just before the halfway point. 'He even stood aside to let me pass,' says Damian, betraying how in awe he was of the American, even as he was overtaking him. 'That was exciting. It really spurred me on.'

Near the end, he caught up with another of his heroes, Zach Miller. 'I'd actually bumped into Zach a few days before in a cable car,' he says. 'It was funny, because we were both being followed around by film crews.'

He said he passed Zach walking up a hill. 'I don't think he recognised me,' he says. 'His eyes were glazed and he was talking about stopping. Normally I would encourage someone, even a rival,' but he looked so bad I thought, "Yeah, you're not safe up here."'

I ask Damian about his run of results: thirty-first, nineteenth, twelfth and now fifth. Can he do even better? Will he be back?

He says he doesn't know, though he certainly won't be back next year as he has promised his wife he will skip it. 'This has been a difficult year for my family,' he says. 'I sacrificed a lot. I missed friends' weddings, my dad's seventieth birthday. But I don't have this thing nagging at me any more. I could happily never run again and be content with what I've achieved.

'It shows, though, that if you obsess about something, if you really work at it, and do everything you can, you can achieve it. There's something very satisfying about that.'

Among the other runners I knew in the race, Sondre

Amdahl, Elisabet's partner, and Magda Boulet from California, also dropped out. It's a race that can eat even the best alive.

One man who seems unstoppable is the British soldier Tom Evans. He was doing the shorter CCC race, but it was still an extremely competitive field, and he came home in first place, passing the Chinese runner Min Qi on the last descent. Hoka will be rushing to offer him a new, improved deal, I'm sure.

And so it's home to Devon and the end of this two-year journey into ultra running. The first question people always ask me is whether I plan to carry on and do another one. Right after I finished the UTMB – or rather somewhere on the path between La Fouly and Champex Lac – I would have rather cut off my hand than agree to run another ultra marathon. But perhaps in the same way women forget the pain of childbirth, the pain of a race soon dissipates. Even up each hill it happens. Every long climb seems to go on for ever, getting tougher and tougher until I'm thinking this is insane, stupid – and still it goes on. But as soon as you're over the top and moving down the other side, if you look back, you think: 'It wasn't that bad, actually.'

So, a day or two after the UTMB, I'm thinking maybe I could do another ultra. Not 100 miles, but perhaps a shorter one. Some people forget even quicker. Rachel says she is already looking for another 100-mile race, looking to gather the points for the UTMB next year. What about the pain? I ask her. Do you really want to go through that again?

'I don't see it as suffering,' she says. 'For me the experience of an ultra doesn't even begin until about 80km. At the start I have too much energy, but when I get tired, everything melts away and it's just me and the running. That's what I love about ultras, the feeling of the breath, the movement, experiencing the world on your feet. It's empowering.'

It reminds me of the marathon monks of Mount Hiei in Japan who run a thousand marathons in a thousand days.

'The idea behind the constant movement,' one of the monks explained to me, 'is to exhaust the mind, the ego, the body, everything, until nothing is left. Then something, pop,' (and he mimes a bubble popping) 'something comes up to fill the space.'

This something, he says, 'is the vast consciousness that lies below the surface of our lives, beyond the limits of our usual, everyday experience. A sense of oneness,' he says, 'with the universe.'

After the dawn broke on the second day, I did begin to experience a sense of peace, a oneness with the world. I felt then as if I could go on for ever. The pressing call of the watch, the need to get to Chamonix by a certain time, was gone, and all that existed was the present moment, the sound of my feet on the ground, the quiet murmur of the mountains. On the last day, safe in the knowledge that I was going to make it, I relaxed, and it really was, for those last 15 miles or so, a wonderful, joyful experience.

In the end, ultra running is not simply running a long

way. In some ways it is not even running. A few days after the UTMB I see the footage of Zach Miller and Xavier Thévenard at Champex Lac, sitting side by side in the aid station, 75 miles into the race. The intensity in their faces is incredible. People are talking to them, helping them with their bags, but they are somewhere else. I was the same at that point. In an ultra marathon, and particularly one of 100 miles or more, you get to a place, a state, that you never go to in the rest of your life. A tiredness so extreme that you're now just surviving, trying to stay alive. Of course, you have a get-out, you know you can stop, but to keep going, you are faced with an extreme reality.

Most of the time we exist in a constructed world where everything is designed to keep us comfortable, keep us away from the rawness of life. But we evolved to exist in an environment that would often be tough, difficult, danger-ous, and deep down I think we long for a connection to that ancestral existence. In his book *Feral*, George Monbiot talks of how in the modern world we have become cut off from our nature, but that inside we have a deeply buried need to experience the wildness of life. He describes hunt-ing fish with a spear, and carrying a dead deer he found by a river, carrying it slung across his back. He says in both cases it awoke a 'genetic memory' in him, a feeling of his wild instincts coming alive, and he says it made him want to roar.

This is being human, and it brings an intense feeling of existing, which in the rest of life we rarely glimpse. Usually we're caught up dealing with practicalities, navigating the world we have built around us, with all its roles, its relationships and its entertainments, its sideshows for the mind. But after 24 hours in the mountains, these things cease to exist. The whole task of life becomes simple and singular: just get to the finish. Keep moving, nothing else. Here the only distraction for the mind is the watch. And it doesn't help. That's why I stop it.

I remember when I first began thinking about ultra running and I started looking at races to enter. I wanted the outcome, not the process. I wanted to be that person arriving triumphant at the finish, arms raised, having passed the test. But the oblivion I would have to go through to get there scared me. Even at Champex Lac, it still scared me. Yet it is the best bit. As Kartik told me at the track race in Tooting, that's the point at which things start to get interesting. Afterwards, when you finish, you get a sense of achievement and accomplishment, but in some ways it is a let-down, an anti-climax compared to the feeling of being totally alive that you get in the midst of the storm.

Rachel tells me that the first time she ran a race in the UTMB festival, one of the slightly shorter ones called the TDS, as she neared the finish in Chamonix, and she could hear the town, and the people cheering in the distance, she started to go slowly; she sat down; she walked. 'I didn't want it to end,' she says.

It's not exactly enjoyable, but in the heart of the crisis, everything is so real, you become so aware of your vulnerability, and of your strength, and ultimately, there on the edge of survival, you become fully aware of your existence. And it is there, deep in the pain cave, as they told me all along, that the fun really begins.

ACKNOWLEDGEMENTS

Firstly, a huge thank you to Marietta for holding the fort while I was out training, racing and flying off around the world doing research. Also, for her wonderful company and calm, steady crewing. And for being the person I most wanted to see at the end of every race.

Also to my children, Lila, Uma and Ossian, for being so kind and loving in my moment of crisis.

To my Mum and Dad for their endless care and concern.

To my brothers, Jiva and Govinda, for their encouragement. It's just a shame Govinda had to spoil it by beating me in my first long trail race.

To Betty and Robin for their support and kindness, which seems to know no bounds. I'm eternally grateful.

To Tom Payn, a brilliant athlete and a special person who helped me in countless ways, and to Rachel for her insights and for letting me gatecrash her train out of Champex Lac.

To Elisabet Barnes for showing me the ropes in the early days.

To Damian Hall for six-hour bimbles in the rain-soaked hills.

To Tia Boddington and everyone at the Miwok 100K in California, especially to Gary and Holly Gellin for looking after me in their wonderful home in Mill Valley. Thank you also to Hal Rosenberg for the lift to the race, and to Magda Boulet for the ride home.

To Craig Dennill in Durban for his hospitality and for getting me on the inside at the Comrades Marathon. Also to Bob de la Motte for sharing his stories and contacts.

To Conyers Davis for getting on board with the East African ultra runners idea – it wouldn't have got off the ground without his energy and drive.

Thank you to Joe Kelly for being such a font of knowledge and for staying interested in my projects. To Gary Ward for fixing my Achilles injury. To David Weinstock for helping Gary to fix my Achilles. To Jae Gruenke for an introduction to Feldenkrais and running. And to Shane Benzie for taking the time out to find more room for improvement.

To Tom Craggs for being a brilliant and understanding coach whose sessions and encouragement helped get me through all this.

To Zach Miller, his sister Ashley and her husband, Nathan, up at Barr's Camp, in Colorado, for a wonderful few days.

To Quentin and Bing at the Ring O' Fire race in Anglesey. To Lowri Morgan for helping the miles pass so quickly with her stories.

To Shankara Smith and the wonderful lap counters at the Self-Transcendence 24-hour race in Tooting, south London.

To Kate Carter for training runs and for commissioning race reports from many of these ultras.

To Robbie Britton for linking me up all over the place and for being brave enough to express opinions on the darker side of the sport.

To my agent Oli Munson for his continued brilliance, and to Laura Hassan and Fred Baty at Faber for picking this up and editing it into shape.

Thank you also to all the people who took the time out to talk to me about ultra running, and to the following people for taking time out from their lives to help me in one way or another: Charlotte Etridge, Jason Koop, Francis Bowen, Risper Kimayo, James Elson at Centurion Running, Eric Schranz, Michaela O'Sullivan and Andrew Venning, Anke Esser, Kirsty Reade and Pete Aylward, Lee Procter at Inov-8, Ben Abdelnoor, Deborah Vincent, Juan Esteban Usubillaga in Boulder, Andy Nuttall at *ULTRA* magazine, Malcolm Anderson, Jessica Vinluan and Jonathan Litchfield.